THE COMPLET
SCREENWRITING FOR CHILDREN'S FILM & TELEVISION

By
MOTTI AVIRAM

Editing: Nano Shabtai
Translation: Yael Valier
English Editor: Suzanne Klein
Illustrations: Dudy Shamay
Professional Counselors:
Ayelet Amit (M.A.) - Educational counselor
Yoni Goodman - Animation director

Special Thanks to:
Sesame Workshop (& Rechov Sumsum)/ HOP TV /
IET - Israel Educational Television / Noga
Communications / BFTV – Baby First TV / PitchiPoy
Animation / Rony Oren / Hanoch Piven / Puppet
Productions

© 2010, Hebrew Edition by Motti Aviram
mottiaviram@gmail.com

Produced by Notssa – www.notssa.com

Table of Contents

Motti Aviram

INTRODUCTION

I assume that most of those involved with writing and directing children's shows recognize the following question: "So... when are you going to start writing shows for adults?" This legitimate question is usually asked by friends and family members. Unfortunately, quite a few distinguished professionals in the television industry regard children's television as merely the first stage in the evolutionary development of the television or film world. Some of them regard the children's television niche as inferior to the niche of adult-oriented shows. In their view, children's shows belong at the bottom of the creative path, while at the other end of the path, at the top, "real" things are being done: the "important" adult shows.

Obviously, this is completely incorrect, and in many ways the opposite is true. Creating excellent shows for children calls for more professional knowledge, more sensitivity, and more astuteness than when creating shows for an adult audience.

Russian writer Korney Chukovsky[i] chooses what is, in my opinion, a wonderful point of view from which to observe this young nation of viewers. He argues that the human race reaches its most distinguished intellectual milestones during the early years. At no other stage in a person's life does one gain as much knowledge as that gained by a child in the first four or five years of life.

Chukovsky compares infants to a race of aliens: a highly intelligent race of aliens that reaches our planet with no previous knowledge that is forced to understand, in a relatively short amount of time, what this world is about and its laws. The aliens need to quickly understand that the mixtures of sounds the humans around them use for interpersonal communication are divided into words that add up to sentences, creating a strange thing called *language*, which they must decipher and learn. In addition to language, they must recognize and learn many other things, like facial expressions, which are a part of this interpersonal communication system.

Chukovsky dismisses those who try to compare the learning of a first language by an infant to the learning of a second language, no matter how difficult, by an adult, because all languages basically respond to a similar set of rules. All languages consist of syllables that add up to words that make up sentences. Our little newborn alien, who is still unaware of these principles, is required to exhibit much deeper comprehension skills — he is forced to learn what language is in the first place and the context within which it exists.

Chukovsky's way of viewing the nation of children as a highly intelligent group of aliens is very helpful for understanding and appreciating this target audience.

Chukovsky presents typical questions asked by children:

— Mom, tell me… who was born first, you or me?

— Why do they put the pits inside the cherries?

— So… the knife is the fork's husband?

In his view, these questions, often regarded by adults as signs of charming ignorance, prove the exact opposite. They point to the complex, winding, and intelligent road the *alien infant* goes through on the path to understand the surrounding new and complex world.

This book recommends its readers, first and foremost, regard young viewers with the utmost respect: appreciate their skills, understand their conceptual environment and their temporary limitations, and find a way for us, as creators, to enjoy this fresh, non-cynical group of viewers that settles in to watch our shows and movies.

In addition to knowledge of screenwriting, writers for

movies or for television shows must gain a great deal of additional knowledge and understanding in varied fields, such as developmental psychology and education, which are vital in understanding the young target audience's abilities and needs. And since most children's television shows involve puppets, animated characters, or other types of unrealistic environments, gaining technical knowledge in these fields would clearly be very helpful to those who wish to write for children.

The knowledge needed for the creation of children's shows is generally not studied in film and television classes at universities or at other formal educational institutions. New writers and creators for children go through their initial education in internal workshops that usually exist within production companies that specialize in children's content. As a result, this precious information remains out of reach to people outside these production units.

This book attempts to gather all of the *worlds of knowledge* needed for writing quality children's shows and movies, and to present this information to anyone who is interested.

When I try to illustrate the characteristics of an ideal creator of children's shows, I always think of a good friend of mine, an economist who has nothing to do with the world of children's writing, but any child who has met him has been taken in by his charm. An anecdote that perhaps illustrates some of his magical connection to children occurred a few years ago, before he had children of his own.

One evening, the two of us were invited to a party at the house of mutual friends. Our hosts had three children, aged three, five, and eight. All of the guests tried to have a polite conversation with the people next to them in the living room and in the backyard. My friend did not find much interest in this customary social activity, and so he walked alone, bored in the backyard.

When he met a group of little locals playing soccer in the backyard, he asked them if he could join their game, and they immediately agreed.

It is important to understand that his request to join the soccer game did not originate from an adult wish to entertain children; it was a wish that came from his true preference to kick a ball rather than to walk around a garden with a wine glass in his hand, nodding and pretending to smile at people he hardly knew. At first, the children were slightly anxious because they did not know him, but quickly the anxiety ended and the game began. The four of them divided themselves into two groups: the five-year-old and the eight-year-old versus my thirty-five-year-old friend and the three-year-old little sister. The game continued with my friend and his little partner beating the other team significantly. The losing team protested at first because "It's not fair," and "He's big and we're small."

My friend explained that it was not his fault he was bigger than them and that he was a better soccer player. "And what do you suggest?" he scornfully asked. "That I let you win because you're small?" This solution certainly did not appeal to the group, and the game continued the same way it began. I continued watching from the sideline, amazed at this phenomenon: an adult who showed genuine interest in a game with three children, never using a superior viewpoint but relating to this situation from the same point of view of the children. At the same time, he obviously exhibited an adult sense of responsibility. He did not kick too hard, to avoid hurting the children, and every now and then, he cautioned them when he thought they were acting in a dangerous way.

The implication of this soccer game to the creation of movies for children leads me to the ideal approach for creating content for children: the creation of content from the children's point of view while the show's creator gains genuine joy from the creative process, and at the same time, maintains the maturity and the responsibility of a person who knows he is creating for an audience different from him, while being aware of their needs and limits.

Creating content for children burdens the writer with no small educational responsibility. Our young viewer still lacks critical skills, forcing us to avoid presenting content that might hurt the viewer, her friends, or her surroundings. But more importantly, even before the *educational responsibility*, children's writers must develop an awareness of the inherent difference between the world of adults and the world of children: the level of a child's comprehension is different, the way a child becomes happy is different, and so are the contents and the worlds that interest a child. The implications of this gap between the children's and the adults' worlds are numerous and will be presented later in the book.

By watching a young child build a tower with building blocks, we discover she may think nothing of destroying the tower just before the last block is placed, then start building the tower from the beginning. An act like that may frustrate the viewing adult because adults are used to result-oriented thinking, but for the child at this stage of life, the result is not necessarily important. The drive to build, to put together, and to glue exists but so does the drive to destroy. This impulse fills the child with a feeling of satisfaction, for when she takes something apart, she learns what this object consists of, while creating for herself an opportunity for renewal.

Between these two extreme drives, the child simply enjoys the process. It is only at a later age, with the development of constructive thinking, that the child begins to show more interest in the end result.

We, as creators, give a lot of weight to the point of the story, and we dedicate a lot of effort to inventing the point, while we forget that children think differently from us, as well as the fact that children often watch their favorite shows again and again. After the first viewing, the point becomes meaningless, but they enjoy watching the movie again. The path of the main character is a much bigger source of curiosity than the end result. If we do a good job internalizing these and other facts, we will be able to create better and more suitable content for our target audience.

This book will attempt to provide for its readers knowledge of young viewers' comprehension skills and preferences. Which genres do children prefer? What makes them laugh? Which characters take hold of their hearts, and why?

I believe that good movies, like good literature, are supposed to be good for each and every living soul, and the proof is that works like *Alice in Wonderland, The Wizard of Oz, The Little Prince, Winnie the Pooh, Peter Pan,* and others were all created for children, but at the same time, they have brought great joy to adult readers as well.

Motti Aviram

KNOWING OUR
TARGET AUDIENCE

When it comes to knowing our target audience, it is important to understand that it is impossible to relate to our class of young viewers as a homogeneous group. The world of a child whose life experience includes just one winter is completely different from that of a child who has experienced two, three, or more winters. We must understand that at this point in their lives the gap between someone who has experienced one winter and someone who has experienced two is significant since the child who has spent twice as much time in this world is twice as wise as his younger, less experienced playmate.

This life experience expresses itself in many spheres, some of which are easy to describe and quantify, like vocabulary, for example: a two-year-old's vocabulary includes a few hundred words, at most, compared to that of a four- or five-year-old's, which already includes several thousand words. Vocabulary size, of course, affects a child's ability to cope with more complicated content, and this is just one of the differences that exists in the target audience that is generally named, *children.*

This leads to the first given that we have to accept in our process of getting to know our different target audiences:

They are divided into age groups.

Developmental psychology divides our target audience into age groups based on their stages of maturity in various developmental areas: cognitive, motor, verbal, emotional, and social. I will lay out here one of the accepted developmental models from the beginning of a child's life until adolescence. According to this approach, the child's life is divided into six main stages (From *Psychiatry of the Child and Adolescent*: Tiano 2005):

1. **Newborn** — until the age of two months
2. **Infancy** — from two months to one year of age
3. **Toddlerhood** — from one to three years
4. **Kindergartner** — from four to six years
5. **School Age** — from seven to eleven years
6. **Adolescence** — from twelve to eighteen years

Children in these developmental stages are assessed, as previously mentioned, according to their degree of maturity in a variety of developmental areas, and for anyone to whom these labels are new, here is an explanation.

Cognitive Development

This describes the development of thinking skills in a child: memory, grasp, the manipulation of information, the ability to come to conclusions, problem solving, planning, spatial abilities, and more.

Motor Development

This category is divided into two skills.

Gross motor skills involve the muscle tone of the large muscles and includes mechanisms of stability, balance, and movement in greater body processes such as walking, running, jumping, and riding a bike.

Fine motor skills involve fine muscle functions such as cutting with scissors, holding a writing implement, grasping and assembling small items, etc.

Emotional Development

This describes the abandoning, in stages, of an egocentric point of view, understanding the separateness of the primary caregiver (usually a parent), the ability to express and explain emotions, and the beginning of self-control over emotions, which includes the beginning of the ability to defer gratification and the ability to cope with frustration in nonviolent ways.

Social Development

This describes the child's ability to create connections with family members and group equals (others in the same age group) for the sake of shared play. Social development is tied to the ability to make friends (socialization), which includes, among other things, the ability to internalize rules of fair play, moral development, the ability to categorize, and more.

Verbal Development

This describes the process of understanding and producing meaningful language. Language serves as the connection between the child and his social environment. One of the expressions of the child's understanding of conversational context is his ability to copy and impersonate language and to role play.

It is clear that for us, the producers of TV and film for children, the cognitive development of our youngest viewers, who are in the first stages of maturation, is of prime importance since in these stages they are developing their ability to cope with the complexity of language and with more complex content.

If we are not aware of young children's limits or of their current cognitive abilities, we are at risk of creating content that will not match their level of comprehension.

Understanding the thinking skills of very young viewers is the foundation stone of writing for that age group. Through familiarization with and understanding of the complexity of the thought processes and behaviors of this target audience, we will learn to produce appropriate and enjoyable content.

Since TV is a completely open medium in which it is not possible to target broadcasts for very limited or defined audiences, TV program producers often try to pitch to wider audiences, keeping in mind the different cognitive abilities of the members of that wider audience. The supply of a single product to a wider group of children is made possible when a program is built from a number of independent layers, each of which appeals to a different segment of the target audience. For example, the design of the program (the appearance of the characters and the set) can appeal to one audience segment, the plot can appeal to another, while a third can be entertained by jokes and situations which are woven into the action.

A good example is the *Sesame Street* series, whose main target audience is children in the three to five year age group, which has successfully used this method for many years. In addition to its primary target audience, the program tries to appeal to an additional group — the parents, whom the producers consider to be an important part of the parent-child viewing process and who are therefore the target of not a little relatively grown-up humor. This humor entertains the viewing parent without impacting the content that is pitched to the program's target audience. Hence the reason why some of the series' characters are inspired by the world of adult content, like *The Count* for example, who is based on the noble Transylvanian vampire, Dracula. Children are entertained by his strange accent, his singularity and colorfulness, and his superpowers, while parents are entertained by the humor contained in the idea that Dracula, the romantic and noble vampire, spends his time teaching children how to count on *Sesame Street*, and by the double meaning in his name.

In his book, *The Secret Language of Film,* Jean-Claude Carrière[ii] describes the screening of a film to an audience of African children at the beginning of the cinematic age. The African audience, who was not trained in the understanding of consecutively screened pictures and was not familiar with western cinematic culture, had a hard time understanding the film. Therefore, it was the custom at that time to use an *explainer* (explicador) — someone who stood next to the screen and explained the story and the action to the viewers. The comparison of our young audiences to audiences of children at the beginning of the twentieth century may be exaggerated, but it is raised here to emphasize the fact that just like those children, our young viewers are likely to find it difficult to understand the language of cinema. Therefore, as producers of content for young children, we must learn to understand the world of our viewers in a way that allows them to understand and enjoy a film, without needing an explainer while they watch.

In my opinion, the best way to grasp the comprehension skills of very young children is, first and foremost, by practice. No theoretical knowledge can stand in for the experience of watching children watch TV programs, films, or children's theater. No explanation, as detailed and organized as it could possibly be, can replace the thing itself.

The most fruitful learning happens when you are the one who created the segment that is being watched, and, of course, there is no greater satisfaction than watching a group of kids rolling in laughter at a comic moment that you wrote or directed yourself. On the other hand, the greatest learning in this area comes when your audience chooses not to laugh at the comic moment you created, loses interest in the action, understands the plot differently from the way you meant it, or doesn't understand it at all. You can rely on this target audience for one thing: Its members will answer your questions absolutely honestly and won't do you any favors. Children will get up in the middle of the screening of your program, without being bothered by your presence at all, if, in their opinion, it doesn't justify an extended separation from the red truck that they left in the sand box a few minutes ago.

In an attempt to understand if, or how much, we had managed to correctly identify the tastes of our target audience, we once screened a pilot for a new kids' series in a kindergarten. The purpose of the screening was to hear what the kindergartners thought of the heroes of the new series.

We had to stop the first screening right at the beginning because the children showed no interest in the screen. They talked among themselves and barely looked at the screen at all. When all was said and done, it seemed that they preferred to go out to the yard to do things that interested them much more. We were shocked by the children's reaction. We had not supposed that the series could be that bad, but the kindergarten teacher made us feel better. She explained that in a few hours, one of the kids in the class would have a birthday party and that the birthday boy had told the others that morning, "in secret," about the party surprises that were awaiting them. This secret information excited the kids very much, and so there was almost no chance that they would be able to concentrate on this or any movie.

After a week, we came back. This time, the kids were

willing to give us their full attention. They watched the episode with interest and agreed to answer questions as soon as it was over. But here too, we were in for a big surprise. All in all, they liked the plot and the characters. They liked the supporting character, a good-hearted and naive puppy, very much, and described him as "cute," but they almost unanimously described the hero of the series as "not nice" and said that they "don't like him at all." We were very surprised by their reaction because we had thought that they would like this character most of all. The character was that of a witty, sneaky, cheeky crow who liked to get in to all sorts of hanky-panky and usually got tangled in his own web of intrigue.

The kindergarten teacher, who listened to our conversation with the kids, suggested different wording for our question. "We have two more episodes here," she said to the children, "one with this cheeky crow and one with the cute puppy whom you all liked. Which one would you like to watch now?" And then, to our astonishment, almost all of the children asked to watch the episode with the cheeky crow.

The teacher solved the riddle of the kids' unexpected choice for us later. She explained that, in her opinion, the crow was perceived by the children as a mischievous and impudent hooligan, as opposed to the good-hearted puppy. She guessed that it was hard for the children to admit to themselves, and even more to us, that they liked the character of a brazen hooligan because it would reveal them to be of similar character. The question, "What would you prefer to watch?" freed them from the problem of their own self-perception, and/or our perception of them, and allowed them to express what they really thought of the character.

We can learn about the gap between the way children express themselves and the way they really see their world from a random morning assembly that I joined once in a pre–kindergarten class for two- and three-year-olds. During the assembly, the teacher, together with the kids, dealt with subjects like the seasons, holidays, family events, and even unusual news events that it was reasonable to suppose the kids had heard about at home and about which they were curious.

The subject of that morning's assembly was personal hygiene. The children and the teacher talked about the importance of personal hygiene and about the different actions we take in order to keep clean. The teacher showed the kids different items we use to keep clean: soap, shampoo, toothbrushes, towels, sponges, and the like, and everyone was supposed to contribute something they knew to the conversation.

As an observer, it seemed to me that the kids were not that interested in the subject, or that they didn't really understand what was being said. One or two kids participated in the conversation, and the rest looked around the room or at the teacher, despite her attempts to get them to talk. It looked to me like they didn't really know what she wanted from them.

At a certain point, she suggested that each child go to the dolls corner to choose a doll so that the children could brush their teeth and wash the doll's with the hygiene supplies that she had shown them previously. From that moment on, it was a different show. The kids ran to the dolls corner, carefully chose dolls which appealed to them, and started to enthusiastically brush their dolls' teeth exactly the way their teacher had shown them during the assembly. They brushed up and down and then side to side, exactly according to the book. They washed their dolls' hair, made sure no shampoo would get into their eyes, and explained to the dolls why it was so important to be clean. Afterwards, they dried their dolls off, enjoying the whole process immensely.

If I had had to estimate how much they had understood of what the teacher said based on their minimal verbal expressions at the beginning of the assembly, I would have said that they had understood nothing at all. But the transition to the practical showed me that they had absolutely understood, beyond my expectations.

Among the two- and three-year-olds, there was a particularly small little girl, one and a half years old (!), who didn't speak at all and preferred crawling most of the time. She was not a regular member of the kindergarten. She had joined for a few days because her regular caregiver was sick and the teacher, who knew her parents, came to their aid and let her spend time in the kindergarten until her caregiver got well.

Obviously, this little girl did not participate in the morning assembly. During the conversation, she sat alone in the dolls corner, busy with her own matters. When all the children got up in order to wash, brush, and shampoo their dolls, she did not participate and did not show any interest in the goings on. But as soon as the teacher announced the end of the activity and let all the kids out to play in the yard, the little girl got up and ran to the corner, now empty, where all the hygiene supplies were and, with great care, started to perform all the cleaning actions that her older counterparts had performed. She brushed her doll's teeth, washed its hair, dried its hair, and combed it. All this showed that although she appeared to have taken no part in the conversation or the activity, and although she couldn't speak at all yet, she had nevertheless understood very well what had been said and done.

Another experience which taught me to have faith in the

thought processes of two- and three-year-old children happened during a visit at another kindergarten when the teacher told the kids why their friend, Luke, had not come to kindergarten for the last week. She explained to the children that Luke was in the hospital following a bad burn that he had sustained when boiling water from a pasta pot had spilled on him. The description of the accident caused me to flinch, but the children seemed almost indifferent to the teacher's words.

The teacher stopped talking, and then a conversation started when one boy wanted to tell about a time when he got a shot and "it hurt." Another child told everyone that he knew the name and address of his family doctor by heart, and one girl told the class that she knew how to swallow pills like a grown-up, with a glass of water, and that it isn't hard at all to swallow pills when you're sick, etc.

And then, when I was absolutely certain beyond any doubt that the incident of Luke's horrible burn didn't interest the kids at all, and the teacher wanted to end the morning conversation, one boy brought up the subject again and asked, "So when will Luke get better and come back to kindergarten?" From that moment on, all the children started to ask precise questions that were completely on target.

- Why didn't his mother watch him?
- Did it hurt?
- Does he have bandages?
- I miss him.
- Does he have a sore?
- Can we visit him?

These questions showed me that the children had understood everything they had been told and had apparently internalized and processed the information they had heard about Luke's injury, but because of the egocentric thought processes which characterize children of that age, they first had to place themselves in the center of the action, and only then could they relate to the problem which had been put before them and to its particular subject.

Incidents like this one led me to realize that it is best to use an informal approach when trying to get to know the way children think. This approach allows us to get as close as we can, and as deep as we can, into the world of our target audience.

Having said that, and despite my warm recommendation that you regularly observe or hold conversations with your target audiences as the best way to really grasp their abilities and comprehension skills, it is important to be very wary of listening to random children's conversations, or of surface observations.

Surface observations of children can sometimes lead us to facile and mistaken conclusions. It is important to remember that a deeper understanding can be developed chiefly through personal conversations with individual children (excluding group conversations) on whatever topic is on the agenda.

And indeed, the vast majority of good screenwriters with whom I have spoken have told me that when they write for children, they usually imagine a child whom they know well, or several specific children of the right age, so that they can assess exactly what is funny or moving to them and what will arouse their curiosity. It can be supposed that for exactly that reason, many writers discover the world of writing for children with the beginning of their journey as parents. The daily connection with their children sharpens their awareness of the needs and language of that age group, improves their expertise in the subjects that interest their target audience and challenges them as parents to create high quality content for their own children, and through them, for all children.

It is true that parenthood helps us as writers, but clearly it is not absolutely necessary. A significant portion of the talented children's writers with whom I've worked hadn't even started dreaming about kids when they wrote their excellent children's programs, and only when they had become parents, some years later, did they discover how well they'd hit the nail on the head when it came to their own young children's preferences.

Writers of content for children are able to satisfy kids' needs more exactly as their understanding of the range of children's needs increases. On the experiential, informal front, writers of children's content should have a store of experiments in their *experiment bank* that helps them in predicting children's reactions to various content. By spending time with children while they watch movies or TV programs, writers of children's content will come across situations where the children don't laugh at all at content that seems funny to an adult or situations where the children lose interest in content that seemed fascinating, or vice versa.

Relatively easily, an experienced kindergarten teacher can point out a song, story, or movie that will speak directly to children, and, on the other hand, she can veto content that has little chance of scoring highly among them. Children seek to fill their needs in all sorts of ways: in conversations with their friends or with adults, in games, in stories, in picture books, in songs that they hear, and of course, in television, plays, and films. Children are busy with infinite questions and their ways of learning are free of all the assumptions to which we are already bound. They are explorers without trails. Their innocence and curiosity leads them to be sharp and creative in their questions and evaluations.

Aristotle said, "Philosophy begins in wonder." When a child observes the world, its order and creations; its people; animals; mountains and rivers, he asks himself, "Where did all these forms come from? From where are these creatures? These entities? And how did they get ordered and organized the way they are?" Wonder is the basis of all questions whose goal is to understand deeply. And children, as opposed to adults, have an easier time with wonder.

- Can I stop thinking?
- How do I know I'm not dreaming right now?
- Where does the sun go at night?
- Why do we get old?
- Why can't cats talk?
- Why does it hurt?

The pattern of *why questions* that children love to ask is embedded in hundreds of well-known children's songs and stories.

One day I thought, in my innocence, that it would be a good idea to find the sixty most common *why questions* and to make them the basis of an entertaining television program that would provide answers to the questions that interested children so much. To my great surprise, in light of an investigation we launched, it turned out that there is no such thing as the most common *why questions* because children only ask such questions in the here and now. From their point of view, the point of the query is to find an answer to an immediate question, to the problem that is bothering them at the moment that they are asking. A child who has been forbidden to jump from a point high off the ground wants to know **right now** why children can't fly. A child who is trying to zoom his bike around the yard but can't because there is a big tree in his way wants to know **right now** why trees can't move. A child who has fallen and gotten injured wants to know **right now** why it hurts. Children have no interest in a collection of answers to *why questions* in the absence of situations which caused them to ask the question in the first place, and they have absolutely no interest in *why questions* that were asked by another child in another place or at another time. We adults are the ones who grouped *why questions* into a category and then named it. From the children's point of view, the question is just another query necessary to their infinite process of information gathering on life and the world around them.

In my attempts to learn more about my target audience, I once read a description of a fascinating study (De Vries, 1969) in which very young children were introduced to a friendly cat. In the first part of the study, the children got to know the cat and call it by its name. Then, in the second stage of the study, a mask of a dog's face was put on the cat. When the kids were asked, "Who is that?" they unhesitatingly answered "dog." This phenomenon is typical of children in the first stages of development, when children still have a hard time distinguishing between the external appearance of the thing and the thing itself (the preoperational stage, Piaget's Theory; see explanation in Chapter 4).

I admit that I would not have known what to do with this theoretical piece of data had I not been present, a short while later, at a kindergarten where a little show that reminded me of the above study.

It was a one-woman show. The actor put three cardboard boxes, on which were drawn three houses with three different colored roofs, on the table. "In the first house — the one with the black roof — lives wicked Mr. Mad," said the actor. "He is an awful, scary, and dangerous man with a black hat," she continued. "In the second house — the one with the green roof — lives Mr. Muddled. Mr. Muddled has a green hat, and as his name suggests, he is terribly muddled. And in the third house — the one with the red roof — lives Mr. Chuckles. Mr. Chuckles has a red hat and funny things always happen to him because he is a funny man."

With that introduction, the show began. Each time the actor appeared, she was wearing a different colored hat. Apart from the change in hat, the actor looked exactly the same, yet from the children's point of view, every time she emerged with a new hat, she was a completely different character. This came to a climax when she put on Mr. Mad's hat and threatened, "If I (Mr. Mad) get a hold of that Mr. Chuckles, he'll be in for it!"

When the actor emerged again, wearing Mr. Chuckles' red hat, the children screamed in complete hysteria: "Mr. Chuckles! Mr. Chuckles! Run away, quick! Be careful! Mr. Mad is looking for you..."

Some of the children actually shook in fear and anxiety lest Mr. Mad catch Mr. Chuckles any second.

For those of you who wonder if Mr. Mad actually caught Mr. Chuckles in the end, fear not; he didn't appear again. And for those of you who are disturbed by the naivety of our target audience, you can also be tranquil; they weren't naive at all, or, at least, they were a lot less naive than they appeared.

At the end of the show, I interviewed some of its young viewers as to their level of understanding of the threefold role that the actor played. To my astonishment, it turned out that the children understood absolutely that Mr. Mad could never catch Mr. Chuckles or Mr. Muddled. Everyone understood that an actor had played all three roles using three different hats. So what happened here? Before I answer, here is another example:

During a different visit at a different kindergarten, I met a boy who was playing with a small truck. His mother had just come to pick him up and she said to him, "Put the truck back in its place because we're going home." The boy picked up the truck, lay it down in a little doll's bed and said to it, "Good night, truck. I'll see you tomorrow."

"You know that trucks don't sleep in beds," said his mother with a smile.

"I know," said the boy, "but I'm playing now."

I assume that everyone has happened upon a child with arms outspread, pretending to be an airplane as he runs around the room making incessant engine noises. There is no need to worry; he doesn't actually believe that he is a plane any more than he believes that he can eat the "delicious" mud pies that he just "baked" next to the faucet in the yard.

The behavior of the children who watched the show I described, and the answer of the child who put his truck to bed, "I know, but I'm playing now," show us how central and important imagination is in the lives and development of children. Imagination, at this stage in their lives, is a playing tool exactly like dice, toy trucks, or the bent nail that they found one morning on the sidewalk. They are completely aware of the borders between the imagined and reality. Yet in their imaginative play, the more they are able to ignore the real world around them, the greater their pleasure.

In his book, *Playing and Reality* (1971), Donald Woods Winnicott describes "the transitional phenomenon," the phenomenon of imagination and play in children. Every creative action, according to Winnicott, is under the rubric of a *transitional phenomenon*, which helps the child cope with the daily trauma of the meeting with reality. Through imagination and play, the child intertwines elements of his inner world with physical, external objects and places, and imagination with concrete reality. In this way, the child experiences control over reality through play in the *transitional space* — the area between one's inner reality and external reality. Additionally, through play, the child becomes creative. Using his imagination in the context of play allows him to express himself. This feeling of control over reality and self-expression is fundamental to his healthy emotional development.

Uri Rapp, in the book, *The World of Play* (1980), claims that one of the most important elements of play is that people build for themselves a world that they, and not an external force, control. And what could be a better response to the needs of a child than a world devoid of parents to tell him when to go to bed, devoid of a kindergarten teacher who tells him what to do and when, and devoid of an angry adult who forbids him to make noise during rest time. In the world of play, the child is entirely responsible for what happens and when.

And indeed, the most intense period of play occurs in the kindergarten years, between the ages of two and six, which is why this age is called *The Age of Play*. Many kids regularly venture out with dinosaur or monster dolls, fire trucks with ladders, or some kind of hero figure. At all available moments, they engross themselves in play in which they see themselves as the super-powerful protagonist, embodied in the person of the small toy doll in their hands. For these moments of play, they are all-powerful. They are the strongest, the fastest, the scariest, or the most beautiful. In the world of play, there is no limit to their powers and nothing stands in their way. Everything is under their unique control, and they are the ones who decide what will happen.

Nevertheless, it is important to remember that most of the activities that a very young child experiences are a form of play, and not all forms of play at this age are necessarily bound to the imaginative faculty.

Daily activities, like getting dressed, eating, putting dishes into the dishwasher, etc. are perceived by children as play. Play is an important element in the education of the child. Through play, the child develops independence, self-esteem, social skills, motor skills, and more.

Daydreaming can be put into the same category as play. It helps children cope, through their imaginations, with different situations, and, sometimes, even with extreme, disturbing existential questions. Children are absorbed by many difficult issues such as the fear of hunger, life and death, being orphaned, sibling rivalry, fear of a stepmother, and the fear of abandonment. With the goal of shielding children from these difficult subjects, and with the intent to keep them safe, many parents avoid bringing them up around their kids. Nevertheless, children think about these things.

It turns out that one of the best ways for children to deal with these subjects are through good old fairy tales. Tens of fairy tales begin with the death of the king or the queen and more than one begins with the words, "When the king was about to die, he called his sons, the three princes, and said to them..." Subjects such as death, being orphaned, hunger, sibling rivalry, and fear are central themes in fairy tales and lead these stories to be riveting to children.

In his book, *The Uses of Enchantment: The Meaning and Importance of Fairy Tales* (Knopf), Bruno Bettelheim dissects the best of the most famous fairy tales and explains how they help children cope with the difficult questions that absorb them. Through fairy tales, which present these issues in the most basic ways, and with the help of colorful characters such as witches, princesses, knights and dragons, children can lay bare these engrossing questions for themselves.

Fairy tales are awash with stories about witches who steal children from the protective embrace of their parents or who turn people into animals. They present characters like the Genie in the bottle, who, with one wave of his hand, is capable of emptying a house of its inhabitants, such that when the hero, Aladdin, comes back, he discovers that he is alone in the world.

The bitter tears that children shed when they are left in kindergarten by their parents every morning usually arise from their fear of abandonment, which is absolutely concrete and which, from the child's point of view, is almost no different from the abandonment of Hansel and Gretel in the forest.

Just like fairy tale heroes, who find themselves in lonely isolation until the story's happy ending, so a child feels during some of the difficult moments with which he has to cope every day in his imagination. He is busy with questions such as: To where do his parents disappear when they leave him in kindergarten and go to work? Or, what could the old woman who lives next door, and looks like a dangerous witch, do to him? And how does one cope with the fear of the threatening neighborhood dog who is much more frightening than any fire-breathing fairy tale dragon? From the point of view of the child's emotions, there is not much difference between his mother, who won't let him go outside to play with a friend, and the wicked queen, who locks her daughter up in a tall tower.

Beyond dealing with the anxiety-producing problems we have already listed, like death, becoming an orphan, the fear of abandonment, sibling rivalry, etc., fairy tales answer different needs too, like the need to be accepted and to belong, the need for warmth and love, knowledge, laughter, and more.

The point of departure of many fairy tales reflect the way children see themselves in their everyday lives. Sometimes, a child feels neglected in favor of a sibling, like Cinderella, or she feels unappreciated, just like the ugly duckling. In this way, fairy tales implant hope in the heart of a child, hope that one day, everyone will recognize his worth, the kingdom will be his, the princess will fall in love with him, and the king will allow him to marry her and to rule the kingdom. And when he has finished dreaming, he can go back to his everyday games with his friends, full of energy and hope that one day, they'll all see who he really is...

Media industries discovered children's interest in tales of bravery, or in heroes with superpowers, a long time ago. And so Superman, Spiderman, Batman, and other superheroes whose superpowers allow them to do wondrous things, have joined the good old Genie in the bottle. They're strong, fast, smart, and invincible. Through identification with these heroes, and through their imaginations, the children make up for all their lacks, real and imagined. They can imagine themselves rising to the skies, just like the hero, beating giants; rescuing the weak; changing shape, size or appearance; and coming out of it all with the upper hand.

A thorough knowledge of the world of fairy tales affords creators of content for children a deep understanding of the way stories can answer the needs of children and provides a source of inspiration for new plots and exciting characters.

Just like stories and fairy tales, movies and television programs aimed at children provide them with an arsenal of magical characters and fantasy worlds in which they can unleash their imaginations. Our job as creators of children's content is to combine the understanding and awareness of children's needs with the creative power we have, and with these, fulfill their needs and expectations appropriately.

A sampling of various television series or current media figures can help us with this.

Bob the Builder's design, for example, reminds us of Playmobil characters and various other current doll characters with whom children play. Furthermore, Bob is a character whose profession is one that fascinates children. He is not any kind of superhero — he doesn't have any particular superpowers — yet nevertheless, just like a firefighter, police officer, pilot, bus driver, and other revered people, Bob has abilities that children would very much like to have themselves. He has a crane, a tractor, and a concrete mixer, and he builds buildings and roads by himself and therefore serves as a model for identification and emulation by his viewing audience. Bob is like a child who has superpowers, in his own field, and children see him as a fellow — like a child who has the abilities of an adult, and even more.

Children (and adults too) are usually enthralled by giant tractors that uproot boulders or by huge cranes that easily move enormous loads of bricks. Bob the Builder provides his viewers with a great amount of interesting knowledge in the fields of building and heavy machinery, and in addition to that, he excels at solving problems through positive thinking with which he always manages to resolve the difficulties he faces. Bob is seen by the child as a character with whom he can identify, and this leaves the child with strength and confidence.

The series, *Dora the Explorer*, also satisfies a long list of children's needs in various areas. Dora's nature is to be investigative and adventurous. Though she also doesn't have superpowers, she provides children with a riveting interactive experience. Children who watch Dora are asked to react out loud, to stand in front of the screen, and to perform all sorts of actions. These actions help Dora, as it were, to get out of the sticky situations in which she finds herself.

This interactive viewing experience, in which children feel themselves a full partner in Dora's adventures on the screen, strengthens children's self-confidence. Dora's curiosity and adventurousness parallels the natural curiosity and adventurousness of her viewers at this stage in their lives. Dora also answers the child's need to gain knowledge. The viewing child takes part in the adventure, and, among other things, gains vocabulary in another language.

A further example is the series, *Brum*, whose main character is a unique kind of superhero: a toy car. Brum looks like a real toy car and has a unique personality. He identifies injustices, chases bad guys, fights them, and wins! All children who hold a little toy car in their hands can draw confidence from their imagination, from which they can send the car out to defend them against anyone who would even think of harming them.

As opposed to the writing of content for adults, where writers are chiefly motivated by ideas around which they weave plot and character, the basis of most successful children's programs are motivated by the real needs of children. When creating this content, writers have to understand which real need is being met by their writing, and how the child will use, and enjoy, the result.

THE PRINCIPLES
OF
WRITING
FOR CHILDREN

The difference between writing for adults and writing for children stems, first and foremost, from the essential difference between the characters of these two audiences.

When writing for adults, the writer focuses on an audience of equals — an audience with similar life experiences and with associations and insights similar to his own. However, when writing for children, the writer must put himself in the shoes of the young viewer and adjust his writing to an audience with a limited understanding, distinct content needs, and different tastes and preferences. Understanding these three fundamental principles is the foundation for writing for children and distinguishes this type of writing from any other.

It is very important to understand that for children, content is the response to a real need! And what is the most fundamental desire of children of all ages? **To be grown up!** More than anything else, children want to be big — and as soon as possible. Therefore, from their very first moments of awareness, they are preoccupied with the fact that they are small and wish this were not true more than anything else. Naturally, children are therefore greatly interested in any content that can help them along the path to this glittering goal. Content that will provide them with as much information about the world as possible. Children want to know everything — exactly like all the adults around them, who seem to them to be all-knowing.

Therefore, children's content must conform to three basic principles that characterize writing for children and differentiate this writing from any other kind.

- **Understanding the cognitive capabilities of young children** — Writers for young children must be familiar with the cognitive limitations of the various target audiences and understand the changes that occur in their comprehension skills at different ages.

- **Content as the fulfillment of a need** — Content, of course, responds to a need. Therefore, the writer must be sure that the content she writes actually responds to a real need in the target audience.
- **Familiarity with the content repertoire that children love** — Writers for children must be familiar with the worlds of content that children love: princes, monsters, witches, fairies, superheroes, and other characters and worlds that enchant this target audience.

These three fundamental principles are the basics of writing for children. These principles, combined with writing skills and screenwriting know-how will no doubt yield excellent content for children.

This book was originally written for writers familiar with screenwriting or directing, with the goal of expanding and deepening their knowledge of writing and directing scripts or plays intended primarily for children. Screenwriting in general requires wider know-how, available in writing workshops or other forums, and requires quite a lot of practice. This book does not profess to teach screenwriting in general, but in order not to neglect readers unfamiliar with this art, I will try to explain, in a nutshell, a few basic principles that hold true for screenwriting in general.

LIMITATIONS OF A SCRIPT

The first principle that a content creator for television, film, or stage must be familiar with is the Limitations Principle. Unlike literary writing, in a film or play, communication with the viewer is limited to only two channels: the visual channel and the audio channel. The viewer is exposed solely to what he sees on screen (or on stage) and what he hears during the film or show.

Although this seems self-evident, this is not the case. Anyone who has started to write a script experiences the huge difficulties in translating latent messages into script situations.

All the descriptions that convey the sentiments of the characters, their conflicts, desires, disappointments, fears, joy etc. have no place in screenwriting. Scripts are based mainly on dialogues, and people tend not to talk about their innermost feelings. The role of the screenwriter is to create situations that enable his characters to act is such a way that will enable the viewer to deduce what the characters are feeling at any given moment.

Let's assume, for example, that Greg and Danny are characters in a film. At a certain point in the film, Greg wants to visit Danny, but Greg doesn't want Greg to come because he is mad at him but doesn't want to say so openly. In a novel, you can convey this information using the description of the omnipotent narrator, and the author can preface this by writing that although Danny and Greg are great friends, an event that occurred today in school made Danny want to take a time-out from this friendship.

In a film, on the other hand, viewers must understand these types of situations on their own and draw conclusions based on what they see on the screen. This is why the most important skill that screenwriters must cultivate is their sophisticated cinematic expression skill, including visual expression skills through which it will be possible to take advantage of the cinematic expression limitations and convey, using these limitations, more complex content messages.

These messages can be conveyed using directions that will be followed by the actors.

EXAMPLE:

The phone rings in Danny's home. Danny is wearing a comfortable sweatshirt and is engrossed in a computer game. Danny answers the phone.

Danny:
(**Overly pleased**) *Hey, Greg... It's great you called...*

Greg:
Are you home? Great! I'll pop by cause I want to —

Danny:
I'm home right now, but... (**Lying**) *I'm just on my way out with my parents.*
You caught me at the door...

Greg:
Really? What a shame. I really wanted to come over — where are you going?

Danny:
I... I... (**walking around the empty house**) *we're going... to visit my aunt in the hospital...*

The viewers see, with their very own eyes, that Danny is lying. Danny had no intention of going anywhere, and when he tells Greg the lie, it is because he doesn't want him to visit right now. Danny tells Greg: "I'm just on my way out..." but based on the fact that he is wearing a lived-in sweatshirt and slippers, the viewer can deduct that Danny had no intention of going out. He even said that he was just going out with his parents, while the audience clearly sees that he is home alone. These facts give a different meaning to the words he says. The viewers must look at the scene and draw conclusions based on what they saw. What they saw is the final result of a visual decision made by the screenwriter when writing the script. This decision conveys to the viewer that the words being said have a different meaning. The viewer understands that despite what Danny says, he is not interested in Greg's friendship right now, although this is never verbalized.

When writing scripts, as opposed to writing literature, there is no place for verbal descriptions of emotions. The viewer must understand the emotions based on the visual representation. Sometimes background narration is used as a means to convey messages, but narration is usually perceived as a *literary* means and is typically used as a last resort. Typically, a writer must find situations and actions that illustrate the hero's sentiments to the viewer without these being stated explicitly.

ANOTHER EXAMPLE:

Let's assume that a certain screenwriter wishes to demonstrate to the viewer how hurt her hero is that none of his friends came to his birthday party held at his home. In the film, we see the image of a beautifully decorated birthday room — a birthday table laden with treats and delicacies, and a birthday cake decorated with whipped cream and a colorful marzipan figure. In the marzipan at the center of the beautiful cake, we see the smiling face of the boy (the hero), sculpted in colored marzipan in honor of his birthday. And then, at a certain moment, we hear an intercom buzzer. The boy runs joyously to the intercom, but from the conversation, we realize that someone pushed the wrong button. Our disappointed hero glances at his watch and realizes that no one is coming. He takes a fork and angrily squashes the marzipan face created in his image. He demonstratively throws the cake into the garbage can, and then, one after the other, he throws away the rest of the birthday treats. It is clear to the viewer that there was no need to throw the cake away, but due to the blatant action of crushing the cake and his marzipan image, the viewer understands the boy's emotional turmoil.

Many books dealing with the principles of screenwriting divide the action on screen into three parameters: space, action, and sound. The image that the audience sees includes two of these components — space and action — with sound being the third, unseen, component.

According to this approach:

Space — refers to everything seen on the screen. The location, appearance of the characters, hints about the season, day of the week, etc.

Action — refers to everything that happens on the screen — movements of the heroes, camera movements, and everything else that happens on the screen.

Sound — refers to the dialogue, music, and all the sound effects that the viewer hears throughout the film.

These are the three basic tools at the screenwriter's disposal. With proper handling, these tools can convey a story that includes time, plot, actions, wishes, and emotions.

THE CLASSIC SCREENWRITING FORMULA

There are many ways to write scripts. The options available to communicate a story are diverse. However, and especially for someone who has never written a script, familiarity with the "classic script formula" is essential.

The American screenwriter, Robert McKee, considered the ultimate guru of screenwriters the world over, defines a good script as "a good story that is well told." His basic assumption is that writing is an art based on enduring and universal principles and forms that are familiar and accessible to us from as long ago as when Aristotle wrote *Poetica*. The art of writing requires not only meaningful and original content but also skill in its formulation, that is, reciprocal relations between form and content. But first of all, a good story is essential.

WHAT, IN FACT, IS A GOOD STORY?

A classic story is fundamentally a series of events based on a fascinating turn of events in the life of the hero. This turning point is usually referred to as an inciting incident: something unexpected that happens to the lead character that diverts him from his course, thus starting the story.

The story is a voyage that the hero undergoes as part of his attempts to return his life to its previous course or to accept the change in his life. The life of a character can change suddenly due to an infinite variety of unexpected turning points — learning about a life-threatening disease, finding out that a spouse is cheating on him, unexpectedly winning one million dollars, an unforeseen encounter with a robber, some kind of fault, a task the hero took upon himself and cannot complete, etc. Nearly anything unexpected that happens to a hero can contribute to a good story.

It was Archimedes who said: "Give me a lever, and I will move the world," and I say: Find yourself a good turning point, and you have the makings of an excellent story. Writing for children is also driven by good turning points.

A basic difference between writing for adults and writing for children lies in the differences in content and therefore also in the nature of the turning points. While the plots of the adult world are driven by turning points such as falling in love and betrayal, crimes, losing a job, illnesses, etc., much smaller and simpler turning points are sufficient for plots in the world of children. Examples include, "Where has my collection of pine cones disappeared?" or "My best friend didn't come to kindergarten today," or "I can't do something that older kids can do." The difference between plot-driven writing for adults as opposed to children is only in the content repertoire that is suitable for different target audiences. Yet other than this, the writing technique is identical.

Evidently, enchanted turning points will lead to enchanted plots. It is clear that turning points such as smelling a magic flower that turns the person smelling it into a colorful butterfly, or an unexpected encounter with a chick that has lost his mother, or with a flying pony will result in turning points beloved by our target audience. Writing for children, like writing for adults, also requires a turning point, but these turning points must take place in unusual locations and facilitate encounters between their heroes and special, unexpected, and magical creatures, if possible.

The inciting incident, which is the first turning point, is the plot's driving axis, with the plot being the story of the process by which the hero confronts the changes in his life produced by the first turning point, whether it is the firing of a businessman who loses his job or a kitty that has forgotten how to speak Catish.

Usually, at a more advanced stage of the plot, an additional turning point occurs, called the second turning point. It is thanks to this turning point that the hero begins to take the high road, and the script reaches its third part called the resolution. I'm sure than anyone who's ever heard a lecture about screenwriting is familiar with the *classic screenwriting formula*:

Exposition › First Turning Point (inciting incident) › Plot › Second Turning Point › Resolution

This formula is also known by the name of *three-act plot structure*:

- **First Act**
Introduction, exposition — introducing the heroes, defining the story's timeline, background, and location, and initial introduction of the conflict.
- **Second act**
Body of the plot, in which we are exposed to the hero's course of action, to who can disrupt this course of action, and to the film's breaking point or turning point, which will lead the plot to its climax in the third act.
- **Third act**
Resolution of the conflict, relief of dramatic tension, and conclusion of the film.

The definitions of the various types of formulas are of no great importance, since the structure is actually identical.

The *classic screenwriting formula* or the *three-act plot structure* exist in most feature or television films. I'll use an amusing story that once happened to me to demonstrate the classic screenwriting formula in a simple and enjoyable manner.

One summer evening, I was sitting with Shelly and Jean, two writing colleagues, in a small café. The meeting dealt with the development of a new television series for a children's channel. Our original decision to meet in this specific café can be viewed as the exposition to the story I am about to tell. This is because all the plot events that the hero himself chose occur during the exposition, and had the hero not chosen them, things would not have happened as they did, and the plot would not have developed.

While we were holding our writers' meeting in the café, at around four o'clock, the waitress asked us if we'd like anything else, since "the café will be closing very soon" (because it was located next to businesses and offices that closed in the afternoon). We thanked her politely, paid the check, and continued to sit for a while. After about twenty minutes, we got up to go, each of us in a different direction. It was then that we discovered, to our amazement, that the café was empty, the front door was locked, and we were, in fact, locked in. The café's staff had gone home and accidentally locked us in.

Initially, we were amused by the idea. Shelly said that the nice waitress had probably heard us talking about the inciting incident and decided to give us an instructive practical lesson in inciting incidents. Our being locked in a café met all the conditions of an inciting incident, since it was obviously unexpected, and it prevented all three of us from continuing the course of our lives as planned. All three of us were supposed to wrap the meeting up at four thirty and head out, each on his or her own way.

Shelly was supposed to pick her son up from day care. Jean was supposed to go to her dance class (where latecomers are not let in), and I had another meeting scheduled on the other side of town, but we were all locked in and couldn't continue with our lives as planned. At a certain stage, like in any good story, the new situation was no longer amusing, and we realized that now, as a result of the inciting incident that changed the course of our lives, we must start to deal with our own plot. And exactly like in any plot, and like all the heroes in all the stories, we must try to put our lives back on their original track, in other words, we must find a way to escape from this café.

The first escape plan was to jump over a fence surrounding the café's garden. We went out to the garden and examined the fence, but it was too tall and prickly. Next we checked if it was possible to go out through the kitchen. We were glad to find the door to the kitchen open, but the kitchen's back door that led to the service parking was locked with a heavy padlock. We lost heart for a moment, but then our hope that someone would return and open the door revived, because all the signs indicated that someone had left intending to return — some of the lights were still on, and the sound system was still playing. We waited for a while, but none of the café workers returned. The situation began to seem serious.

Shelly's daycare manager told her over the phone that her son was crying, and she should come pick him up quickly. Jean's class was about to start, and I was pleading over the phone, asking the people waiting for me on the other side of town to be patient, hoping that I could still make the meeting. Then... while we were deep into the plot, our story's second turning point occurred. The second turning point is the one that usually advances the heroes of the story to the plot's resolution stage.

Jean suddenly discovered a large key hanging on a nail in the wall. A plastic tag attached to the key read: Merchandise Door. We agreed that if the event we were in the midst of truly fit the classic structure of a script, then Jean's finding the key was the second turning point and all that remained was to resolve the plot — in other words to use the new element she found, the key, to find the corresponding door and to gain our freedom

The second turning point usually occurs at the point in time in which the third part of the story begins. At this stage, something happens due to which the hero finds a solution or the path to a solution that will rescue him from the situation he finds himself in, from which he wishes to be rescued. At this turning point, the hero is supposed to learn, to discover, or to understand something new, and throughout the resolution stage, he must use these new insights that he discovered in the second turning point. In this case, Jean found a key with *Merchandise Door* on it, causing us to assume that it belonged to a door. A door that, when we found it, we would be able to open and reach freedom. It was clear, therefore, that all that we had to do was find the door that the Merchandise Door key opened. First we tried to open the metal door leading to the service parking lot, but the key didn't fit. The key also didn't open the front door to the café, and then suddenly we saw it! At the very end, deep in the kitchen, next to refrigerators, hidden behind a pile of potato sacks, we saw a small door. The door's width was normal, but it was only about 40 inches tall. It was a tiny service door that was apparently used to bring merchandise into the kitchen on a trolley. We moved the sacks out of the way and discovered, to our amazement, that the door wasn't even locked. This is exactly in line with Robert McKee's theory that a script must always finally satisfy the audience's expectations but not exactly the way the audience expects it… because the audience loves an ending that is both expected as well as surprising. And this indeed was the case. We found the door to freedom, and even the key to this door leading to freedom, yet unexpectedly the door was not locked… which meant we could have exited the café through the door without any key.

Needless to say, we all managed to make up the lost time and return to our daily routines. The fundamental question that remains is, does this story of being locked in the café contribute to the understanding of the rules of writing by this book's readers, since this is the only reason I told this story?

The next section presents a sample of a script that was part of a program developed for a children's channel. It is followed by an analysis of the script according to screenwriting principles.

The following scene that takes place in the apartment of Grandmother Rona and Grandfather Gene is a conversation between the neighborhood crow, Chuck (a puppet, of course), who likes to visit from time to time, and grandmother Rona. The two are discussing Bali the dog (also a puppet), who lives in the neighborhood and also likes to visit the grandmother and grandfather's house often.

MEASURING LOVE

Interior / Day / Home of Grandma Rona and Grandpa Gene

Grandma Rona is busy in the kitchen. Attached to the refrigerator door with magnets are three new childish drawings. Chuck the Crow arrives with his wings spread, panting.

From left to right: *Grandma Rona, Bali, Chuck and Grandpa Gene*

Chuck:
(**Panting**) *Hello, Grandma Rona.*

Grandma:
Hi… hello, Chuck.

Chuck:
I just popped in for a minute. I was thirsty and remembered the wonderful lemonade you make. So I dropped by.

Grandma:
Got it. I'll pour you a glass of delicious, refreshing lemonade.

Chuck:
Thank you. (**Notices the drawings and is impressed**)
Wow! Not bad!
Not bad at all. Very nice drawings. Who drew them?

Grandma:
Bali.

Chuck:
(**Jealous**) *Yeah... Well... sure, I should have known...*

Grandma:
What should you have known?

Chuck:
I should have known that in this house you only hang Bali's drawings and no one else's. (**Hurt yet noble**) *But that's okay as far as I'm concerned!*

Grandma:
Why do you say that, Chuck?
Did you ever give me a drawing that I didn't put up?

Chuck:
No, cause I don't even like to draw!

Grandma:
(**Sounding like a detective**) *So maybe that's why there's no drawing by you on the refrigerator, Chuck.*

Chuck:
(**Unaccepting**) *Maybe.* (**Explodes**) *So why did Grandpa Gene only take Bali fishing yesterday? And why did you only buy Bali a stamp album for New Years?*

Grandma:
(**Carefully**) *Grandpa only took Bali fishing because Bali asked him to, and you didn't. And we only bought Bali a*

stamp album because Bali collects stamps, and you don't.
But you forgot that we only bought you a model airplane kit,
and we only took you to the kite competition last week.

Chuck:
Yes... that's true. So why do I always feel that you love
Bali more than me?

Grandma:
Chuck, we don't love Bali more. We love both you and
Bali just the same.

Chuck:
That's not true. You love him more!

Grandma:
Chuck, you're wrong. We love you just the same.

Chuck:
Really? How much?

Grandma:
How much what?

Chuck:
How much do you love me?

Grandma:
How much?

Chuck:
How much do you love me, and how much do you love
Bali?

Grandma:
We love you very much and also love Bali very much.

Chuck:
I understand... but I'm asking how very much?

Grandma:
Look Chuck, there is no such thing as how much love. I can't say that I love you twenty-two. You can't count love.

Chuck:
I understand. So assuming you love me twenty-two, then how much do you love Bali?

Grandma:
What I'm trying to say, Chuck, is that love can't be measured with numbers or quantities. Love is something you feel in your heart and can't be counted. And my heart is so full of love that it is enough for both you and Bali, as well as for other people that I love.

Chuck:
You're just saying that.

Grandma:
No I'm not! (**She has an idea**) *Say, Chuck, who you love more, Grandpa Gene or me?*

Chuck:
(**Confidently**) *Grandpa Gene.*

Grandma:

(**Stunned**) *Ah… What? Really? You don't say… Why do you love Grandpa Gene more?*

Chuck:

Cause he takes me to work with him in the garden, and you don't.

Grandma:

Ah… well yes, that's true. But I always read you the stories you love.

Chuck:

(**Recalling**) *Right! You do read them really funny, with all the voices… yeah, so I probably love you more.*

Grandma:

Well thank you… but what about the wonderful cheese sandwiches that you say only Grandpa Gene knows how to make?

Chuck:

Oops… thanks for reminding me. I forgot all about them. So I must love Grandpa Gene the most.

Grandma:

Really? And who sits with you every evening before you fall asleep because you don't like to be alone?

Chuck:

You do! Only you. So it is you that I really love a lot more. (**Confused**)

But actually no… Grandpa… no, you… actually, it's Grandpa…

Grandma:
It's alright, Chuck, each time you love one of us a little more, but in general you love both of us.

Chuck:
That's true. I love both of you, I mean… you're both okay.

Grandma:
And I also love you as well as Bali, and I'm sure that Grandpa Gene feels the same way.

Chuck:
(**Contemplating**) *Does that mean that if I draw you a picture, you'll hang it on the refrigerator?*

Grandma:
Of course! (**Gives him pencils and paper**)

Chuck:
Really? Great. Thanks. I just… don't really feel like drawing right now… but some other time, Grandma Rona. Thanks for the wonderful lemonade. (**Flies away**) *Bye bye.*

This dialogue between Grandma Rona and Chuck the Crow was obviously written for children. It is written based on the three fundamental principles used to write scripts intended for children: it speaks their language, deals with things that interest them, and includes a magical character — Chuck the Crow who exhibits childlike behavior patterns. But otherwise, there is no essential difference between the writing technique used in this script and the technique used to write any dramatic script for adults. If we try to *insert* the *Measuring Love* script into the classic screenwriting formula, we'll discover that it fits perfectly.

Exposition — Chuck the Crow is suddenly thirsty and decides to visit the home of Grandma Rona and Grandpa Gene to drink a glass of cold lemonade. This is a plot development that is not forced upon Chuck the Crow. Chuck chose this course of action, and it is clear that had he not chosen this action, the entire episode's plot could not have occurred.

Inciting Incident — When Grandma Rona takes the jar of lemonade out of the refrigerator for Chuck, he notices and is surprised to see that the refrigerator door is covered with Bali's drawings, causing him to worry that perhaps Grandma Rona prefers Bali over Chuck.

Plot — Chuck tries to confront the new information that *stares him in the face* and changes his life axis that day. Originally, he had intended to stop at Grandma's and Grandpa's house to drink a cold glass of lemonade and then fly away. Yet this new revelation prevents him from continuing on his way, until his standing in the eyes of Grandma Rona and Grandpa Gene is restored.

Second Turning Point — At this turning point, as you may remember, something happens, thanks to which the hero *stumbles* on a solution or direction for a solution that will help him out of the situation into which he was driven, and from which he wants to be freed. In this screenplay's second turning point, Grandma Rona suddenly asks Chuck whether he loves her or Grandfather more.

Resolution — Chuck gradually realizes that Grandma Rona doesn't prefer Bali over him. He understands that just like he loves Grandma Rona and Grandpa Gene about the same, this is exactly what they feel toward him.

From the *Measuring Love* script presented above, and from many more scripts that were a great success among the young audience, it is possible to learn that, in principle, there is no essential technical difference between writing for adults and for children. This does not hold true when writing for toddlers, which requires a slightly different plot approach, as will be described later.

So what prevents any screenwriter from also writing for children?

Technically, the answer is clearly absolutely nothing. However, from my experience as the head writer of many children's series, I know that some people find writing for children easy and natural, while others find this genre very difficult.

I believe that the most basic and central characteristic essential for writers for children is to be interested in the content repertoire that children love, to remember how these worlds of content captured our imagination when we were children, to reconnect with these enchanting worlds, and most importantly, to enjoy this work — or in other words — to connect to your inner child.

WRITING FOR THE VERY YOUNG

It seems that there is no real difference between the plot structure of scripts written for adults and those written for children; yet this is not an accurate statement. As I noted in chapter 2, all young television viewers should not be considered a uniform group. The plot structure presented in that chapter does indeed address the needs of children aged about three and older, yet younger children seem to enjoy simpler plot structures much more.

We are all familiar with the first books that young children love. These are usually plot-less stories, in the classical sense of the word plot. An example is the story about a young puppy dog going for a walk in the neighborhood and making new friends — animals it has never met (*Where is Pluto* by Leah Goldberg). Pluto meets a frog, and then a bird, and later a butterfly, a horse and a cow. The children listening to the story can already identify these animals, yet to the puppy, the story's hero, these animals are brand new.

Young listeners enjoy celebrating their superiority over the young puppy, and enjoy the story tremendously, although it does not conform to the outline of a classic story. Another example is *Egg in Disguise* by Dan Pagis, the story of an egg that didn't want to be an egg. It tried to become a flower, and then a mushroom, then a vase, and even a clown, but to no avail. Finally, it was content and happy to resume life as an egg. All these stories do, of course, have a plot structure, but it deviates from the classic plot structure .

This is a voyage-type structure. A repetitive voyage centered on a recurring pattern. At the beginning of the story, the child understands the nature of the voyage and its purpose. In the case of the *Egg in Disguise*, for example, the egg did not want to continue to be an egg, and that point marks the start of a series of encounters between the frustrated egg and characters and events that are very similar to one another, except for one very clear element that changes every time, and this is, of course, the focus and subject of the encounter. During its voyage, the egg that wants to become something different encounters a flower and decides that this is what it wants to be.

When it is uncomfortable being a flower, it continues on its journey and meets a mushroom, and decides that this is definitely what it wants to be, and then it wants to become a vase, and then a clown. This continues until it reaches the final, inevitable decision that the best thing would be for it to remain an egg.

The constant element here is the journey that continually advances along a single axis, as well as the egg's behavior, which follows a fixed pattern in all the encounters with the characters. This is just like the puppy in the first story described here. The puppy leaves its home and meets more and more animals it has never encountered before. Here, also, the pattern of encounter remains fixed and only the animals change. The reason is that for children of this age, the "plot," according to the accepted definition, is of no importance. They are only at the very beginning of their ability to deal with content, and the content-based satisfaction that they need at this stage is much more basic.

Until about the age of two, children enjoy consolidating a sense of their own control of language and content to which they are exposed and, therefore, the simpler the plot structure, the easier it is for them to master the elements in a story.

It is no coincidence that children enjoy shows in which the actor speaks to them in half-words or half-sentences, like an act composed of funny stories I saw in one of the kindergartens I visited.

Funny Dunny is a clown who tells stories in kindergartens, and the children anxiously await his weekly visits.

SEGMENT FROM THE ACT:

Dunny: *Hello, chil…*
Children: *…dren!!!*
Dunny: *How are…*
Children: *you!*
Dunny: *Want to hear a st…*
Children: *…ory!*
Dunny: *Wonderful. Today I'll tell you a story about someone who walks around with this thing on her head. (Shows them a crown)*
Children: *Princess…*
Dunny: *Exactly. That's right. A princess. This is a story about a princess and also… oops… I forgot the name of the animal in this story. I just remember that is goes quack quack…*
Children: *Duck!!!!*
Dunny: *That's right, a duck. How could I have forgotten such an easy word? Oops… it's unbelievable, kids, but now I forgot the sound a duck makes…*
Children: *Quack quack!*
Dunny: *Right, quack quack, thanks for reminding me. So here is the story. Once upon a time, in a faraway land, lived… (shows a crown)*
Children: *Princess!!!*
Etc.

Children enjoy Funny Dunny's stories because he fulfills the need patterns of very young children – texts that enable them to anticipate and predict. Predicting strengthens the children's confidence in their knowledge and gives them a sense of successfully deciphering and controlling the content.

Most books and scripts written for very young audiences use various writing techniques that facilitate prediction: rhyming, accumulation, repeating patterns or rhythmic beats. These help children predict the end of the word or sentence, which reinforces their sense of control of the content, which greatly enhances their enjoyment.

Rhyming is one of the simplest methods of content prediction. It is based on repeating a similar sound at the end of various words, usually at the end of a line. When the child internalizes the recurring sound at the end of the lines, he or she can predict the end of all the lines in a poem or song:

Once upon a time there were three little foxes
Who didn't wear stockings, and they didn't wear sockses,
But they all had handkerchiefs to blow their noses,
And they kept their handkerchiefs in cardboard boxes.
They didn't go shopping in the High Street shopses,
But caught what they wanted in the woods and copses.
They all went fishing, and they caught three wormses,
They went out hunting, and they caught three wopses.
They went to a fair, and they all won prizes—
Tree plum-puddingses and three mince-pieses.
They rode on elephants and swang on swingses,
And hit three coco-nuts at coco-nut shieses.

(From *When We Were Very Young* / A. A. Milne)

At first, the children enjoy identifying the recurring sound. Later, from the second time onwards, they enjoy the information they have already acquired and the ability to anticipate the sound at the end of each sentence. Their ability to say the sound even before it is read out loud gives the children great joy and, as in the case of this poem, even added delight. Their delight stems from the deliberate use of certain words, such as: sockses, pieses and shieses.

However, although rhyming at the ends of lines encourages a sense of control and enjoyment in children, rhyming is not enough. When writing rhymes for children, we should take several additional parameters into consideration, such as visualization, simplicity of content and meter, and avoidance of adjectives .

Visualization – a young child finds it difficult to internalize rhyming words that lack visual meaning. Rhymes meant for children should have graphic images. When the child hears the rhyme, he or she should be able to conjure up a clear image (even if it is a nonsensical image): caught three wopses, tree plum-puddingses, coco-nut shieses. Clearly these rhymes describe something extremely visual. From a young child's point of view, a rhyme that is not visual is meaningless.

Simplicity of content, musicality and meter – another consideration to be taken into account when writing rhymes for children is to create content that is easy to grasp and remember. Children love to repeat lines and rhymes that are read out or sung, so it is necessary to make sure that the rhymes consist of simple and easily remembered words taken from the child's world. This is also true of musical rhythms; these too should be simple and easily understood so the child can actively participate with hand clapping or leg stamping.

One idea per line – it is important that the textual (or visual) idea be completed within one line, and not extend over one and a half or two lines because, from the child's perspective, the rhyming syllable marks the end of the sentence, and it is difficult for him or her to understand that the words coming after the rhyme may be linked to the same idea.

Avoid the use of adjectives – adjectives typically bore children. Learning language begins with learning nouns, then verbs, and only at the end do adjectives join in. It is for this reason that adjectives are suitable for slightly older children.

Use of onomatopoeic sounds – the integration of onomatopoeic sounds into texts for children offers a wonderful advantage, as long as the sounds are directly linked to the song's content. *Choo-choo* train, Old MacDonald had a farm, *EE-I-EE-I-O*, etc. are sounds that children love to make. This is also true of names that are derived from the names of animals – a mouse named Mousy, a dog named Doggy Dog, etc.

PRINCIPLE OF ACCUMULATION

According to this principle, a child internalizes a basic, simple plot structure that is later repeated with slight additions. With each repetition, a small layer is added to the basic plot. The child develops control of the basic plot structure, enabling him or her to predict changes in the plot's development. This is evident in the stories I described at the beginning of the chapter, as well as in the story *Cat on the Mat and Friends* (Brian Wildsmith), a story in which a nice cat sits on a mat and, on the next page, is joined by a dog, and then a cow and, finally, an elephant. The basic plot is simple and, from this point on, the child is free to focus on the list of characters that join the cat on the mat. One of the most well-known stories that demonstrates this technique is *Chicken Little (The Sky is Falling)*.

Chicken Little is walking in the woods one day when suddenly, as he innocently passes under a tree, an acorn falls and hits him on the head. The little chick is frightened and cries out: "Oh no, the sky is falling! I have to run and tell the king!" Chicken Little runs to the castle and on the way meets a Hen. The Hen is on its way to the forest to hunt for tasty worms for breakfast, but Chicken Little calls out: "Hey Hen! Don't go into the forest. I was just in there and the sky fell on my head. Come with me to tell the king, he must be told." The Hen joins Chicken Little. And so both of them set out, and on the way they meet a Rooster on its way to the forest to find tasty seeds for breakfast. "No, Rooster", cries the Hen, "Don't go into the forest, the sky is falling. Come with us to tell the king, he must be told."

The Rooster joins them, and on the way they meet Mother Goose on her way to the forest to find tasty blueberries for breakfast. "No, no, Mother Goose," cries the Rooster, "Don't go into the forest, the sky is falling. Come with us to tell the king." Mother Goose joins the three, and all four set out to tell the king. Chicken Little, Hen, Rooster and Mother Goose walk down the path leading to the king's castle...

Unlike classic plot structure where plot development is characterized by twists and turns or a complicated story line, in an *accumulating plot*, it is extremely easy for very young children to predict the rest of the storyline, giving them a sense of control of the language and plot, which is so important to them at this stage of their lives.

Recurring patterns – recurring patterns are small content patterns that constitute part of a story. The child encounters the familiar pattern that he can identify and predict over and over again throughout the story. An excellent example is the recurring pattern in Goldilocks and the Three Bears:

The recurring pattern is Large – Medium – Small, an

identical pattern used to describe the items in the bears' home:

- Three porridge bowls: Large – Medium – Small
- Three chairs: Large – Medium – Small
- Three beds: Large – Medium – Small

Recurring patterns appear in children's stories in various forms – sometimes as a recurring object, sometimes as an identical sentence repeated by the hero, and at other times as a fixed method the hero uses to escape from situations, and more.

NARRATIVE METERS

Meters are typically used by writers of songs or poems, and less often in writing stories or scripts. A meter is a fixed rhythmic beat on which words of a song or recitation "sit." A text written according to a meter is based on fixed intervals of time, as if to the sound of an invisible, monotonous metronome, thus creating a recurring rhythmic meter that is not necessarily related to content or rhyme. The child identifies this internal beat, which helps him or her repeat the words of the song or poem and take control of the content. "T'was the night before Christmas, when all through the house, Not a creature was stirring, not even a mouse; the stockings were hung by the chimney with care, In hopes that St. Nicholas soon would be there" (*T'was the night before Christmas* by Clement Clarke Moore). The meter stems from the rhythmic structure of the text. Sometimes it is also used in literary texts and even in scripts.

In *The Cat in the Hat* (by Dr. Seuss), the meter plays a central role in the children's enjoyment of the text and helps control the content of the plot:

And then something went BUMP!
How that bump made us jump!
We looked!
Then we saw him step in on the mat!
We looked!
And we saw him!
The Cat in the Hat!

Like the other techniques described above, the meter also gives a child a sense of success in deciphering and controlling content, because even if he or she has not yet achieved total mastery, identification of the rhythmic pattern offers partial positive reinforcement.

Most of the examples presented above originate in children's literature, since these writing techniques are used primarily by writers of literary content for children. Yet understanding these literary *prediction boosting* methods provide scriptwriters with tools that enable them to create a script that is more appropriate for the needs of the viewing child, and principles such as accumulation, recurring patterns, rhymes, or rhythmic meters are easily integrated into dialogues in any script written for very young children.

The use of literary *prediction boosting* techniques is less accepted in scriptwriting, yet the use of these techniques in scripts for young children aged two to three years significantly increases their enjoyment of any program they watch. The reason, as already explained, is that young viewers enjoy plot structures that are much simpler than plots for their older friends aged four and up.

Below is an example of a screenplay which makes use of heavy foreshadowing. This screenplay is aimed at a particularly young audience.

IT'S COLD OUTSIDE

Lilly peeks out her bedroom window. The wail of a strong wind and the sounds of children playing outside are heard. Pieces of clothing — a sweater, a coat, a hat, and gloves — are hanging on the clotheshorse in Lilly's room.

<u>**Narrator:**</u>
Nelly and Jeff, Lilly's friends, are playing outside. Lilly wants to join them.

Lilly runs out the door. A gust of wind is heard and Lilly comes back immediately.

<u>**Lilly:**</u>
Oh no... Lilly is very cold outside.

<u>**Narrator:**</u>
Lilly says that she is "very cold outside." What could Lilly do so as not to be so cold?

Lilly looks at the clotheshorse and ponders. The camera focuses on the sweater.

<u>**Lilly:**</u>
Lilly knows. Lilly will wear a sweater and then Lilly won't be so cold.
Lilly puts on the sweater and goes to the door again. She opens it and returns immediately.

<u>**Lilly:**</u>
Aaah... Lilly is still very cold.

Narrator:

Hmm... It seems that Lilly is still cold. What else can Lilly do so as not to be so cold?

Lilly looks at the clotheshorse and ponders. This time, the camera focuses on the coat.

Lilly:

Lilly knows. Lilly will wear the coat and then Lilly won't be so cold.

Lilly puts on the coat and goes to the door. She opens it and again returns immediately.

Narrator:

Hmm... Lilly is wearing a sweater and a coat, but she is still cold. What else can Lilly do so as not to be so cold?

Lilly looks at the clotheshorse and ponders. This time, the camera focuses on the hat.

Lilly:

Lilly knows, Lilly knows!! Lilly will wear a hat and then Lilly won't be so cold.

Lilly puts on the hat, goes to the door, opens it, and returns again.

Lilly:

Ugh... Lilly is still a little cold outside.

Narrator:

Hmm... Lilly is wearing a sweater, a coat, and a hat, but she is still cold. What else can Lilly do so as not to be so cold?

Lilly looks at the clotheshorse and ponders. This time, the camera focuses on the gloves.

Lilly:
Lilly knows, Lilly knows! Lilly will wear her gloves and then Lilly won't be so cold.

Lilly puts on gloves (the last items on the clotheshorse) and walks out the door. The sounds of Jeff and Nelly happily greeting her are heard coming from the outside.

Narrator:
Lilly put on a sweater, a coat, a hat, and gloves. And now she is not cold anymore.

It is fair to suppose that the current reader had no trouble identifying the elements that were foreshadowed in the above screenplay. The principles of accumulation, rhythm, and repeating pattern were very plainly realized in this screenplay. The watching child is made aware of all the items of Milly's clothing on the clotheshorse and can easily predict her actions.

Below is another example of a screenplay for very young children. This screenplay also clearly makes use of foreshadowing. As this screenplay is aimed at three-year-old children and older, its writing is more sophisticated.

As opposed to the screenplay, *It's Cold Outside*, this screenplay makes use of classic plot structure, in a similar way to the screenplay, *Measuring Love,* which was presented earlier in the chapter. The action is motivated by an event, which includes several turning points that move the plot forward. With that as a given, here the screenplay uses textual structures which answer the need of the very young viewer for foreshadowing.

WE DON'T WANT TO GO TO SLEEP

From left to right: Zoom, Peewee, and Milly

Evening... a farmyard. The series' heroes are three chicks. (Feathered, yellow, chick-shaped body puppets. The puppets are operated by actors who wear them as body suits.) The three chicks, Zoom, Peewee and Milly, are sitting in the sitting corner in the yard and are finishing their dinner, which they are eating from colorful bowls. In the background, the sky is dark. It is sunset. Milly wipes her beak with a napkin. She gets up and stretches, yawns widely, and says:

<u>Milly:</u>
Okay, that was delicious. I'm tired, so goodnight everyone. I think I'll go to sleep. **(She turns to go.)**

<u>Peewee:</u> **(He also gets up and yawns.)**
Yes, I'm really tired already, too. I'll also go to bed.

(The two go toward their sleeping baskets.)

Zoom: **(sniggers out loud)**
What?! You're already going to bed?

Milly:
Yes, we're tired.

Peewee:
Very tired.

Zoom:
What? Really? You're such babies. *I'm* not tired at all!

Milly: **(stunned)**
You're not tired? It can't be. It's late, and we're always tired at this time of the evening.

Zoom: **(with exaggerated confidence)**
Yes it can be. It can be with ice cream on top.

Milly:
Not even a little tired?

Zoom:
Not even a little.

Peewee:
I'm sure you're a little tired because I saw you yawn before. Three times!

Zoom:

Oh... no... I just opened and closed my beak three times!
I'm not tired at all! I'm so not tired that I think I'll go to sleep
very, very late tonight.

Milly:

Very, very late?!

Zoom:

Very, very late!

Peewee: (with admiration)

Wow... to go to bed late...

Milly: (going back to the sitting corner)

Okay, I can also go to sleep very, very late if I like.

Zoom:

What are you talking about? You always fall asleep
before everyone else.

Milly:

So what? I can stay awake a long time, if I want.

Zoom:

No way!

Milly:

Yes way! And you know what, tonight I'm also going to
go to sleep very, very late!

Milly fixes Zoom with a competitive look.

Zoom:
Really? Let's see you do that.

Milly:
Let's see you do that.

Peewee:
What? So now both of you are going to go to sleep very, very late?

Zoom and Milly:
Yes!

Peewee: (also sits down)
Really? Then I also want to go to bed very, very late, like you both.

Zoom gets up and stretches. Peewee sits down again and all three are quiet. Milly and Zoom look at each other with great suspense, as in a *staring competition* and nervously drum with their fingers on the tabletop.

Peewee:
Ah, going to bed very, very late is really tiring.

Peewee stares at Milly and Zoom. Slowly his head nods, and he rests it on the table and falls asleep. Milly and Zoom don't give up; they keep staring at each other and drumming with their fingers.

Zoom:
You look a little tired to me, Milly.

Milly:
Tired? Me? No way. Don't make me laugh. If anything, you look a little tired to me.

Zoom:
Me? I couldn't be more not tired! I'm so not tired that I think I'll look at this picture book. Or maybe I'll look at two picture books.

Zoom takes a book and starts to look at it.

Milly:
Oh yeah? So I'll also look at a book. Maybe I'll even look at three!

Milly takes a book and starts to look at it. Milly and Zoom tensely turn the pages and keep checking to see if the other one has fallen asleep. Zoom flips pages fast and then slams his book shut, waking Peewee in the process.

Zoom:
Okay. I finished looking at my first book.

Peewee: (bleary)
What? What happened?
Zoom:
Everything's fine, Peewee. You can go back to sleep.

Peewee: (tired)
To sleep? I wasn't asleep. I was awake the whole ti....me.

Peewee goes back to sleep in the middle of his sentence. Milly closes and puts down her book.

Milly:

Okay. I finished looking at three books. (**She gets up**)
*Seems to me like it's very, very late now, so good night
everyone.* (**She turns to go but sees that Zoom is still
sitting. She turns to Zoom.**)
What? You're not going to bed?

**Zoom picks up a new book and raises it so that it
hides his eyes.**

Zoom:

*No! I'm not going to bed, because I'm not at all, at all
tired yet!*

Milly: (astonished)

*You're not tired yet? That can't be because it's very, very
late now, and we've never gone to bed so late.*

Zoom:

But I'm not tired at all! I'm not even a little tired!

Milly:

Not even a little tired?

Zoom:

Not even a little tired.

**Milly sits down again, and she also takes a new book
from the pile and raises it so that it hides her eyes.**

Milly: (exaggeratedly)

Okay, so I'm also not even a little tired!

Silence. Milly and Zoom are hidden behind their books. It looks like they're reading but their heads are slowly nodding. The books come down slowly, and they both fall deeply asleep. Now all three chicks are sleeping. Suddenly, Peewee wakes up in alarm and wakes the others up when he shouts.

<u>**Peewee:**</u> **(jumping up)**
It's the big balloon! It's chasing us! We have to run faster. **(He sits back down)**

<u>**Milly:**</u> **(waking up and arranging herself in dismay)**
What? What? I was awake the whole time!

<u>**Zoom:**</u> **(also arranges himself quickly)**
Yes... me too!

<u>**Peewee:**</u> **(talking in his sleep and returning to his dreams)**
Mmmm... Milly... be careful of the balloons.

<u>**Milly:**</u>
What funny dreams that Peewee has.

Peewee keeps sleeping, and Milly and Zoom look at one another.

<u>**Zoom:**</u> **(tiredly)**
This is... easy peasy!

<u>**Milly:**</u> **(wiped out)**
What's easy?

Zoom:
Not sleeping!

Milly: (with great effort)
Oh! Right! It's so easy that I think tomorrow, I won't sleep all night.

Zoom:
Yeah? I think that I won't go to sleep all night tomorrow night ... or the next night... maybe even all week.

Zoom's head starts nodding but he catches himself immediately. Then Milly's head begins to nod, but she also wakes up immediately and sits straight up in her chair. In the end, she breaks and rests her head on her arm, on the table.

Milly: (in a conciliatory voice)
Zoom.

Zoom:
What?

Milly:
Are you really not tired?

Zoom:
Why, are you tired?

Milly: (in great fatigue)
No. I just thought that... I thought that maybe instead of today... maybe tomorrow we won't sleep all night?

Zoom: (leaping at the opportunity)

Tomorrow? Yes. Great idea! I was thinking exactly the same thing. It's really an excellent idea, Milly!

Milly:

So that's settled: Tomorrow we won't sleep all night!

Zoom:

Right! Tonight we'll go to bed, and tomorrow we won't sleep all night!

Milly: (getting up and yawning)

So are you coming to bed?

Zoom: (getting up)

Yes.

(They go slowly. Zoom turns around to call Peewee.)

Peewee. Peewee, come to bed.

Peewee: (completely asleep)

Yes, I'm coming. One minute... in just a little bit.

Milly and Zoom go to their sleeping baskets slowly and with great fatigue, yawning all the while. Then Mr. Mortimer the Mole comes out of his molehill and clears his throat. (Mortimer is an adult mole who serves as an understanding adult character who is the responsible one in the series.)

Mr. Mortimer

Peewee: (waking up in dismay)
Huh? What? Who is that?

Mr. Mortimer:
Peewee?! What are you doing here at this very late hour?
Why didn't you go to sleep?

Peewee: (rubbing his eyes)
Um... we, we had a competition tonight to see who could
go to bed the latest.

Mr. Mortimer:
Oh, in that case, I think you have a winner!
Peewee:
Really? Who?

Mr. Mortimer:
It looks like you, Peewee. And I suggest that you go to
sleep right now in your basket. Good night, Peewee.

Mr. Mortimer goes back to his burrow, and Peewee looks around.

<u>**Peewee:**</u> **(tired)**
Milly? Zoom? Did you see? I won? Yes! I won! Woo hoo!

He sinks down again and falls asleep.

In the screenplay, *We Don't Want to Go to Sleep*, it is possible to discern quite a few writing principles which respond to the needs of the young viewer — for example, the principle of accumulation and repetition (as in, "very very late..." etc.). There is no doubt, however, that this screenplay was aimed at older kids than those who would be entertained by *It's Cold Outside* and a little younger than those for whom *Measuring Love* was written. *Measuring Love* was written in classic form and is aimed at the oldest population of children who can still be called very young, in other words, for kids four years old and older.

In summary, it is important to understand and relate to the significant differences in comprehension skills of the different groups in our population of viewers and, similarly, to be aware of and tailor the level of the script — the language, plot design, and writing principles — to those populations.

.

WRITING COMEDY
FOR CHILDREN

Browsing comedy-related bookshelves indicates a wide selection of guides for novice comedy writers: ***The Principles of Comic Writing***, ***Writing Comedy in Stages***, ***The Comic Writer's Toolbox***, ***Comedy Writing Techniques***, and so on. Yet, I have never heard of a comedian who acquired his comic skills at a college or by reading a comedy writing manual. A peek into the biographies of the greatest comics shows that none of them started making people laugh after reading a textbook. They all started making others laugh when they were children. They made their families laugh, they made their kindergarten friends laugh, they continued making their school friends laugh, until eventually their natural preoccupation with comedy became a way of life.

Each and every famous comedian or comedy writer (and there are many) lays out his own personal comedy experience.

Woody Allen, in Melvin Helitzer's book, ***Comedy***, is quoted as suggesting a potential comedy writer should watch dozens of comedies. Comedy writing reminds him of playing jazz music, because he thinks jazz is just as impossible to learn. Of course, you have to learn to play the instrument well, but in order to really know how to play jazz music, you must continuously listen to jazz music until the moment comes when you realize you can do it. Milt Josefsberg (one of the head writers of ***All in the Family***), in his book, ***Comedy Writing for Television and Hollywood***, argues that a childish nature is a prerequisite for comedy writing. Most of the comedy writers he knows (including himself) are childish, and their childlike view of the world stands at the center of their comic writing. Robert McKee, on the other hand, argues that a comedy writer ought to be a bitter and angry person because angry people, by nature, have a cynical worldview and tend to be tougher critics of society, which is reflected in their comic writing.

I believe they all have a point. There are those whose excessive immaturity moves them to create comedies and those who use comedy to sublimate aggression and anger, but it is clear that the vast majority of those involved with comedy react first and foremost to an inner voice that calls on them to want to make everyone laugh, at all times, and at all costs.

Despite the different ways comedy writers view the act of comic writing, it is likely that, in the end, they see more things alike than differently, and that most of them share common views of the creative process and of the way they think comic writing should be treated.

Most of them tend to mention Sigmund Freud's view of humor and Henri Bergson's famous essay, "**Laughter**," which was written in 1901 and is still considered a milestone of comedy theory by those involved in the field. According to Freud, humor is almost an existential necessity. He describes humor as humanity's best defense mechanism — a psychological mechanism that helps people deal with tough situations, fears, and prohibitions.

I have not looked at the minute biographical details of famous comedians in order to examine whether their lives actually included those unfortunate childhood events that pushed them into the tickling hands of humor. However, even those who were not natural-born comedians can understand the way comic mechanisms work and the way to create them, or at least to avoid standing in their way. One thing is universally acknowledged: when something is funny, the viewer laughs!

THE COMIC PERSPECTIVE

There are some who argue that children laugh between 300 and 400 times a day, while adults laugh between fifteen and one hundred times a day. It seems that adults think laughter is not serious enough, which is certainly not true. But to understand what makes children laugh, we must first understand the mechanics of humor in general.

Miriam Ruth (***Literature for Early Childhood***) defines humor as "[The] spiritual ability of people; to discover, to express, to understand or appreciate strange elements to the point of absurdity." This means that to be able to laugh at something, a person must be able to understand and appreciate the strange element in the situation he is presented with. Of course, there is no way to understand the different and the absurd unless the person already knows the *normal* or the *acceptable*. Since *the humorous* is a distorted version of the acceptable and the serious, it's clear that only those who know the way things operate in the real world could understand and identify the funny or the ridiculous, which are at the center of the comic situation.

Henri Bergson (a French philosopher who is considered by many to be the father of the theory of laughter, 1859-1941) defines comedy as "the gap between our expectations about the way the world works and the way it works in a comic situation." Thanks to this gap, we enjoy watching a policeman who is intently examining a train set displayed at a toy store window, while behind him a procession of cars drive through a red light. In this case, humor is found in the gap between our expectations from the policeman and the way he is supposed to act in this situation, and his actual actions.

A DISTORTED REALITY
AND EXAGGERATION

A good illustration of the comic perspective is the distorting mirrors in a carnival funhouse. You never see in those mirrors anything that does not exist in reality around us. Everything reflected in the mirrors exists in reality, but the act of distorting the reality is what makes us laugh. We are able to see ourselves in the distorting mirrors as short, fat, deformed, or ugly, but we can never be offended because we know we are perfectly fine, and it is just the distorted mirror that reflects that version of ourselves. The same is true for the world of comedy. Even if the reality in a comedy reflects our patterns of behavior, we can identify it without getting hurt, knowing that after all, this is only a comic *reflection* of ourselves that allows us to see what is funny, and it is clear to us beyond doubt that even when the comedy deals with issues we hold dear, we are fine, and it is just this particular perspective that makes us funny.

Comic potential, then, always exists in close proximity to a realistic world and on account of realism. Comic reality stretches everyday reality, distorts it, and takes it as far as it can. Comic reality can exist in every space, if we are able to stretch it and exaggerate it to the point of humorous. In comedy, the characters act in an exaggerated way, and the events they go through are similarly exaggerated.

If you examine TV comedy shows, for example, you will find that in most cases, their secret is a familiar world that has been distorted to the point of being funny. Family sitcoms, for example (like *All in the Family*, *Married With Children*, or *The Fresh Prince of Bel-Air*), take the familiar nuclear family — a common family hierarchy, in which parents provide and care for the children, who are in turn obedient or rebellious — and turn upside down the familiar and expected reality and set of values to create a new, comic reality.

BETWEEN DRAMA AND COMEDY

There are seemingly no differences between content that feeds drama and that which feeds comedy. Basically, the same content can certainly feed both genres, with one small difference: the writer's perspective. Writing from a dramatic perspective is aimed mainly at emotions and is written with the goal of arousing feelings such as love, hate, frustration, hope, despair, happiness, disappointment, anger, jealousy, or embarrassment, whereas writing from a comic perspective actually aims first at reason and logic, and through that, at emotions. In order to understand drama, of course one must have certain levels of knowledge and experience, but understanding comedy is truly a logical operation that calls for prior knowledge and a multi-stage processing operation.

Take, for example, the joke about a large sign hanging off the bars of an ostrich's cage at a zoo. The sign reads, "Warning! Do not scare the ostrich — the floor of the cage is made of concrete." To enjoy this joke, the listener must recognize the conventional wisdom that says when an ostrich is scared it usually buries its head in the sand, and then imagine the frightened ostrich trying to bury its head in the concrete floor of the cage.

Or the joke about the rabbit that meets a running, naked turtle. "What happened to you?" asks the rabbit. "Never mind," answers the turtle. "I couldn't take it anymore. I ran away from home." Here, too, the listener must perform an intellectual act to understand the double phonetic connotation — to understand that a homeless turtle seems naked and then to enjoy the contextual absurdity inherent in the phrase, "I ran away from home," since normally one runs away from home because of someone else: the parents, the partner, and so on. So, the turtle cannot have a reason to "run away from home."

Comedy transfers reality via a prism, which calls for a processing operation done by the listener in order to understand the underlying idea behind a joke. Only after this understanding is done, enjoyment can follow. For instance, we can examine the following jokes, aimed primarily at children.

- A mother says to her son, "Let's see if you know arithmetic. If you had three pieces of candy and your brother asked for one, how many pieces of candy would you end up having?"
  "Three!" the boy replies confidently.

- What does the cat say when it sees a giraffe for the first time?
  "Meow…"

- A kid tells his mother, "The teacher was mad at me today for something I didn't even do."
  "What was it?" asks his mother.
  "Homework," he answers.

- How does an elephant get out of water? Wet.
  How do two elephants get out of water? One after the other.

-

In order to understand the first joke, a child must have a basic knowledge of arithmetic. The child must know that three minus one equals two and not three and that the child's answer to his mother is not derived by mathematical calculation but is due to the relationship he has with his brother.

The second joke is a nonsensical one, based on the obvious. The listener is supposed to enjoy the fact that contrary to expectations, the cat that saw a giraffe for the first time did not say, "Wow, it's so tall," or "What is this animal?" The child who hears this joke actually knows that cats cannot say anything other than "Meow," but the way the joke is being told distracts the child's awareness of this information, and so the cat's "Meow" sounds funny and surprising.

The third joke requires knowledge of language. The child should enjoy the fact that usage of the phrase "something I didn't do," when it involves the teacher-student relationship, usually means something negative, while in this instance it is the not-doing that is negative and therefore amusing.

Understanding jokes, then, requires from the listener the ability to perform analysis based on a certain level of previous knowledge. Incidentally, this is the reason comedies, unlike dramas, are less suitable for wide audiences and are usually targeted at a smaller number of viewers.

Another example can be found in children's humor based on one of their primary worlds of knowledge: the language. Jokes that use this knowledge make children laugh, but of course a French- or a Spanish-speaking child cannot enjoy jokes based on a double-meaning of words in English.

For example:

Q: How does a skunk call home?

A: On his smellular phone.

Q: Why was six afraid of seven?

A: Because seven eight nine!

Q: Where does a cat go when he loses his tail?

A: The retail shop.

A movie that uses these types of jokes reduces its target audience to that of children who speak the language, which is the basis for the joke. When it comes to comedies aimed at adults, this phenomenon is even more striking, even if language is not the main obstacle. Comedies aimed at adults usually deal with social phenomena like stupidity, ignorance, hypocrisy, prudery, indifference, corruption, and so on. For the comic distortion to be effective, the comedy focuses on a specific world. Consequently, if a movie makes fun of military life (*Catch 22*), disaster movies (*Airplane!*), or science fiction (*Spaceballs*), viewers will not be able to enjoy it unless they know the social phenomenon or the milieu the film deals with.

LAUGHTER / HENRI BERGSON

French philosopher, Henri Bergson, analyzed the phenomenon of laughter in his essay, "**Laughter**," which was written over a century ago, and as mentioned, is considered a formative essay in the field of comedy — a milestone, according to most of those involved with the genre.

It is important to understand that Bergson's essay had

been written about twenty years before the birth of cinema and the first comedies screened there, and about forty years before the start of television broadcasting. This essay was written at a time when no one could have predicted the enormous volume electronic media would take in our lives, let alone the importance comedies would have within these media (sitcoms, variety shows, sketch comedies, and so on). Naturally, then, Bergson deals with humor manifested mainly in books, in plays, in caricatures, or in social situations typical for the time of the essay.

And yet, I think it makes sense to present some of the conclusions Bergson reached in his essay, and which I find to be still relevant today. Whereas contemporary scholars of comedy examine the subject from a practical perspective, Bergson traces the roots of comedy and examines comedy from a primary perspective that first and foremost appreciates the phenomenon of human laughter. Presenting the highlights of his writing can assist any writer in the stage of developing comic situations and characters that are also addressed to children.

Bergson counts three basic conditions for the creation of comedy in general:

- Comedy always deals with people. An image of a landscape, for example, cannot amuse us unless it has something to do with humanity.
- Comedy cannot coexist with emotions because when a person identifies emotionally with the subject of the comedy, he will not laugh. No one will laugh at a person slipping and falling after stepping on a banana peel if he identifies with the person's pain.
- Laughter is primarily social. A person does not tend to laugh when there is no one else around.

In addition to these three basic conditions, Bergson

presents a series of comic principles he divides into three situations:

- Comic situations that stem from a comical shape or posture of a character
- Comedy stemming from a certain situation or text
- Comedy stemming from the character's nature

COMIC SITUATIONS STEMMING FROM A CHARACTER'S COMICAL SHAPE OR POSTURE

The Comedy of Shape — What is a comical expression? Bergson ponders this question of what makes a funny expression and what is the difference between funny and ugly. After all, sometimes people laugh at others' defects. He reaches the conclusion that defects that can be mimicked by full able-bodied people have comical potential. He examines this idea through facial expressions and reaches the conclusion that a facial distortion by a person, in a way that shows him as if he is holding an emotional or a physical state for a long time (as in crying, or in distorting the face in an expression that looks like an endless whistle), has comic potential. The same is true when it comes to distorting the entire body or a part of it. Holding a facial expression or a movement is a form of human caricature. Actor Rowan Atkinson, who plays the character of Mr. Bean, makes wide use of external comic distortion. He sometimes walks with his belly extended when he imitates the walk of a very fat man, and when he wants to appear like a little child, he walks with his legs bent. He often uses extreme expression, and he certainly can make people laugh that way.

The Comedy of Mechanics — Bergson argues that human actions that seem like simple mechanical movements are usually funny. A person repeatedly performing a physical action that makes no sense and only produces a type of mechanical action should be funny — for example, a character walking, then every once in a while lifting a leg or an arm in a peculiar way, then walking a few more steps normally, and then going back to the strange mechanical movement. Also, a group of characters who supposedly have nothing in common and "randomly" perform seemingly similar movements: let's say they all suddenly scratch themselves, or they all bend down to tie their shoes at the same moment. Bergson argues that a fixed mechanical action, or a mechanical action of a group of people acting at the same time, will be amusing because it reminds us of a group of marionettes supposedly connected to each other by invisible wires. This essentially clownish principle is used in many comedies based on physical humor, like Laurel and Hardy movies, where the two "coincidentally" decide to make the same movement at the exact same moment (like scratching their heads), or a similar object each of them is holding "coincidentally" slides off their hands at the same moment... and not to mention their mutual "coincidental" attempt to pass through a door at the same time.

Comedies Stemming from the Contrast between the Physical World and the Spiritual World — A physical event that bursts the bubble of spirituality is usually funny. A speaker who sneezes in the middle of an important speech, a queen forced to take her tight shoes off while on a royal visit, a soldier who must loosen his belt slightly while standing at attention, and so on. Bergson defines these as situations in which "the body takes over the soul." This is like the comedy that arises from the contrast between the physical Sancho Panza and his master, the spiritual Don Quixote. Bergson defines it as the gap between the body and the soul. This type of humor is actually used extensively in comic situations targeted to children, where they tend to burst the bubble of the "important" adult through a physical event, thus diminishing his importance in the eyes of the child. For example, an adult school or kindergarten teacher who runs away from a tiny mouse, an angry neighbor who scolds children but is afraid of a small dog, or an adult who teaches children to act politely but cannot control himself when he sees a tempting cream cake, running in front of everyone else to grab himself a slice.

Comedies Stemming from a Person Masquerading as an Inanimate Object — With this definition, Bergson talks about those situations in which a human adopts the behavior of an object. For example, a man is shot out of a cannon at the circus and adopts the behavior of a human bullet; a man stands on all fours covered by a tablecloth, pretending to be a table; or a hypnotized man believes he is a tree or a bush and tries to act accordingly. Clowns often use this type of humor. The humor comes from the clown's attempt to dress like an object and from the reaction of another clown, who supposedly believes he is facing a table, and so he places a vase with flowers on his friend's back.

COMEDY STEMMING FROM A CERTAIN SITUATION OR TEXT

Repetition — When discussing the principle of repetition, Bergson relates to a phenomenon reminiscent of a rolling snowball. The more a snow ball rolls, the faster it gets, which increases the comedy. The phenomenon of repetition can be expressed in one repetitive event (similar to the comic term *running gag*). As an example, Bergson describes a situation in which a person is walking down the street and by chance meets an old acquaintance he would have rather not met. There is nothing funny about this meeting, but if throughout the day, the person will go to many other places, and in each place he will meet that same acquaintance *by chance*, at a certain point these "chance" meetings will begin to be funny. In addition, Bergson recognizes the phenomenon of repetition in more complex structures, which stand at the base of comic plays, where the series of chance meetings may turn into a chain of mishaps that lead from one to the next. The series of mishaps becomes the center of the comic plot. For example, a guest enters a lounge and accidentally bumps into a woman. She then drops the cup of tea she had been holding. The tea on the floor causes another guest to slip and hit the window. A plant that was placed on the window seal now falls down to the street, where it lands exactly on a policeman's head. The policeman calls the entire police force to the scene, and so on. The repetition mechanism is a comic instrument capable of moving many plots.

Order Reversal — Bergson also treats the principle of *order reversal* as the force behind many comic situations. The principle of reversing order is manifested when characters' roles or audience expectations are reversed: a robber chasing a cop, a kid scolding an adult who did something bad, a defendant lecturing morality to a judge, and so on. Reversing plot order also belongs to this category — meaning a plot with a structure reversed from what is expected. For example, a plot in which one character lays a trap to catch another, and eventually the character that laid the trap is the one caught in the trap. According to this principle, a chaser becomes the chased, a scam artist will be scammed by his intended victim, and so on.

Interlocking Plots — This principle applies to a large number of plots that intertwine to create a single plot in a play (main plot, secondary subplot, and so on) — plots that seemingly have nothing in common content-wise, other than *a single comic common denominator* they all share. This common denominator moves each of the plots in a different way, meaning, a type of a comedy of errors, where each of the characters sees only a part of the truth and acts accordingly. Bergson treats writing comedy with interlocking plots as a highly challenging task, because every now and then the subplots and the characters within them are supposed to intersect, and even at that time, each of the characters will only see their truths. This principle has many expressions, since some of the plots are supposedly not comical at all, and the intersection is what creates the comedy. On the other hand, some of the subplots are comical by themselves. The sum of all the subplots is bigger than its parts. Some of the subplots are mixed with others, when the characters in one subplot hide information from those in another, and sometimes it is "by accident" that certain information is withdrawn from a character in one of the subplots, and this lack of information creates the desired comic developments.

The Comedy of Words — Bergson examines the *comedy of words* in relation to two aspects: the aspect of content and the aspect of presentation. Bergson finds that comic content comes in two basic forms: comic-dramatic content and comic-witty content. These two forms of content fit with two different forms of presentation: comic-dramatic presentation and comic-witty presentation. Comic-dramatic presentation stems mostly from emotions and is mostly dependent on the quality of the actor's performance because comic-dramatic content is a result of a situation. For example, when someone says or does things he did not mean to say or do, but did anyway because he was being distracted, or any other comic situation that is a part of a comic event. Comic-witty content depends mainly on words. Wit is achieved using various means of language, such as taking an issue and enlarging the idea behind it to the point of absurdity, or saying something in a tone entirely in opposition to the original intent behind the words. A witty presentation has more to do with the mind. It always reflects the personality of the performing actor, so the actor's personality has an important role. Bergson compares a witty presenter to a poet reading his poems, since in this case the importance of the poet does not fall behind the importance of the poem he is reciting.

COMEDY STEMMING FROM
THE CHARACTER'S NATURE

Comic Nature — The concept of a *character's comic nature* is the essence of comedy, and the concepts Bergson terms (repetition, order reversal, mechanics, and so on) are merely tools used by the comic characters on their comic journeys. The character's nature has an important role in drama as well, but unlike its storytelling dramatic sibling, the comic character, by definition, is there to provide for the essential needs of the viewer. People, by their nature, are motivated by drives, needs, wants, wishes, attractions, and desires that the rules of society and morality prevent them from fulfilling. Since we cannot do everything we want to do, the comic character does it for us. The role of comedy is to free the spirit! Comedy allows us to take revenge on the society that limits us. It tears the veil off our daily social norms. Laughter, according to Bergson, is highly reminiscent of our excrements, which if left inside the body, would poison and kill us. In the same way, comedy clears our souls from the poison of thinking. Modesty, for example, which many people tend to feel pride in having, is driven to a large extent by our fear to be seen as ridiculous by others. For this reason, comedy usually deals with these traits that make people laugh at others: avarice, arrogance, hypocrisy, laziness, obsessive punctuality, gluttony, cowardice, or stupidity. The main axis that drives a character in a drama is the motive. Comic characters have motives too, but comedy is usually expressed by the way the comic character deals with its motives. This is usually expressed through comic gestures like posture, way of speaking, movement, and other physical gestures that reveal the main character's soul, and gives the viewer tools with which to understand the character's hidden goals, so to speak. Many comedians call this comic device, *transparency*. That is, acting that allows the viewer to see, in a manner of speaking, the comic character's wheels of thought. It's important to remember that an essential condition for the existence of a comic character is its lack of awareness to its own traits — traits only the viewer or other characters are supposed to see. Bergson adds that successful comic character traits are those that can be easily translated into clear physical gestures, which can be identified and imitated by others. Comic acting is the development of this type of behavioral gestures that would seemingly cause the viewers to see a giant label of the character's traits glued to its back.

HUMOR IN CHILDREN'S WRITING

Funny television shows or movies targeted at adults are defined as comedies. Of course, comedies for adults are divided into types of comedies, such as slapstick comedies, satires, or parodies, or into genres like sitcoms, sketch shows, black humor comedies, romantic comedies, and so on.

Unlike comedies targeted at adults, children shows have no comic genres, and in general, there is no such thing as a comic show or movie for children. Comedy in children's shows and movies is usually merely a tool meant to increase the child's enjoyment of the content. Children's TV shows and movies are usually designed to deliver an educational message, and the plot is usually scattered with comic characters or situations which make it more fun for the children, thus helping to deliver the messages.

Although comedy is used as a tool when writing for children, comic writing for children is not essentially different from comic writing for adults. Both require first and foremost, a *comic tune-up*, and indeed, the gap between comic writing for children and comic writing for adults lies in the particular nature of this target audience. With comic writing not intended for children, the writer turns, as stated, to an audience of his peers, and is not required to view the content from an angle different from his own. With comic writing for children, the writer is required to be acquainted not only with the worlds of content beloved so much by children (like princes, monsters, witches, fairies, superheroes, and so on), but also with the suitable types of humor that speak to their hearts.

Surprisingly, it has become clear to me that most of Bergson's principles can be applied to all audiences, regardless of age. If we take, for example, a part of Bergson's definition of the comic character, and change the word *humans* with the word *children*, we will discover that his principles seem to have been aimed from the beginning at humor meant for children:

Children, *by their nature, are driven by impulses, needs, lusts, attractions, and wishes that the laws of society prevent* *them from achieving. Since **the child** is prevented from doing as he pleases, the comic character does it for him. The role of comedy is to free the **child's** soul. Comedy allows the **child** to use it to take revenge on the society that limits him.*

This passage, of course, refers to the humor that helps us, as humans, deal with the hardships we face, by responding to the various limitations imposed on us daily by morality, law, and society.

However, this definition seems even more suitable for comic characters starring in shows or movies meant for children, since the child, even more than the adult, feels trapped in a stock of prohibitions and restrictions imposed by the adult world. The child often thinks of adults as a nation of giants that prohibits loud noise, mess, revelry, using swear words, and many other "wonderful" and forbidden things. Indeed, children's favorite comic characters are those that act with ignorance, in opposition to the known behavioral set of rules. The dumber these characters are, or the more insolent they are, the more they will provide enjoyment and laughter for the children, since the character, *unlike him* (the child), does not really know or understand the rules of the world and the way it operates, which causes the character to frequently make mistakes, be confused, get to the wrong places, do forbidden things, be unable to accomplish the simplest tasks, and accidentally anger the authoritative characters around it.

These characters work for the viewer on two levels: One — they give the child a sense of superiority. The child's world of knowledge comes out victorious when compared to the character's foolishness. Two — the child feels comforted by the character's situation, which reminds him somewhat of the lack of control he feels when it comes to certain subjects. However, even this comic perspective is different and constantly changing with age. Things that make a three-year-old laugh will not necessarily make a six-year-old or a nine-year-old laugh. The way of viewing the world changes with every age, and comic understanding is determined by this view of the world. There is a clear link between types of humor, on the one hand, and the viewing child's cognitive developmental stage and his ability to understand and enjoy humor with different levels of complexity, on the other hand.

Since children's knowledge and life experience are fairly limited in their first years, their range of comic understanding is obviously equally as limited. Certainly they can identify, understand, and laugh at many comic situations, but only as long as the basis for these comic situations is found in the short life-experience they have acquired and in the pool of knowledge they already have.

The book ***Children's Humor*** by Paul McGhee and Antony J. Chapman, describes an interesting experiment that looks into the comic comprehension of very young children (two-year-olds and younger). As part of this experiment, a mechanical toy was given to a few groups of under-two-year-old children. The children learned to play and to operate the toy for some time.

Later, the toy was replaced by a toy that looked identical but had one difference: when switched on, the toy acted differently. Indeed, it turned out that when the children operated the new toy, with its new and different function, they began to laugh. The long time the original toy was in their possession allowed the children to gain confidence in their knowledge about the way to operate the toy, and in addition, they already had a vast toy-related life experience that taught them toys did not change their characters. And yet, when the familiar toy suddenly acted differently than expected, the children found it to be hilarious.

The ability to identify and to enjoy basic humorous situations depends, as stated, on the viewer's prior knowledge. A joke that illuminates how essential prior knowledge is to the understanding of jokes (and which children find very amusing) tells about a tortoise and a hare that competed to see who would reach the ocean first. The joke teller asks, "Guess who won?" And the answer is, "The tortoise, because it had a car." The child is already supposed to know the tortoise could not have a car and that driving a car is an action that is borrowed from the human world.

Humor, as noted, serves humans when it comes to dealing with things that scare them or are difficult for them to endure, and there is no difference when it comes to children. Their initial fears come from their motoric functions: getting up, walking, and so on. Therefore, a child who has just learned to walk will very much enjoy laughing and making those around him laugh about this issue. For example, he will put himself in a position of near-falling (like a baby who is still unable to walk) and enjoy the apparent sounds of fear his parents will make when viewing this "dangerous stunt" he has made, and the laughs he will earn when they understand he threw himself on the floor on purpose.

Later on, when children are two to three years old, enjoyment and laughter come mainly from the sounds of words and their rhythm. They enjoy rhyming words, like skies / flies / eyes / spies / and fries, and making connections between the words, even if the results are nonsensical, and especially if they are asked to take part in making up the rhymes. At the same time, as mentioned, the children begin to enjoy jokes that revolve around swear words and images of various excretions: poop, pee, farts, burps, runny noses, and so on, and its use is generally forbidden (*toilet humor*, as it is generally known).

When children begin to develop language fluency, the nonsensical humor becomes more sophisticated. The previous jumble of words that rhymed but were otherwise meaningless makes way for literal humor based on puns, word games, and rhyming sentences with double meanings, which make the listener laugh due to the intended lack of logic within them: "I ate a fruit that tasted like a boot," or "I was feeling content so I flew in a tent."

Their awareness of the errors hiding within those nonsensical sentences makes them doubly happy, when they understand the hidden absurdities in the silly rhymes they have just heard. And so, gradually, they enjoy a more verbally sophisticated type of humor, founded on the knowledge base and the associations they have already acquired.

When children are in their preschool stage, they aspire mainly to control language and the knowledge they have acquired in various fields. By then, they enjoy a relatively diverse verbal humor, which is also based on their vocabulary. Humor has an important role in the process of social development. It connects between the joke teller and his audience, and just like it is for adults, it operates as a shield in social relationships and helps children build confidence in themselves and in their knowledge, as well as gain attention, acceptance, and approval by their surrounding peers.

At this stage, they truly enjoy humor that presents adults as confused and wrong. Children have a great time identifying adults' mistakes, since the ability to recognize those helps the children feel like they truly know the laws of this world. Korney Chukovsky's **Right and Wrong** describes a father who draws for his daughter. In his drawings, the father confuses facts and fiction. He draws, for example, an uncle sitting in a doghouse while a dog is sitting at the table, or a house floating on the ocean waves while a boat is placed on land. Throughout the book, the girl scolds her father and corrects him. This type of humor, which

deliberately confuses the natural order of things and creates ridiculous imagery in the kids' minds, is one of their favorite types of books. This type of humor also develops the comic skills of the kids themselves, motivating them to create their own funny stories and have fun with the rules of their newly acquired world of knowledge.

However, it's important to remember this is not exact science, since in quite a few cases, children at a very young age were observed and found to have enjoyed a relatively complex humor for their age, and vice versa, namely older children who did not laugh at all when they heard jokes that were supposedly suitable for their cognitive developmental level.

In their book, ***Children Humor***, McGhee and Chapman divide the fields of children's humor into several groups:

Absurd and Nonsense Humor — This type of humor appeals to a very young audience through its silly absurd jokes, like "I ate a fruit / That tasted like a boot," or "I saw a dog / Dancing with a frog," and so on, or through more sophisticated absurd and nonsensical jokes that appeal to an older audience, like "Why is the tomato red and round? Because if it were yellow and long, it would have been a banana." Or "If a sheep gets into the water with its front legs, how would it get out of the water? With wet feet."

Naughty Jokes — Jokes that deal with issues revolving around poop, pee, farts, and burps, are all beloved by children, because they legitimize the so-called breaking of daily taboos.

Failure Humor — This one, which is mostly visual humor, describes slips and slides, or it presents authority figures or other regular adults who fail at knowledge or at actions (this type of humor gives the child a jubilant sense of superiority).

Linguistic Errors — This type of humor is based on linguistic errors, like a person asking for noodle soup and the waiter gives him a doodle soup, later giving him a poodle soup, and so on (words that sound the same).

Humor Based on the Element of Surprise — This is based on the gap between expectations and realization. The surprise-based humor is expressed initially at a very young age with the *peekaboo* jokes, where something is hidden, and for a short time, the child thinks it has disappeared, or jokes like *Little Piggy*, where the last grandchild without oatmeal suddenly gets tickled. With older children, this type of humor is expressed through unexpected events, such as a child calling his dog that has gone missing behind the bushes, but in its place a turtle comes out; or someone who thinks he put sugar in his drink but finds out it was salt.

The Humor of Mismatch — This type of humor is expressed mostly through content that jumbles the ways of the world, like an adult sleeping in a baby's bed, a train sailing in the ocean, a cat barking, and so on.

COMIC CHARACTERS

By reviewing Bergson's principles, we discover that many of them are applied in plots and in comic characters children enjoy and that we all know very well. For example:

A character with a shape that's opposed to its character: a person with an angry face, who is timid and kind (The

Comedy of Shape); an amusing robot that looks like a human, but every now and then, freezes in the middle of a movement or a sentence (The Comedy of Mechanics); a character who used to be an animal or a tree before a magician turned him into a human (Comedy Based on a Human Masquerading as an Inanimate Object); or a kid trapped in an adult body (like in the movie *Big*) and vice versa.

The comic characters in most children's stories demonstrate Henri Bergson's principles. A young lion cub who has never tasted strawberries, decides one day that strawberries are his favorite food, and that he is unwilling to taste anything else. Unfortunately, strawberries do not grow in the woods where he lives, and his mother the lioness does not know what to do. Her cute little boy refuses to touch the soup, the rice, or the fries, and all day demands to eat only strawberries. One day, kids with strawberries arrive at the forest. The kids, who planned to have a picnic there, get scared when they see the innocent lion cub and run away, which finally gives the lion the opportunity to taste the coveted strawberries, only to realize then that the strawberries he wanted so much do not taste good to him, and that he probably does not even like strawberries.

This is, of course, a children's story with a moral. This is not a comedy, and yet the figure of the lion makes children laugh, and that's because of the gap between the characteristics they expect to find in the lion, which are usually strong, frightening, and dangerous, and the figure of the lion in this story: a whiney, spoiled baby. (Bergson's principal of Order Reversal).

Another children's story that makes children laugh a lot is *Caps for Sale* (by Esphyr Slobodkina). It tells the story of a cap peddler who wears his merchandise on his head, meaning that on top of his cap, he wears a tall tower of caps for sale. One morning, after he is unable to sell even one cap, he decides to rest under a large tree. After a short nap, he wakes up to realize the enormous tower of caps that was on his head has disappeared. When he looks up toward the tree branches, he is astonished to see a smiling group of monkeys sitting on the tree branches, each wearing a cap. The peddler looks at the monkeys in anger, and the monkeys look back at him with anger. He waves his fists at them, and the monkeys in return wave their fists at him. He stamps his feet, and the monkeys imitate his stamping, and so on, and so on, until finally the peddler angrily throws his own cap on the ground. Of course, the monkeys do the same, and that's how the peddler gets his hats back. If we examine the comic incident that takes place between the peddler and the monkeys, we will be able to identify quite a few Bergsonian principles, such as the principle of mechanics, reflected by the behavior of the monkeys, and the principle of repetition, expressed through the repetitive imitation. In addition, children may see the monkeys as a group of kids who rebels against the angry adult, thus allowing the children, according to Bergson, to take revenge through comedy at the society that restricts them.

If we continue to examine more funny stories, like the famous children's book, ***The Story of Ferdinand*** (by Munro Leaf), we will find that Bergson's principles of comedy apply here as well.

Ferdinand is a young Spanish Bull, destined from an early age to become a fighting bull in the arena. However, unlike his other bull friends, Ferdinand prefers to just sit around and breathe in the scent of the flowers. The other bulls love to head-butt each other, to jump, to run around, and to be heroes, but none of that interests Ferdinand. Of course, one day he is taken into the arena to fight the brave bullfighters, and there, to everyone's surprise, he sits quietly at the center of the arena and begins to smell the flowers on the hats of the ladies in the stands. The bullfighters try in vain to make him stand up and fight, but Ferdinand just sits and smells the flowers, breathing in, and breathing in, and breathing in.

Ferdinand is undoubtedly a *comic character* as well, according to Henri Bergson's definition, and what happens in the ring is inherently comical since there is a clear reversal of order.

If we take the process of creation of comical situations for children's scripts from a practical level and examine their process of creation in a simplistic way, we will find that coming up with a comical situation is seemingly not that complicated. We come up with a character with a funny face, doing funny things, saying funny things, and experiencing funny events.

Of course, there is no need for all the parameters to come true at the same time. It's definitely fine to implement together only one or two parameters. But in order to understand the process of creation of comic content for children's shows, we shall try to examine the four parameters and see how they come to be expressed in practice.

Funny-looking characters are, of course, familiar to us all at their fundamental shape, reflected in the characters of the classic clown. The clown makes us laugh because of his exaggerated appearance: gigantic shoes, large pants with (usually square) excessive cloths hole-covers, a massive red nose, and hair with unrealistic colors, like green, red, or blue (with or without bald hair). Even the objects the clown uses have unrealistic measurements: a giant comb the clown uses every once in a while, or a tiny suitcase into which the clown will try to put large objects.

Creating comic characters for children's shows involves a great deal of the principle of clownish exaggeration, characters like the confused man who wears different shoes on each foot, with his pants inside out, with the pockets sticking out, with the undershirt over the shirt instead of underneath, and wearing a sock on his head instead of a hat. Obviously, the confused man mistakes forward and backward, right and left, and up and down. With the *exaggerated mirror* approach, the character's inner traits are expressed externally with exaggeration, like in the character of a superhero that was featured on a children's TV show I had created. Here was a superhero with no superpowers. Like other superheroes, he indeed could use his cape to fly anywhere a person was in trouble, but when he actually got there, his ability to help was no different from that of normal kids, so he had to get children around him to help. In addition, the crises for which he was usually called were mostly trivial: a flower that needed water, a cat that was lost and unable to get back home, a kid who couldn't remember what his mother asked him to bring from the grocery store, and so on. The superhero's appearance was exaggerated, of course: a colorful cape on his shoulders, shiny boots, tight pants, and a mask. These clothes were designed as a mixed caricature of many known superheroes blended together.

Another character with a clear comic appearance is the One Man Band, with the giant drum hanging off his back, the cymbals between his knees, the harmonica stuck to his mouth, and the guitar in his hands. Obviously children will only consider visually comic characters as funny if they understand what is behind their appearance. They need to understand that a man who wears a sock on his head instead of a hat, and an undershirt on top of his shirt instead of underneath, is dressed like that because he is confused, and that the reason our superhero wears shabby and eclectic clothes is that he is not really a superhero but only likes to think of himself as such. They must also understand that the reason the One Man Band is funny is that it's one man who is essentially a whole group of musicians, which usually includes three or four musicians.

Funny actions are actually verbal jokes that have been translated into actions: planting a bar of chocolate in the ground with the hope that a chocolate tree would grow there in the future; pushing a stroller in the playground with a baby plant (a sprout) in the stroller instead of a real baby; or a man sitting on a watermelon as if it is an egg that will hatch. This list of actions and similar ones will amuse children only if they can recognize the absurdities within them.

Saying funny things, of course, means the things the character is saying are funny, assuming these things take into account the types of humor children love. Starting from nonsensical humor through understated handling of issues the child thinks of as taboo (noise, rowdiness, challenging of adults, and so on), and texts that allow the child to enjoy his ability to understand lies behind what is being said: Why is the main character wrong when he suggests his friend use a rope to tie his bike to a cloud? Why shouldn't a cat be left alone to guard a bowl of milk? Or why can't the comb eat, even though it has teeth?

Behind the funny things that may happen to the main character lie hidden all the children's favorite slapstick jokes: cream cakes that land on the face, slipping, falling, unexpected meeting, and all the other things that stand at the basis of the Failure Humor. This type of humor is suitable for the stage they are in. The have only recently learned to walk, and now they are at the stage of refining their motor skills. Visual humor that involves slipping and falling or humor that shows authority figures or other adults who fail at doing things, gives, as mentioned, a feeling of control and superiority that is very enjoyable to children.

Another comedy category which can be a frame for the comic characters, and which children favor, is the tall tale. The tall tale, like the comic character, is enjoyable to children because it gives them a sense of superiority over the story teller. Here, though, exists a double emotion: on the one hand, the child's enjoyment from having no doubt that the tale he's being told is illogical and cannot happen in real life, and on the other hand, the joy of being drawn into a fictional world filled with inventions. It is important to understand that making up tall tales is fundamentally different from just making up lies, since the tall tale is not a lie but an absurd exaggeration. When it comes to tales and to listeners of tales, there is a kind of an unwritten agreement between the story teller and his audience, in which everyone knows and agrees that this is a type of fun meant for enjoyment.

In a story-telling contest, described in one of the *Wise Men of Chelm* stories, five Chelm residents sit around on the eve of Passover and compete to see who can tell the most wondrous thing that has ever happened to them. The first talks about his uncle's giant apple tree. The apples on this tree were so big, that one time it took him three years to finish just three apples. The second tells of a giant turkey his father brought for the Passover meal. They cooked half of the turkey, and the amount of meat was enough for a meal of fifty people! The other half was left in the yard, where it continued to lay eggs. The third stands up and tells of his relative who lives in a city and built such a tall house that if anyone wanted to reach the top floor on Passover, they had to begin climbing the stairs on Purim!

The five Chelm residents who tell their wondrous tales do not doubt each other's tales. Each story always ends with full agreement from the five, who say, "Yes... there are wonders in the universe."

Enjoyment of tall tales depends on the teller's ability to believe his own stories and to tell them without batting an eyelid, as if these things really happened.

The world of tall tales always revolves around a small nucleus of realism. For example, a teller of tall tales is holding a small apple, weaving together an entire story around it. Apparently, only a few hours earlier, the man had eaten an apple, which was, of course, a different apple from the one he's holding. While he was eating that apple, he accidently swallowed one seed. At first he did not feel a thing, but then the seed began to sprout inside his stomach and suddenly out of his belly started growing a beautiful enormous apple tree, filled with juicy red apples. Of course, the storyteller could not walk around with such a tree growing out of his belly. Luckily for him, all this happened right next to the house of a famous surgeon, who brought down a surgery bed to the street and removed the giant tree from the man's belly. With that, everything returned to normal, aside from the wonderful apple he is holding in his hands as proof and souvenir from the apple tree that used to grow out of his belly. As mentioned, the joy children get out of listening to this storyteller's stories comes from their knowledge that he is making up the stories and also from their readiness to sail with him into the world of tall tales and imagination.

A kindergarten-teacher-turned-children's-writer recounts the stormy winter day she left the kindergarten to bring something inside but got delayed on her way back. When she returned to the kindergarten, the children asked, "Where were you? Why didn't you get back here?" and she amusingly answered, "I tried to return, but the wind was so strong that it lifted me high up into the sky, far, far away from the kindergarten, above other streets and places, and I yelled, 'Hey... get me down... please... I have to get back to the kindergarten,' until finally a few good people threw a rope at me and managed to get me down from the sky."

"The children were in shock for a moment," tells the writer, but then they all began to laugh, telling her, "Tell us again how the wind blew you up into the sky." and then they began to make up similar tales by themselves, about how the wind blew them away into unexpected places.

It is important to understand that while Bergson's theory of laughter, Freud's theory of humor, or any of the other "laughter theories" can help us understand the phenomenon of laughter, from my experience I know that it is impossible to use them to make up even one good joke. I have already mentioned at the start of the chapter that dealing with comedy is usually a way of life. Most of those involved with comedy have developed through the years a comic perspective of the world. Still, it is, of course, possible to use these theories. Another way of developing this kind of perspective is, among others, a daily use of the question, "What would have happened if..." What would have happened if the dog that has just run in front of me had asked me, "Excuse me, where can I find a darned tree in this neighborhood?" What would have happened if Tom had caught Jerry for once? What would have happened if Goldilocks didn't like porridge?

THE COMIC ACTOR

Needless to say, the choice of actor for the comic role in a children's movie is of crucial importance when it comes to the quality of the comedy being produced. The actor's comic abilities are a prerequisite for the creation of the comic situation.

I have already mentioned that for the viewer, the comic enjoyment is usually formed as a reaction to intellectual activity that happens in his mind. In order to enjoy the comedy, the viewer is supposed to understand something that he hasn't been told explicitly, and through the comic abilities of the actor, the viewer can understand this thing that hasn't been mentioned explicitly in the text. Let's assume, for example, that a comic character is attending a dinner party, and the hostess is serving her a cake. She finds the cake tastes awful, but out of politeness, this character praises the outstanding taste of the cake. As viewers, of course, we enjoy identifying the true feelings of the character. The actor's ability to say the cake is excellent while at the same time letting us understand through acting that she's tormented by every bite is seen as a comic ability. This ability, in addition to comic timing, are the two qualities that distinguish between actors with comic abilities and those without. Comic timing refers to the ability to present comic text at the right time, or the rhythm of the actor's movement while making a comic gesture in a way that makes the audience laugh. Some define comic timing as the ability to create a short pause before serving the punch line, in a way that allows the audience to anticipate the punch line and enjoy it more.

As creators of comic content, we must also fully understand the secrets of comic acting, so we could create amusing content that gives the performing actor ideal conditions for comic acting.

I mentioned at the beginning of the chapter that children usually laugh between 300 and 400 times a day. It is our job, as creators, to give them high-quality reasons to do so.

A VERY SHORT
(BUT EXTREMELY IMPORTANT)
INTRODUCTION TO
THE NEXT THREE
CHAPTERS

The essential difference between writing for children and for adults is based, as I explained, on three fundamental principles. These principles are basic to writing for children and distinguish this type of writing from any other.

1. Understanding the cognitive capabilities of young children — writers for young children must be familiar with the cognitive limitations of the various target audiences and understand the changes that occur in their comprehension skills at different ages.

2. Content as the fulfillment of a need — Content, of course, responds to a need. Therefore, the writer must be sure that the content she writes actually responds to a real need in the target audience.

3. Familiarity with the content repertoire that children love — writers for children must be familiar with the worlds of content that children love: princes, monsters, witches, fairies, superheroes and other characters and worlds that enchant this target audience.

Mastery of these three principles lies at the very foundation of writing for children. This foundation, combined with writing skills and know-how relating to scriptwriting, will no doubt yield excellent content for children. However, it is important to note that these principles are not of equal importance in the writing process. Understanding the cognitive capabilities and didactic needs of these audiences is of great importance during the writing process. However, it is clear that their importance is not equal to that of the creative skills required of writers for these audiences.

The ability to love and identify with content that children love, to invent plots that capture their hearts, devise magical worlds, make them laugh, to surprise and fascinate children — these are essential skills for writers of content for young children. The other two principles have their own place of honor, but remember that they originate from the academic fields of education and psychology and are primarily work tools used in the writer's creative process. They are tools that help writers to adjust the content they create to children's levels of knowledge and understanding.

However, the ability to identify, to create a repertoire of content that addresses the child's needs, and to expand the boundaries of the imagination — all these stem from the writer's creativity and require originality and imagination that can connect with and speak to the worlds of imagination of the target audiences.

In no way should this be perceived as detracting from the importance of understanding a child's cognitive abilities or educational needs, yet real writing talent is undoubtedly expressed mainly in the process of inventing these magical worlds of content, which evoke the very essence of writing for children. Since the fields of cognition and education are, as said, only tools in the process of writing for children, we will try to provide these tools in the course of the next two chapters, so as to make them available for the central creative process.

COGNITIVE
ABILITIES
IN EARLY
CHILDHOOD

Cognitive development in early childhood involves a range of comprehension skills. The aptitude that children develop in the course of early childhood includes skills in a wide variety of fields. These include cognitive, motor, social, and other capabilities, though as writers of children's content, we will ostensibly focus on understanding the cognitive skills of our viewers, since these include most of the competence required for understanding, assimilating, learning and, principally, enjoying the content that they watch on screen. If so, how does one create content for the screen that is suited to the cognitive abilities of children in their early childhood years? In particular, this question refers to content that is created specifically for children, since it is almost certain that any child, in any age group, can find something interesting in random sounds that come from the screen, or in tempting visuals that are broadcast from it, such as moving patches of color, landscapes, people, animals, and, of course, movies meant for an older audience.

As writers of content for children, it is important for us to be aware of the cognitive developmental stages of our viewers.

Since a great number of developmental theories rely heavily on the research of **Jean Piaget**, (1896—1980), I think it appropriate to open with a presentation of the principles of his research.

Piaget established that in the course of cognitive development, a child examines and researches her environment incessantly. She asks questions, identifies problems, and searches for solutions. Piaget found many parallels between the physiological and the cognitive development of children and points out these parallels. In the same way that a child labors without end to acquire control over her body's motor functions and to succeed in rolling over, crawling, sitting, standing, and walking, so too does she labor without end to make connections and to understand her environment.

Piaget divides the process of child development into four basic stages:

COGNITIVE DEVELOPMENT, (SOLBERG 1996)

1. Sensorimotor Stage — Birth to eighteen months

In this stage of life, the child learns her immediate surroundings through her senses in the here and now. She uses her senses of touch, smell, taste, and hearing. Toward the end of this stage, she also manages to grasp the concept of *object permanence*. That is, at the age of about eighteen months, she finally manages to understand that objects exist even when they are hidden from sight. We all know the famous game of Peekaboo in which a parent hides his face from the child with the aid of a pillow, for example, and then peeks out and hides again. FROM the child's point of view, when the parent is hidden, the parent simply does not exist, and he comes back into existence at the moment of his reappearance.

2. Preoperational Stage — eighteen months to seven years

In this stage of life, the child still thinks in concrete terms (that is, she still apprehends the world through her five senses) and in egocentric terms, in which she sees reality from her point of view only. Not only does she not see things from a different point of view, she does not even understand that other points of view exist. During this stage, the child sees herself as the center of the universe. She believes that all phenomena around her exist and are aimed for her benefit only. (Solberg 1996; Tiano 2005) Animism is another form of thinking that defines the preoperational stage. At this stage, children have trouble differentiating between animate beings, plants, and inanimate objects. From their perspective, inanimate objects are alive with will and desire. As a result of this belief, children tend to anthropomorphize objects, and of course, plants and animals, too. (Katznelson 2005) As such, their capacity for self-criticism is limited.

Piaget divides the preoperational stage into two stages:

1. Preoperational Stage — two to four years

In this stage, the child begins to use symbols in three areas: language, imaginative play, and delayed impersonation, that is, impersonation of something that is not present in real time. At this stage, the child still finds it hard to understand the difference between the external appearance of a thing and the thing itself. For example, the child will not be able to correctly identify a close family member in a police officer's or firefighter's uniform given that she is used to seeing the relative in regular clothing.

2. Intuitive Stage — four to seven years

In this stage, the child is developing the ability to classify objects according to their characteristics (size, color, shape, etc.), though only according to one criterion at a time (for example, by color or shape but not both at the same time).

3. Operational Stage — seven to eleven years

In this stage, the child's grasp is expanding. Her thinking begins to be more internalized, and she is beginning to use logical operations such as conservation, categorization, and classification. She is also beginning to understand the concept of reversibility (the understanding that objects can be changed and then revert back to their original state) and to develop flexible thinking. At this point, the child understands that a ball of modeling clay, which has been rolled into a sausage shape, for example, can revert to its previous shape and dimensions.

4. Formal Operations Stage — eleven years and older

In this stage, systematic, objective, and abstract thinking is developing. The child can see things from a different point of view. She can be self-critical and can come to conclusions and make estimations.

With that, many education professionals with whom I have spoken say that, from their experience in the field, they can witness to the fact that most children are ahead of the developmental stages as they appear in books. Nevertheless, sticking to the formally accepted developmental stages ensures that we satisfy the demands of the lowest common denominator.

Therefore, before we begin to write content for very young children, I will examine classic television content, which has already proven itself, and try to figure out which cognitive skills a child needs in order to understand the segment.

Language skills - It is clear that the child must have semantic abilities and control of a vocabulary that includes the words spoken during the program, and similarly, to understand the hidden meanings of those words from both the semantic and the social point of view.

Awareness of the *rules of conversation* - The child must be aware of unwritten rules of conversation, without which she is at risk of missing the real meaning of the words spoken in the film. This refers to things such as tone of speech or expression which can sometimes radically change the meaning of words.

Understanding of abstract concepts - The child must comprehend basic abstract concepts such as *over, under, inside, behind, next to, a lot, a little, big, small, love, sorrow,* etc.

The ability to process information and to draw conclusions - The child must be able to process information that she sees on the screen. She must also be able to predict an outcome before it occurs (for example, what will happen to the plate when it falls) and to understand the order of basic functions or events, like the seasons of the year, etc.

Understanding the language of film - The child must have an initial intuitive grasp of the rules of the language of film. He must be aware of the connotations behind the occasional filming of the protagonist in extreme close-up and then in wide shot and understand the plot elements which proceed from these frame sequences.

Plot memory - Of course, *memory* here does not refer to the child's ability to remember. As we know, children are born with excellent memory — they have simply not yet developed memory strategies. In other words, they have not developed habits or memory templates such as those belonging to adults who know what is important to remember and what isn't.

In the course of a film or a play, there are plot situations which demand that the viewer remember a particular event. This event then serves as the basis for understanding a subsequent plot change. Therefore, sometimes, in order to understand a particular series of events, our young viewer must remember and connect many details which motivate the specific plot events and twists that she is watching.

It follows that in order to cope with basic plots, the child must have acquired these six basic skills. Clearly, these six skills are only a small part of the full complement of skills that a child must acquire at this stage of her life; she must also develop mastery in the various social fields, in the development of motor skills, and more. Given that the goal of this book is to train writers to write children's content, we will focus on the six skills mentioned above at this stage. Understanding them will help us produce better content for children.

To help us see how these theoretical skills become concrete in the real world, let us try to examine them in the defined plot of a television segment. For the sake of this example, I chose a well-known segment that became a classic of children's programming a long time ago. The segment is "Ernie and Bert at the Beach" from *Sesame Street* produced by the Sesame Workshop.

In this segment, Ernie is having fun digging a big pit in the sand when, suddenly, he discovers that Bert, his good friend, has disappeared. Ernie is extremely worried and enlists the aid of the famous detective, Sherlock Hemlock. The detective follows clues in the hopes of decoding them as a means to solving Bert's mysterious disappearance. And indeed, after only a few moments, Hemlock solves the puzzle. It turns out that when Ernie dug his pit in the sand, he inadvertently threw a lot of sand on his friend Bert and buried him. When the frightened Ernie hears the solution to the puzzle, he goes to his friend Bert's aid immediately and begins to dig in the sand on his left in order to extract Bert from under the huge pile of sand... except that during his rescue operation, he throws a lot of sand, this time to his right, which is to say to where Hemlock the detective is standing, and this time mistakenly buries Sherlock Hemlock, the famed detective.

ERNIE BURIES BERT AT THE BEACH

Ernie:

Oh wow! Look at this nice and deep hole I have been digging. Hey Bert? Isn't this a nice hole here? Hey Bert! Bert! Hey, what happened to my friend Bert? He was here just a moment ago. Where did he go? Here's his beach hat but he's gone. Oh no. My friend Bert is lost. How am I going to find him?

Sherlock:

Egad! Sherlock Hemlock here, the world's greatest detective. What seems to be the trouble?

Ernie:

Oh! My friend Bert, he is lost.

Sherlock:

Lost?

Ernie:

Yes. He was sitting right here. See? And I was digging a hole in the sand like this. See? Digging away. All of a sudden I looked around and my friend Bert is gone and all that's left of him is his beach hat sitting right here on this pile of sand.

Sherlock:

Never fear.

Ernie:

Ah! It's terrible.

Sherlock:

I, Sherlock Hemlock, will find out what happened to Bert by examining the clues.

Ernie:

What clues?

Sherlock:

Well, first we have Bert's hat.

Ernie:

That's the only clue.

Sherlock:

Hmm! Wrong. We also have this pile of sand here.

Ernie:

But that's just an ordinary pile of sand.

Sherlock:

Wrong again. It's a talking pile of sand.

Suddenly, the hat moves and begins to emit sounds.

<u>**Ernie:**</u>
Hey how about that?

<u>**Sherlock**</u>:
*Hah! I have it. I have solved the mystery of
"What happened to Bert."*

Sounds continue to be emitted from the hat.

<u>**Ernie**</u>:
What happened, Mr. Hemlock?

<u>**Sherlock**</u>:
*Well, as you were digging this hole, you threw the sand on
top of your friend Bert, who was sitting here,
and you buried him up to his beach hat.*

<u>**Ernie:**</u>
Oh no! That means that Bert is in this pile of sand!

<u>**Sherlock:**</u>
Correct.

<u>**Ernie**</u>:
Oh! Excuse me, Mr. Hemlock.

<u>**Sherlock:**</u>
Sure.

<u>**Ernie:**</u>
*Bert! It's you. Let me dig you out of there. I will get you out
Bert, old buddy.*

Bert:
Ah! Why did you do this?

Ernie:
There we go. Are you all right, Bert?

Bert:
Yeah. Thanks Ernie... Pffff... Thanks a lot, Ern

Ernie:
Oh! Don't thank me, thank Mr. Hemlock here.

Bert:
Who?

Ernie:
Mr. Hemlock here.

Bert:
Where?

Ernie:
Mr. Hemlock? Oh no!

Bert:
Ernie!

Ernie starts digging out Mr. Hemlock, whom he buried while digging Bert out.

Bert:
Ernie, watch where you are throwing that sand!

The above segment is entertaining for viewers of almost all ages, but it is important to remember that is was written first and foremost for very young viewers who were defined from the beginning as its main target audience.

So let us again examine the six cognitive skills defined above with the goal of understanding how the young viewer needs then in order to cope with this kind of television content.

A. LANGUAGE SKILLS

In order to understand words like *sea, sand, hat, spade, pit, to dig,* etc., the viewing child must understand a great number of words, including the words that are mentioned in the segment — words to do with fun at the beach. He has to have fully mastered the semantic and syntactic meaning behind these words, that is, he has to understand them in their different forms: singular, plural, past, present, etc.

The core of human communication is language. The process of language acquisition begins with the emission of sounds. At the beginning, these are sounds without meaning. Afterwards, this turns into the mimicking of sounds and tones, then the forming of solitary words, and lastly, complete sentences.

Many researchers claim that a child's word bank is acquired long before she develops the ability to express the words therein. A wonderful example of this came to me through my son at the time that he was beginning to utter his first words, at the age of about a year and a half. It was a winter's day, at the beginning of citrus fruit season, when the first oranges were appearing on the supermarket shelves. We had taken him to the supermarket and, suddenly, he pointed to the pyramid of oranges in the fruit aisle and cried out,

"Orange, orange, orange!" The only time that we had shown him this fruit was the year before, during the last citrus fruit season, when he did not know how to speak yet. But it turned out that the word had cemented itself in his brain back then, and after more than six months, when he was confronted with an orange again, he was able to refer to it by name.

Learning words is not an easy task for children. They are just like us; we have trouble understanding when one word ends and the next one begins when we first hear a foreign language. In the first stages of life, our speech sounds to them like a continuous mix of noises. Comprehension is made even more difficult by the fact that children, at the beginning of their development, don't understand what language is at all and clearly are not aware that language consists of words or sentences. As opposed to us, they have no previous knowledge of the basic laws upon which language any language rests. The first vowel sounds that they emit in their first experiments with language are instinctive sounds which do not yet try to simulate the sounds and patterns of the language in which they are developing. A proof that these initial sounds are instinctive and not mimetic can be found in research cited in the book, *Child Development: Its Nature And Course* (McGraw-Hill, 1992) where it is shown that children who are born deaf make exactly the same range of sounds that hearing children make at the beginning of their lives. Making these sounds is a purely instinctive act and has nothing to do with an attempt to mimic the sounds heard in the surrounding environment. Only when they reach about one year of age do children begin to try to mimic the sounds and words of the language around them, and they usually only begin to say their first clear words at around fifteen months of age. Several basic physical skills are prerequisite before a child can physically enunciate words.

Technical linguistic skills

Children must develop the technical ability to control mouth and lip movements in order to produce the sounds that the child indeed wants to produce. The child's ability to speak is dependent on the development of the muscles that control her tongue and on her increasing ability to control her vocal chords. She must also have cut her first teeth, since teeth have an important role in the child's ability to make the particular sounds which make up words.

The ability to identify words

Another important ability that a child must develop is the ability to hear — that is, the ability to listen, identify, and then copy a language's word sounds. The child learns to hear and identify an initial repertoire of words that she hears around her. She learns to understand their meaning and slowly learns to make use of them. Obviously, most of the first words children learn worldwide are those related to family: *mom, dad, grandma, grandpa*, etc. Later on, they usually learn to identify clothing items and then objects that are important to them, such as *pacifier (pacy), teddy, light, television,* etc. Children's vocabulary grows incrementally but at an astonishingly fast pace, and studies (*Child Development*, McGraw-Hill, 1992) show that the average vocabulary of a three-and-a-half-year-old child is about 1,222 words, whereas by the age of six, their vocabulary grows to include more than ten thousand words, and some say that the real number is much higher.

It is clear that in order to learn to speak, children first learn to identify single words from within the babble of language around them, and only afterwards do they learn to identify and understand the specific meaning of the words.

At this stage, children learn very quickly that every word has an opposite. For example, fat/thin, tall/short, funny/sad, etc. Therefore, starting from about three years of age, when children learn a new word, they immediately try to figure out its opposite too. From the child's point of view, a word whose opposite she doesn't know lacks meaning. This is almost certainly why children like stories and songs that focus on pairs of words and opposites so much. A good example of this is the song by Batya Ben Dor, *I Am Always Me*. As soon as a child discovers the principle of paired opposite words, she examines the principle incessantly, almost with every word she comes across. This sometimes leads the child to draw conclusions which adults are likely to find amusing, like the child who heard the phrase *running water* and wanted to know if there was such a thing as *sitting water*. This also serves to remind us of the enormous investigating task which children carry out all the time in their heads in the context of trying to figure out the world around them.

It is worth reminding ourselves again that the "amusing mistakes" that children make are negligible in relation to the enormous number of correct conclusions to which children come in the course of their development.

A child's vocabulary building process is, as previously mentioned, incremental. Children usually begin by learning nouns such as *table, chair, house, pacifier, horse,* etc., and then gradually, they move to verbs. Subsequently, they acquire the ability to use adjectives, and then very slowly and incrementally, they begin to understand basic syntactical rules like the use of basic prefixes or suffixes which change a word from singular to plural or from an adjective to an adverb. For example, the child who understood that a person who farms is a farmer, a person who works in the garden is a gardener, and a person who dances is a dancer, therefore came to the reasonable conclusion that a person who delivers letters is a *letterer*. (*From Two to Five*, Chukovsky 1963) There is no doubt that the child in question had well understood the principle that the suffix, *er*, denotes a profession — he simply was not aware of the exception to this rule.

In the next stage of speech evolution, the child understands the structure of a sentence. If, at the beginning of her speech development, she was content to use representative words to get what she wanted — for example, Pacy!, Cookie!, Down! — now she begins to understand the principle of sentences. At the beginning of the process of speech development, if a child wants a banana, she'll point and say, "Banana!" The next stage is when she adds the verb *wants* and says, "Want banana." Next, she will say almost a whole sentence, "I want banana," leading to the uttering of a whole sentence, "I want a banana."

As such, full mastery of language is a basic prerequisite necessary for the child to understand and enjoy dialogue among various figures on stage or screen. Kindergarten-aged children, from three to five years old, already have mastery over the nuances of language and understand speech well. A considered and measured use of slightly more complicated words can absolutely enrich the vocabulary of children, with the condition that their understanding of the overall plot is not dependent on their understanding of the particular *higher* words that the writer chose to use.

B. AWARENESS OF THE RULES OF CONVERSATION

Awareness of conversation rules is necessary in order to understand the following text, for example:

Sherlock: *I, Sherlock Hemlock, will find out what happened to Bert by examining the clues.*
Ernie: *What clues?*
Sherlock: *Well, first we have Bert's hat.*
Ernie: *That's the only clue.*
Sherlock: *Hmm! Wrong. We also have this pile of sand here.*
Ernie: *But that's just an ordinary pile of sand.*
Sherlock: *Wrong again. It's a talking pile of sand.*

A young child, who is not yet aware of the rules of conversation, understands things literally and is therefore not equipped to understand the hidden meaning of things such as, "This is a talking pile of sand," because, on a literal level, a talking pile of sand is a sand with a mouth that can say things. Sherlock is no doubt aware that there is no such thing and when he says, "a talking pile of sand," he is in fact hinting that something else is going on, something strange that needs investigating. Similarly to Hemlock, the viewing child is also supposed to understand this, and this understanding demands mastery of the rules of conversation, as these rules help us to understand things non-literally and differently from their apparent, literal meanings.

Language, on the most simple level of vocabulary, serves as an initial tool which the child needs in order to decode plot elements. Though it is a basic and important tool, it is not sufficient for the true understanding of plot — much more is needed.

Often, speech cannot be understood literally. In order to understand this, children must have a grasp of the rules of speech without which they will not understand what is really being said around them. It follows that in addition to learning phonics, morphology, semantics, and syntax, children must understand other things such as tone of speech and the ability to identify the social context in which a word or sentence is spoken.

Obviously, tone can completely change the meaning of a word or sentence. For example, when you ask someone to do something he doesn't want to do, he can clearly *say* "no" but can also indicate *no* in other ways. He can *verbally* agree to your request but *practically* not respond to it, in which case his negative reaction will not follow from his verbal utterance but from the sarcastic tone in which he responded, as in the following case:

You ask someone who has no intention of going to a party, "Are you going to the party?" and he answers sarcastically, "Of course." It is reasonable to surmise that the hidden meaning of his words is negative, despite the clear semantic indications of agreement. We can conclude that a heavily sarcastic utterance can be understood as opposite to its semantic meaning.

When a man traveling in a train asks his seatmate, "Excuse me, can you close the window," the semantic meaning of the words implies that the man is asking if his seatmate has the physical capacity to close a train window. However, given our mastery over the rules of conversation, we understand that in this situation, a question is not being asked but rather a request is being made. This is another example of the way words can acquire different meanings depending on their social context.

Children begin to internalize the rules of conversation

when they begin to understand that the way they speak with their friends is different from the way they speak with their parents or other adult family members, and that there are different rules when one speaks on the phone or with the kindergarten teacher, etc. For our young viewers, understanding the rules of conversation is almost a prerequisite for understanding dramatic situations since characters sometimes use and respond to a subtext in drama in which the real meaning of the situation is different from that of the semantics of the uttered words. A good dramatic situation is often conveyed via the intention of the speakers, not their words.

Of course, a child acquires mastery over the rules of conversation via her life experience. This is a given that we must take into account when creating content. We must understand that only at the age of about three and a half or four does a child begin to master the rules of conversation, and even then, her mastery is not complete. Therefore, we have to take into account that children often take things literally without understanding double meanings or layers of additional nuance which we intend to convey in the scenarios we write.

C: UNDERSTANDING OF ABSTRACT CONCEPTS

The segment, "Ernie Buries Bert at the Beach," includes a large number of abstract concepts. Words like *mystery, solution, worry, hint, mistake,* and *problem* are words that cannot be conceived through clearly identified objects, unlike the words *table, chair, window, hot, cold,* etc., which all represent objects or clear physical states. In order to understand abstract words, a child must be at an advanced stage of cognitive development.

An abstract concept is one that cannot be apprehended through any of the five senses. In other words, this refers to words that describe things that cannot be **seen, heard, touched, smelled** or **tasted.**

The ability to understand abstract concepts requires a child to be able to draw conclusions. In order to understand what is abstract, the child must make mental connections among several individual pieces of information and, through coming to conclusions based on the common element in all these pieces of information, comprehend the essence of the abstract concept in question. In most cases, children can only understand abstract concepts after they have made connections among a great number of individual pieces of information and have understood the phenomena that influence the information.

For example, only after having seen a car parked in a parking lot **under** the ground, a flower growing **under** a tree and a dog hiding **under** a table, and only after having made a mental connection between all these things, can a child understand the meaning of the word *under.* Abstract concepts, therefore, require the comprehension of different kinds of connections: comparisons (big/small), hierarchies (big/small), sorting (first/second, before/after), and similarly, heights, sizes, distances, quantities, and areas.

If you put your memory to use and recall early episodes of *Sesame Street*, you will be surprised to discover how much effort its creators put into helping children acquire concepts such as over/under, big/small, and near/far. In one segment, Elmo is seen sitting **on** a bench and then **under** it. In another segment, Kermit wonders whether to put his house plant **on** the table or **under** it, and in a third segment, Grover flies **over** a cloud and then **under** it.

The reason for the frequent repetition of segments like these in programs like *Sesame Street* is, of course, that at this age, children need as many examples as possible of the abstract concepts that they are supposed to acquire, given how difficult they are for the child to absorb. Therefore, only after being exposed to many under/over situations will children finally succeed in firmly planting these concepts in their minds and be able to use them correctly.

In the series, *Tweet Tweet,* written for a children's channel, one of the screenplays, "Hop," is written around the concept of *difficult things*. In general, the series centers around the adventures of three chicks who still live in the shells of the eggs from which they hatched. The eggs are located in a small and picturesque yard and each has a door and a window. In the episode under discussion, Zoom, the academic chick, is still sleeping while Peewee, the youngest and most active chick, is awake and looking for a playmate. Milly, the oldest chick, has gone to practice a dance that she has invented and has already warned Peewee, "Don't disturb me today! Unless something **very, very important** happens to you." Peewee was forced to agree — except that, to his distress, he doesn't really understand the concept of *important things*.

IMPORTANT THINGS

At the beginning of the episode, Peewee is wandering around the yard nervously after Milly has scolded him and told him not to bother him, except for *important things*. He wanders around by himself, trying to understand exactly what Milly meant when she said that he could only disturb her for *important things*.

<u>Peewee:</u> (to himself)
I can disturb Milly, but only for important things, only for important things! (**Pause**) *But... how will I know what is important? Hmm, I know. I'll ask Zoom.* (**He knocks hard on Zoom's door**) *Zoom!! Zoom!! Come out! Quick!*

Zoom, a sleeping hat on his head, wakes up panicked and confused and comes out of his egg.

<u>Zoom:</u>
What? What happened?! Peewee! What happened?

<u>Peewee:</u>
Milly told me that I'm allowed to disturb her but just for important things! And I need someone to explain to me what is important!

<u>Zoom:</u> (irritated)
What?? I can't believe that you woke me up for this! I thought that something had happened to you! I thought you needed help! (**He starts to return to his egg**) *Listen, Peewee, when I get up, you can ask me whatever you want, but now don't bother me.* (**He softens**) *Hmm, wait... maybe Milly is right.* (**To Peewee**) *Listen, Peewee, you can bother me, but only for **important things**, okay?*

<u>Peewee:</u>
Huh... important things again? But Zoom... what are important things?

<u>Zoom:</u>
Hmm... Important things are if... if... if... well, let's say something falls on your head! That's an important thing.

Zoom enters his eggshell and slams the door.

Peewee: (wandering around in the yard)
If something falls on my head?
But why would something fall on my head?

Suddenly, a leaf detaches itself from the tree and falls slowly and gently onto Peewee's head.

Peewee:
Huh? A leaf! A leaf fell on my head.! Right on my head.!
Wait, wait! This must be an important thing! Yes, this is a
very important thing!! Hooray! Something important has
happened to me! Now I can call Milly and Zoom. Milly!!
Zoom!! Milly!! Zoom!

Milly and Zoom run to him, panicked and out of breath.

Milly:
What happened?

Zoom:
Are you okay, Peewee?

Peewee: (innocently)
Of course! Everything's fine. How are you both?

Zoom and Milly don't understand.

Zoom:
So if everything's fine, why did you call us?

Peewee: (importantly)
Because something important happened to me.
A leaf fell on me... on my head!

Zoom:
So?

Peewee:
I mean something fell on my head... just like you explained to me, Zoom. So that was an important thing, right? A very important thing!

Milly:
Oh Peewee! We thought something bad had happened to you!

Peewee: (reassuringly)
Oh no... it was just a small leaf. Nothing bad happened to me at all.

Zoom:
Yes, and that's why we're annoyed!

Peewee:
You're annoyed because nothing bad happened to me at all?

Milly:
No, we're happy that nothing bad happened to you, but we asked you not to disturb us unless something important happens!

Peewee:
But it was an important thing! I asked Zoom to tell me what is an important thing, and he said that if something falls on my head, that's important.
And this leaf really fell right on my head!

As you see, in this segment, the writer took a phrase that is usually said in a particular social context, in which it has a particular meaning, and planted it in the mouth of Peewee the chick. In this way, he made it possible for his young viewers to learn the meaning of this abstract concept in a social context and also to enjoy the plot arising from Peewee's mistakes.

D. INFORMATION PROCESSING SKILLS AND THE ABILITY TO DRAW CONCLUSIONS

The ability to draw conclusions is central to the "Ernie Buries Bert at the Beach" screenplay which was introduced at the beginning of the chapter. Sherlock Hemlock, the celebrated detective, uncovers two clues that arouse his suspicion: a hat and a pile of talking sand. Based on these clues, he, and his young viewers, of course, are supposed to come to conclusions about where Bert went. The ability to come to conclusions is a skill that even children in later developmental stages must continue to acquire. To identify a process and understand where it is leading or will lead is not simple at all, but it is an ability without which very young children cannot cope with complicated plots such as the one shown here.

We've already related to the flood of questions young children ask, primarily to their parents in the process of their cognitive development:

- Why was I born a boy and not a girl?
- Why am I sick?
- How do the hands of a clock move?

- Where does rain come from?
- Why doesn't the sea get burned when the sun sets into it?

Research into the cognitive development of children shows that in infancy, babies understand their environment through their sense of touch. Concepts such as *warm, corrugated, prickly* and *soft* are only learned through physical contact with objects. Very quickly, though, children's curiosity grows and they begin to ask questions in an attempt to widen their knowledge base. Their need to acquire new language skills grows with their vocabulary. In parallel with their increasing mastery of language, that is from the age of about two years and on, children try to understand the world on a higher level and want to know:

- How do things work?
- Why do they happen?
- Do some things happen in a particular order?

Even in very early stages, children perceive events and phenomena around them, but only when they reach the kindergarten years do they try to find explanations for these things. Information processing skills and the ability to draw conclusions and understand processes are dependent on a host of prerequisite cognitive skills which they acquire and practice incessantly. An example of this can be seen in their unstoppable quest to identify clear principles and rules that govern the world around them. This, of course, is the stage at which they "invent" all the funny pearls of wisdom that keep adults amused. This arises because every time children run into a principle that is known to them, they check to see if it can also fit into other models. In their role as indefatigable detectives, they examine principles and models and identify logical contradictions when they happen upon them. Therefore, whenever children happen upon a situation which contradicts a model known to them, they will immediately announce this. For example, the child who heard his mother say, "Soon the winter will come" and immediately began to ask, "Really? Winter is coming? How is it coming? Does winter have legs?" Or the child who heard her father say, "I'm dying to see that movie" and asks immediately, "If you die, how will you see the movie?" Or the child who heard his mother say, "Only the devil knows where I got the strength" and responded, "Really? The devil knows stuff like that?"

The difficulties children have with concepts such as these arise from the fact that children understand the world through facts whereas adults have developed the understanding of allegory and symbolism, and allegorical speech depends on the grasping of the abstract. Idioms such as *you're getting on my nerves; get out of my face;* and *I lost my head;* or even the idea of *chocolate fingers;* are hard for very young children to understand at this stage of their development.

In addition to this, one of the critical skills that children must acquire in order to successfully process information and draw conclusions is the ability to sort and order objects and events.

A collection is a group of objects or events which have something in common or are similar in some way. The process of drawing conclusions usually follows the occurrence of several individual events, similar or connected in some way, which lead the child to make a deduction. Similar to the process which leads to the comprehension of abstract concepts, in order to build a picture of events that lead to a conclusion in our minds, we rely on those same sorting, ordering, and cataloguing skills. This is why sorting and ordering skills are such important milestones in the process of learning to draw conclusions. In the next screenplay, we will see an excellent example of a television segment that helps children acquire these essential sorting skills.

BERT AND ERNIE
The Fire Engine

Bert:
Hey, Ernie! Ernie! Ern! Ern!

Ernie:
Hi. Bert.

Bert:
*Oh. Hey, Ernie, I think it's about time that
you put away these toys.*

Ernie:
*Oh well, Bert, I didn't bring all these toys out here.
You brought some of these toys here.*

Bert:
Yeah, well... but you brought most of the toys out here.

Ernie:
*Okay, Bert. I tell you what. I'll put most of the toys away.
Okay?*

Bert:
Okay, Okay, and I'll pick up the rest later, okay?

Ernie:
Okay, fine, Bert.

Bert:
Good. Bye-bye. **(He goes)**

Ernie:
Let's see, er... if I could just group these toys into er... into groups... then I'll put away a group of toys. How about that? Tell you what: I'll put away all the fire engines. Now there's one fire engine here. Let's see, are there any other fire engines here? Don't see any. Hmmm... no other fire engines. Okay, so I'll put away the fire engine.

Starts to go, humming

Oh, but, there are still an awful lot of toys left there. I guess I'd better put away one more group of toys. I tell you what: I'll put away all the big toys. Let's see, er... that's not a very big toy. No. I don't see any other big toys... **(Picks up fire engine)** *Here's a big toy. Look at this big toy here. I'll put away the fire engine.*

Starts to go

Oh, there are still a lot of toys there. I think I'd better put away another group of toys. I'll put away all the... um... all the red toys. How about that... all the toys that are red. **(Picks one up)** *That toy's kind of pinkish, but it's certainly not, not red. You're not red. Are you? No... hmm... red, red toys, any red toys?* **(Picks up fire engine)** *Here's a red toy. Look at that. The fire engine. Okay, I'll put away the fire engine.*

Starts to go again

Oh but there are... there are still a lot of toys here. I'd better put away one more group of toys. I'll put away all the er... all the toys with wheels. How about that? All the toys with

wheels. Rubber duckie, **(He picks it up)** *do you have wheels?
No, he does not have wheels.
Does the horse have wheels?* **(He looks)** *No, the horse
doesn't have wheels. Hey, here's a toy with wheels.* **(Pick up
the fire engine)** *The fire engine. Look at the wheels.
Everybody see the wheels on the fire engine? Yeah, see,
there are the wheels right there. Okay,
I'll put away the fire engine.*

Turns to go

*Er, there are still... there are still too many toys here. I'd
better put away one more group of toys. Umm... I'll put away
all the toys with... with ladders. How about that? All the toys
with ladders. Any ladders on the trombone?* **(He looks)** *No...
no ladders, no ladders. Here's a toy with ladders. The fire
engine. Okay, I'll put away the fire engine. I'm certainly
putting away a lot of toys.*

Ernie starts to go. Bert enters.

<u>Bert:</u>
Hey, Ernie. Ernie.

<u>Ernie:</u>
Yes, Bert.

<u>Bert:</u>
Hey, Ernie.

<u>Ernie:</u>
What?

<u>Bert:</u>
Hey, I thought you were going to put most of the toys away?

Ernie:

Oh, I'm just about to, Bert.

Bert:

Oh, yeah?

Ernie:

*I tell you what. I'll tell you which toys
I'm going to put away. All right?*

Bert:

Okay.

Ernie:

Now, I am going to put away all the fire engines.

Bert:

Good.

Ernie:

And all the big toys.

Bert:

Yes.

Ernie:

And all the red toys.

Bert:

Y...

Ernie:

*And all the toys with wheels. And all the toys with ladders.
Okay, Bert?*

Bert:
Yeah…

Ernie:
Okay.

Ernie leaves with the fire engine. Bert groans.

A skill related to that of sorting, and which demands the development of specific abilities, is that of categorizing, that is, the ordering of objects into logical categories such as large/small, new/old, etc. It turns out that, unlike adults, when children are given sorting tasks, such as the ordering of sticks from short to long, they do not execute the task in a logical way. They do not try to identify, say, the shortest stick, and then the next shortest, etc. Rather, they are more likely to lay the sticks out randomly, observe the result, and then try to correct it to a closer approximation to the desired outcome, in a trial and error process.

It is clear, therefore, that all the skills mentioned above — those of categorizing, sorting, ordering and collecting — are initial cognitive skills which serve as a basis for the development of more advanced logical processes.

E. UNDERSTANDING CINEMATIC LANGUAGE AT A VERY YOUNG AGE

Understanding cinematic language is not a trivial matter. It is not only based on the breaking down of a plot into close-ups and wide shots, but relies on a variety of different conventions — or example, the convention of showing a viewer only part of a process, say, the beginning, and relying on the viewer to fill in the picture. Take a man who throws a cream cake out the window of his house. Only later in the episode do we see the result of this action: a neighbor knocking on the door with a squashed cream cake on his head. In order to understand the plot, the viewer must imagine what happened in the intervening time and enjoy this process of imagining. Or take, for example, the segment in which Ernie buries Sherlock Hemlock in the sand by mistake. In this segment, we see a close up of Ernie who, in his attempts to uncover Bert, is flinging sand to his right. Only afterwards, when the shot gets wider, do we see Hemlock's hat peeping out of the top of a pile of sand. We understand then that the sand flung by Ernie completely covered Hemlock in sand.

On the way to understanding our young viewers viewing skills, we have already learned something about their cognitive abilities. We have learned that they learn new words every day; that they are just at the beginning of the path to understanding the rules of conversation; that they still have difficulty with basic abstract concepts; and that their ability to process information and draw conclusions is very limited. And now in particular, when they are just coming to grips with the basics of human communication, we expect them to show mastery in all the nuances of the language of film — an additional, new, visual rather than textual, language. Delving into the language of film and that of very young children, always reminds me of Don, the three-year-old son of a good friend of mine, and the way in which he watches the Disney series, *Bear in the Big Blue House.*

One of the most important foundations of cinematic language is the division of plot into *shots*. That is to say that every situation is filmed from a number of angles whereby every action or aspect of a character on screen is captured in various fields of view, according to the director's plan and interpretation. When two people converse on screen, it is almost guaranteed that we will see them in two shots, on the assumption that the director gives equal weight to the words of both characters. When one of the two says something particularly important, or particularly emotional, the director will surely decide that this deserves its own shot, and, in order to stress the importance of the moment, will film it in close-up. When the director wants to show a whole group of friends having fun or going somewhere together, it is reasonable to assume that she will show the scene in long-shot, a particularly wide-angled shot, and so on. Just like in any other television program, Jim Henson's series, *Bear in the Big Blue House,* is divided into different shot angles. One day, my friend discovered that his son, Don, had developed a unique way of watching the series. The star of the show is a giant brown bear, and it seems that Don did not feel too safe standing in front of the screen when the bear appeared. He would therefore stand in front of the television, ready for action, at a safe distance from the screen. When the bear appeared on screen in long-shot, he seemed smaller and less threatening, so Don would approach the screen without anxiety. But when the bear appeared in close-up, Don would hurry to put some distance between himself and the screen. At the next long-shot, when Don perceived that the bear had receded to a safe distance again, he would be courageous enough to approach. And so, right through each episode, Don would approach and then retreat from the screen according to the shot angles in which the bear was filmed.

From Don's story and from my own experience watching kids watch programs, we can see that the division of stories into shots is absolutely clear to them, as well, of course, as the fact that children enjoy following the plots of the stories their parents read to them by listening and looking at the accompanying pictures. So from that point of view, children have no problem with scene transitions. Just like in illustrated stories, with the help of the narrative, the children understand that when they see a picture of the protagonist in her house and then one of her in the garden, it means that she started off playing ball in her room and then went out to play in the garden. Similarly, in a televised film, children have no problem following a plot which unfolds in a series of connected scenes. Watching a plot which is told through pictures screened in a film or on television helps them understand the content or plot of a script. So far, it does not seem like cinematic language creates any kind of stumbling block for young children watching stories on film or television. The problem begins, of course, when creators of children's content decide to use more advanced cinematic language, which can include a lot more than a division of plot into scenes and shots.

Quite a few other means of expression exist in the television or filmmaker's toolbox, such as special effects or unusual angles of vision — that is to say, the filming of the scene from an angle different from the eye-level of the filmed characters. Sometimes, movie makers decide to present a scene from a unique angle, such as a bird's eye view, floor level shot, or from the inside of an object. This was done in the famous shot of the placing of a cake in the oven, where the shot was filmed from the cake's point of view, as it were, as it was placed in the oven. Unfortunately, a guide to shot angles, as understood by young children, does not exist, but I am not suggesting that we reduce the editors of our films for young children to using standard shots only rather than special ones. Nevertheless, when we choose our shot angles, we should not forget our young audience and we should therefore choose our shots carefully to suit their cognitive abilities so as to make grasping the story easy.

A children's book illustrator goes through the same process when choosing points of view for her illustrations. In illustrating a book about a farm, for example, she may choose to show a picture from the point of view of a bird on a branch so as to allow the young readers to get a picture of the whole farm and then later draw a flower from the point of view of a little ant. In the same way that a children's book illustrator chooses the best angle from which to illustrate the content placed in her care, we can choose whatever angle seems appropriate to us, on the condition that the plot is served and our young viewers' cognitive skills are up to it.

Clearly, the same thought process is relevant to various intricate camera movements. We must remember at all times that a child watches the action as a viewer from the side who watches "real" action in a kind of arena. Except that instead of the viewer finding himself in the arena of action and choosing himself on what to focus, we make those choices for him. We choose what the child will see at any given moment, and it is therefore important for us to take his desires and level of comprehension into account. To that end, we would not use camera angles and movements that would be on target for adult audiences but would only serve to throw off young audiences and to confuse them as to what is happening to whom and when.

The language of film, like any other language, is a collection of symbols with agreed upon meanings. With the symbols that the viewers have learned to understand in the process of watching movies, they are able to understand the plot created by the filmmakers. Cinematic language consists of plot, which is rendered in sequences that can be further broken down into scenes. The scenes can be broken down into shots, which are filmed at different proximities (from close-ups to medium shots to long shots, etc.) and from different points of view and camera movements.

This is not the place to describe every kind of camera angle and the ability of children to cope with each one of them. But, just like with every other process technique described here, if we try to look at the plot from the point of view of a child, it is almost certain that we will understand by ourselves which techniques to employ and which to give up.

Time, as you know, occupies an important place in the language of film,. beginning with different time transitions (dissolving, wiping, etc.) through editing techniques that show events happening concurrently or plots that include long time gaps or that include switches from time period to time period.

Time is not only an element of cinematic language but will also be mentioned in this chapter as belonging to the category of abstract concepts which are difficult for young children to grasp given that it is not perceivable through any of the five senses. This makes it even harder to grasp when it is translated into the language of film!

Let's imagine, for example, that we were watching the story of *Goldilocks and the Three Bears* on film. In this version, as opposed to how it is usually told, we would show the three bears preparing to leave their house and in parallel, show Goldilocks preparing to leave hers. Then we would show the bears getting farther away from their house in parallel to Goldilocks strolling in the woods and coming closer to their house. In other words, we would try to show our young viewers two events happening at the same time in different locations. And then... the slow return of the bears toward their house when Goldilocks is still tasting the three bowls of porridge. It would make sense for us to edit in fast-paced parallel shots which raises the expectation of the viewer that Goldilocks will be caught by the bears while she enters the bedroom and innocently looks at their three beds.

It is almost certain that filming the story of *Goldilocks and the Three Bears* in this way would prevent many of our viewers from understanding the plot at all. They would not understand who is where and when, and the pleasure they usually get from this story would not be present.

This is the reason that experienced children's production companies are careful to build stories for young children which unfold over one continuous timeline — one thing leading to another and then another until the end of the story. The story is well told and well filmed, and it progresses from scene to scene as more and more plot elements are revealed in different places or new situations, but all this unfolds within one timeline without significant skipping over time periods.

Similarly, it is worthwhile to avoid content that describes events taking place in someone's imagination or in a dream, though that cannot always be avoided since sometimes a story demands this element. In that case, it is necessary to make clear that this is the case, using any useful technique to do so, including stating the fact verbally.

The language of film's toolbox includes an enormous number of techniques, and it continues to develop all the time. If, for example, we watch a thirty-year-old movie, we will see that cinematic language was different from today's. The rhythm is different and even the cinematic syntax is different. In old movies, it was the custom to film the exterior of the building, and sometimes even the street sign, where the action was occurring. Nowadays, we rely greatly on the understanding of the viewer and tend to show only what is essential to the plot.

When a filmmaker approaches the making of a film for young children, there is no reason to use techniques that were popular in the past. All we have to do is to be aware of our young viewers' cognitive abilities and to see the film from their point of view.

F. MEMORY SKILLS IN YOUNG CHILDREN

We have already mentioned that even very young children have excellent memories, but they have not yet developed memory strategies. In their very nature, memory strategies are not similar across the board. The child has to develop different memory strategies for each different domain. These strategies develop as the child acquires greater life experience. If the last time a child went to her friend's house, she was disappointed because she didn't bring a ball or another object, she will develop for herself the strategy of "remembering objects when I go to a friend's house." In exactly the same way, she will learn to understand that she will not comprehend the end of a story, or its punch line, if she doesn't remember what happened at the beginning of the chapter. In order to enjoy the segment "Ernie Buries Bert at the Beach," a child must be able to connect the pile of sand which Ernie throws on Bert at the beginning of the story to the pile of sand which Ernie throws on Hemlock at the end, leading to satisfaction from the segment's humor.

In order to follow an unfolding plot, a child must have developed memory techniques that allow her to remember details. The child must be able to place these details in her memory in order that the connections between plot elements provide a satisfying picture.

When one tells a three-year-old, for example, that tomorrow she is going to the seaside and she should therefore think about the things she would like to take along, it is almost certain that she will instantly generate a long list of objects that she will be absolutely unable to remember the next day. Compare this to a five- or six-year-old, who will not only remember but is likely to prepare a pile of objects, ready for the next day's trip. By the age of nine, it is reasonable to assume that she will take further action to ensure that she will not forget the objects she wants to take on the trip. For example, she may lay the objects in a pile near the door or even make a list.

This example illustrates the process of developing memory skills in children. Three-year-olds do not have the *need to remember* yet, so it is worth building content for them that does not depend on remembering small plot details in order to understand or enjoy the action. For example, it is preferable not to show the protagonist of a story placing her glasses in the fridge at the beginning of a chapter and expect a three-year-old to remember this detail some time later when she subsequently can't find her glasses and blames their disappearance on a naughty, pilfering crow.

At the age of five or six, children have the concept of the *need to remember*, but they do not yet have the skills to do this in a task-oriented way. Only at the age of eight or nine do children develop memory strategies that they can then employ consciously in their learning processes.

Developing memory strategies requires developing some kind of methodological approach. One of the reasons that younger children have great difficulty developing these strategies is that they do not function methodologically in any area.

It is important not to confuse the ability to remember and

the development of memory strategies; children are born with an excellent ability to remember. They remember how things look very well, and if they need an object, they remember where they last put it. But they lack a systematic approach to memory.

In a series of experiments (*Child Development: Its Nature and Course*, McGraw-Hill, 1992), a candy was placed into a sealed container which stood in a line of identical, sealed containers. Children of about three years old were asked to remember the container in which the candy was placed. Because they had not developed memory strategies yet, the children fixed the candy-containing container with a stare in order not to lose sight of it. Unlike adults or other children, the three-year-olds needed to do this since they were unable to generate a different memorizing method, such as counting the number of containers to the right or left of the object or noting its placement with regard to other objects in the room.

In another experiment in which the children were asked to remember details in pictures, they were unable to recall sufficient detail because they had no strategy for doing so.

In yet another experiment, very young children and older children were shown pictures and asked to remember as much detail as possible. During the experiment, the children's eye movements were filmed. Analysis of the eye movements revealed that the older children had developed memory strategies whereas the younger children had not. The younger children were seen to focus their attention on the middle of the picture and to randomly glance at peripheral areas of the picture before returning their gaze to the middle. The older children scanned the pictures from top to bottom in absolutely orderly fashion. Of course, the results reflected these different approaches; as a result of their methodological scanning of the pictures, the older children remembered the pictures in far greater detail than the younger ones.

In a further experiment conducted in order to follow the evolution of memory strategies in young children, a group of children were shown a landscape picture and asked to remember as many details as possible. Another group of children were shown the same picture but asked a number of guiding questions before they saw the picture. For cxamplc, they were asked to answer the question, "In what season do you think the picture was taken?" And indeed, it turned out that these guiding questions resulted in better focus on the part of the children and a significantly higher level of detail recall.

The experiments above confirm that children remember details better as they get older and as they learn the importance of the details of the memories they store.

The development of strategies for the recall of plot details in a story, film, or play also require specific skills. It is well known that children love watching their favorite movies over and over again. Sometimes, they only understand certain plot details on the third or fifth watching. They understand that they will miss the importance of certain details of the action the first time they watch and now that they recall those details, they cast a new light on the entire plot. It is clear that children develop an understanding of the importance of constructing memory strategies as they become more experienced. Later on, they adapt these strategies to the memory of plot details.

I mentioned at the beginning of the chapter that I selected these six skills, out of all the cognitive, social, and motor skills that children have to acquire, in order to determine which functions children must master for the purpose of enjoying the watching of movies or television programs. However, the process of a child's development encompasses the evolution of many more skills of no less importance. This development is dependent on the infinite experiments of trial and error that children practice incessantly. Developmental psychologists describe young children as indefatigable detectives since every object, subject, and word that they have ever encountered arouses their curiosity.

This curiosity causes them to direct an unceasing flow of questions to their parents and the other adults around them. The minds of these "indefatigable detectives" find connections among all sorts of crumbs of information that come their way — and sometimes they make faulty connections leading to amusing conclusions.

Henri, the three-year-old son of a good friend of mine, informed her one day with finality that he had decided to stop eating from that day forward. When she asked why, he answered, "So that I will never die." My friend, who hadn't understood the logic, asked him to explain, which he did: "I need to eat so I can grow, right? And the more I grow, the older I'll get, right? And what happens when we get very old? We die! So if I don't eat, I won't grow, and if I won't grow, I won't die!"

Henri's logical process could be very amusing to adults, though there is nothing more annoying to Henri and children of his age than having an adult laugh at the conclusions they work so hard to draw. The vast majority of the conclusions to which they come are logical and correct. We adults are not aware of the hard work that children put into coming to these conclusions. From our point of view, they say trivial things and sometimes, because of some missing piece of data, they draw incorrect conclusions, like Henri who thought he could stave off death by not eating. Henri simply didn't know that one dies of starvation too, and this led to his mistake. An adult who laughs at Henri simply laughs at a child's temporary lack of a particular piece of information, through no fault of his own. This is genuinely offensive and confusing to a young child who is justified in being hurt at being mocked for his lack of knowledge.

It is important to understand that children learn to comprehend the world around them through their unending deductions, and if some of their deductions lead them to incorrect conclusions, they point to a constantly improving thinking process. Additionally, the amusing mistakes children make (which are usually the only things we remember...) help us to understand their perceptive minds' constant exercising of thinking skills. And of course, those mistakes are negligible compared to the enormous number of correct deductions and conclusions to which they come in their receptive brains.

At this stage of their lives, children acquire basic information processing skills. Their conclusion-drawing skills are not focused, nor do they use any particular strategy. Sometimes they test principles in language, or notice a social or physical principle. In the context of their testing, children sometimes try to draw conclusions in one area that draw from principles in another.

In parents' chat forums, one can often find amusing stories generated when children do just this. For example, a child saw her mother grating a carrot with a hand grater and asked, "Mom, what is that? A carrot sharpener?" Or the child who went on a hike with her parents and was told, "This is a Hazel tree, and this is a Hazel tree, and here's another Hazel tree..." and finally replied in exasperation, "But when are we going to see a Josie tree?" Or the girl who asked her father, "Dad, is a knee a leg's elbow?"

If we ignore the amusing aspect of these stories for a moment, we will perceive the enormous sorting and cataloguing task which children are constantly operating in their minds: A grater really does operate much like a sharpener, and if a tree bears the name of her little sister, Hazel, why shouldn't there be a tree for Josie, too? And it is true that knees and elbows bear a great resemblance. All in all, these three children asked eminently reasonable questions.

The question-asking stage is characterized by those famous, infinite *Why?* Questions. "Why do we have nighttime?" "Why do we have to eat?" "Why can't cats talk?" The *why stage* has inspired tons of children's songs and stories. Some conclusions we can draw from our understanding of this stage is that children are thirsty for knowledge, their comprehension of their day-to-day environment is completely different from ours, and that each crumb of information, however boring or banal in our eyes, is riveting to them.

I ran across an amazing example of this phenomenon during the filming of an episode of *Sesame Street* that I was directing. One of the characteristics of the series was the documentary-like filming of authentic and free conversations between Muppets and children. The children chose to show the Muppet a skill that they had in any area. One child showed off his keyboard playing skills, one his drum skills, and one girl told the Muppet about a particularly scary dream she had dreamt. To my astonishment, when I screened these various accomplishments to a random group of kindergarten kids, they were especially interested in a girl who showed how she could fold a shirt. They asked me to screen that segment again and again, entranced by her folding abilities. I admit to being surprised at discovering again that a simple, everyday act like folding a shirt could mesmerize them more than a child playing the violin or an account of a child's fascinating dream. This example deepened my understanding that learning everyday skills for the world around them is more important and interesting to children at this stage than anything else.

In summary, in order to watch any content on stage or screen, a child must master the series of skills we have discussed: language, the rules of language, abstract concepts, information processing, understanding the language of film, and memory strategies. However, despite everything written here, there is no substitute for experience. No theoretical knowledge can replace watching children watch television programs or stage productions and no explanation, however detailed, can replace the thing itself.

Each of the six categories presented here will take on extra dimensions in your unmediated meetings with children. It is hard to describe in words or to quantify or categorize a conversation with children who just watched a program or film that you created. There is no way to catalog questions about your hero that interest and trouble children, such as:
- When do they eat?
- Where's the shower?
- Where's his mother?
- Doesn't he ever go to sleep?

These questions go to show that they have taken your hero and his world and transferred him into their own world and schedule. At the same time, the children are likely to ask you more questions. Questions that show their astonishingly deep understanding, on many levels, of the segment they watched. You are likely to be surprised to discover that some of the clues you planted in a film for fear that it would be otherwise unintelligible were completely redundant, and that the children understood immediately why the hero failed to achieve his goal and how he will triumph over the plot's pitfalls. In other words: Go to the children, oh sluggard, consider their ways and gain wisdom![iii]

CONTENT
AS THE ANSWER
TO A NEED

I assume that if you are reading this book, you know the famous Aesop's fable, *The Lion and the Mouse*. The story tells of a mouse who climbs onto the nose of a sleeping lion by mistake. The mouse innocently believes himself to be climbing up a pile of dirt when he belatedly discovers himself to be on the nose of the King of the Beasts. Of course, the lion wakes up and is greatly angered by the impudence of the mouse.

"How dare you disturb my royal sleep, you impudent little mouse!" roars the lion as he almost kills the mouse with one swipe of his paw.

"Forgive me," murmurs the mouse, "please forgive me, Your Royal Majesty. Let me go now, and perhaps, one day, I will be able to return the favor."

The lion laughs at the thought that a little mouse could do his royal self a favor, but he is mollified nevertheless, and lets the little mouse go.

Time passes, and one day, hunters in the jungle spread a net and catch the lion. The lion tries to free himself to no avail. The mouse hears the roars of the trapped lion and emerges from his nest to discover the lion, immobilized by strong ropes. The mouse gnaws at the rope with his sharp teeth and manages to free the lion, who comes to understand that even a little mouse can be of service to the King of the Beasts himself.

This is a little story with a big moral. It is a story about the empowerment of the weak, the story about a strong and powerful character who is saved by the small and feeble one. It is told to children with the goal of strengthening their self-confidence and their belief that they have agency in the world, despite their relatively small size and strength compared to those around them.

The concept of *educational values* relates to the moral or

intellectual values that underlie all children's stories — the values which are meant to enrich the knowledge base and qualities of our young viewers.

The educational value that underlies the story of the lion and the mouse is, of course, the empowerment of the weak, and it comes under the guise of the moral at the end of the story. Nevertheless, it is important to remember that a moral at the end of a story is only one way to impart the educational message of a story to children.

The range of educational messages is extremely wide. Sometimes, the acquiring of a new world of knowledge, such as the identifying of colors, is defined as the educational message, in which case, the plot of the story is likely to resemble an adventure involving many different colored butterflies through which children will learn the names of the colors. On another occasion, the acquiring of basic counting skills will be educational message, in which case, the plot may involve, say, the adventures of a child who lives in a skyscraper. In order to get home every day, she must remember her building number, story number, and apartment number and through this, the viewers learn to count. An additional educational goal can be the acquiring or practicing of a new cognitive skill such as the comprehension of abstract concepts. Sometimes, the educational message can be aimed at improving children's social skills, etc.

As we can see, and as I have already mentioned, children show great interest in *anything* that will advance their most cherished goal, which is, of course, to become adults, and as quickly as possible. They are interested in content which will furnish them with as many details as possible about the world and therefore are naturally interested in content which we view as educational.

The acquisition of educational values sometimes happens when we, as parents, teachers and creators, want to teach children *important things*. Children do not choose the content of the books they hear or the movies they watch. Those are choices that the adults around them make. Parents, grandparents, and kindergarten teachers tend to choose books and films for children with educational content rather than content that is *just for fun*. Creators of children's content know this, of course, and so they try, sometimes unconsciously, to meet the demand.

Educational content has always been central to content aimed at children. It has also served as the backbone of folk tales written over the centuries. The moral to the story has served as the basis of hundreds of fairy tales throughout history. Fables and fairy tales had an overt educational and moral purpose and were used by parents and teachers as educational tools, not as fun or simply for pleasure.

Some children's fables included the moral of the story in the body of the text and the story ends with words that summarize the message of the story, such as: "And so the brothers learned that two are better than one," or "...and the moral of the story is that you should never talk to strangers." The overt or hidden messages in children's fables always held their own fascination. A few years ago, I participated in a project initiated by the Sesame Workshop, the producers of *Sesame Street*, in which children's fables were put to special use.

In 2003, the Israeli Sesame Workshop content writers initiated a joint production with the participation of the Jordanian company Jordan Pioneers and Palestinian Television. The central thread of the series was "classic folk tales drawn from the cultural traditions of the three middle-eastern bodies involved in the project." Each episode had as its focus a different, high-quality story drawn from the best of the different national story pools of the Israelis, Jordanians, and Palestinians. All the stories were animated and were used as a reservoir of content for the partnered channels. Each channel developed different screenplays, but central to all the scripts was the reservoir of content we had created, providing a basis for the ideological message of the series, an identical message in each country: peace, brotherhood, and respect of the other.

Through an examination of some of the episodes central to the series, the sharp observer will surmise the educational messages that the creators of the series wanted to impart to the three young target audiences. Examples of stories that stood at the center of the series follow.

"The Kid, the Butterfly, and the Fish"

This is the story of a young goat, a butterfly, and a fish who very much wanted to be friends but had to surmount technical difficulties to do so. The kid and the butterfly could not swim with the fish in the river. The fish and the kid, in turn, could not join the butterfly in fluttering in the sky. Nevertheless, despite their significant differences, the three friends enjoyed meeting every day on the bank of the river to talk, laugh, tell stories, and play games.

The moral of the story: You can be friends with someone who is very different from you.

"Being a Frog Can Drive You Crazy"

This is the story of three frogs who stood at the edge of the swamp and let a little dwarf paint a picture of them. When the dwarf was finished with his picture, the three took a look and were disappointed with their green color.

Suddenly, the color green appeared to them to be banal and boring. And then the dwarf had an idea! He could paint them fresh, new colors with his watercolors. The frogs agreed and the dwarf painted one of them red, one yellow, and one purple. They were very happy... until the stork, who loves to eat frogs, came along and was delighted to fall upon such a deliciously, colorful-looking lunch. The three frogs hurried to hide themselves amid the leaves of the swamp, as was their habit, but this time, due to their bright coloring, the stork had no trouble at all finding them among the leaves. The frogs hurried to jump into the watery swamp and wash off their bright colors, leaving them as green as they had been born. They may have ended up less colorful, but they were certainly a lot safer.

The moral of the story: I am what I am, on the outside and on the inside, and that's good enough (self-concept).

"Hassan and the Ghost"

This is the story of an ancient rumor about a dangerous and awful ghost who lived at the top of a mountain near a little village. The rumor about the awful ghost was well known to all the inhabitants of the village, and they were careful to warn all the children to never approach the mountain, especially at night, because the awful ghost could kidnap them and even eat them. All the children believed the rumors, except for Hassan, who decided to climb the mountain and see with his own eyes whether the ghost existed or not. When Hassan reached the top of the mountain, he did indeed discover an enormous ghost, but he was astonished to discover that the ghost was afraid of Hassan and did not dare to approach him. The two slowly developed a friendship until, eventually, the ghost agreed to accompany Hassan back to the village. And that was how the villagers learned that the ghost was more afraid of them than they were afraid of the ghost.

The moral of the story: Sometimes you are afraid of something simply because you do not know it.

An examination of all the educational messages central to the rest of the stories in this project will reveal that almost all of the stories in the *Sesame Stories* series were written with several key concepts in mind: accepting what is different, accepting myself, and especially respecting others and developing mutual respect. This reflects the motivating idea behind this Sesame Workshop initiative — that of using television as a medium for expressing messages of peace, brotherhood, and rapprochement among children in this area of the world so steeped in conflict. (A similar experiment was carried out in Kosovo.) The overarching goal was to plant in the hearts of the children a belief and hope for a shared life in the future in an environment of equality and respect for the other.

Sesame Stories is a unique example of a television series which makes use of fables and fairy tales as almost its only vehicle for expressing certain educational messages. Only in future generations will we know if this experiment was successful or if it contributed something toward improving the lot of the children of the next generation in the Middle East or in Kosovo.

It is rare for content designed for children not to have any educational message at all, whether it be through a moral at the end of a story or through information of some kind. In the market for content that is not tied to any kind of institution, the educational values come from a need which the writer herself identifies. The writer decides, for example, that encouraging curiosity and questioning in children is a worthy educational goal, or that educating children to be sensitive to their ecological environment is paramount, and so decides to write a plot around this issue.

On the other hand, in the world of children's television, which produces hundreds and thousands of screenplays per year, the concept of educational values is much more institutionalized and systematic — even if only for the reason that it would be strange if five writers for the same series all decided to grapple with the same educational concept at the same time. For this reason, children's channels usually guide their writers to a wide but defined range of educational messages which their educational consultants have already chosen as their educational goal.

It would be a mistake to say that all children's channels work this way, but broadcasting and production companies such as Nick Junior (the producers of *Dora* and *Blues Clues*) or The Sesame Workshop or the children's division of the BBC, and in fact all self-respecting children's broadcasting companies, include education and research departments.

These departments study the changing needs of their young audiences and build an educational or values-based infrastructure for their content creators (their screenwriters, producers, and directors) upon which those creators can develop and expand. These content infrastructures are sometimes called *topic and goals* booklets but the more common name for them is simply *the curriculum*.

These curricula are usually written for new series which are lined up for production and include all the educational messages and values that the writers will need during their writing for the series.

A look at these curricula will reveal a very wide range of educational goals, each of which can easily serve as the basis for an entire plot. These goals can include concepts such as problem solving, self-confidence, a window to science and technology, reading readiness, animals and plants, math readiness, music, etc.

These curricula usually open with an introduction that details the credo of the education professionals who wrote them. The introduction clarifies for its writers what the central tenets of the series should be. There are series whose overarching goal is to strengthen children's belief in themselves; there are series whose goal is to enrich and widen children's knowledge base; there are those that see as their mission the defining of a child's place in her home or in his family, etc. The overarching goal of the series defines the general direction of the episodes, but a series cannot be written on the strength of only one educational or values-based idea. Therefore, the overarching goal is broken down into sub-goals, and these sub-goals, in turn, are broken down into very specific elements that reflect in some way the large number of nuanced subjects included in the more broadly stated goal.

Scriptwriters read these curricula and choose a specific subject which is close to their heart and around which they believe they can weave a plot. At the same time as the plot serves to advance the specific educational goal the writer chose, it also conforms to the overarching goal of the series.

If, for example, the overarching goal of the series is to provide children with a window into science, it is reasonable to expect that a sub-goal of this series will be to teach young children: basic geographical principles, basic physical knowledge, basic astronomy, etc. These sub-goals will be further divided into subjects. A field like geography will be subdivided into subjects like basic world topography — mountains and valleys; forests; the sea — low and high tides, fishing, etc.; or climate — winds, clouds, rain.

Some curricula are more focused and underlie one series only, and some are wider, serving as a basis for an entire channel or network.

In any case, when all is said and done, all curricula deal with the acquisition of knowledge that children are supposed to undergo in their earliest years. This explains why the curricula of so many children's series resemble each other. Scriptwriters are not always clued into the world of young children or their developmental needs, which is why these curricula are so useful to them. I know quite a few writers for young children who use their curricula even when writing for, say, an adventure series that does not need to conform to any particular curriculum. In these cases, their bookshelves full of curricula come in handy when they need inspiration for an infinity of content ideas which must be suited to their target audience.

I have chosen a section from an IETV curriculum which serves as a writers' guide for a daily children's television network for whom I edited and directed a number of years ago.

Here is an excerpt from the first chapter of the curriculum.

EDUCATIONAL CURRICULUM EXAMPLE

General Contents

1. The child within the family and society
2. Music and movement
3. Holidays and festivals
4. The animal and plant kingdoms
5. Reading readiness
6. Math readiness
7. A window to science and technology
8. Ways of life
9. Children and the environment
10. Cognitive skills

1. The Child within the Family and Society

Rationale:

Children are born into two social systems — the family and the wider society around them. At the same time, they live within a nuclear family, an extended family, neighborhood friends, and a network of social and cultural services in which the family functions. It is clear, therefore, that family and social elements make up a part of each child's identity.

Children live and develop within these systems and learn accepted cultural behavior patterns and the mores accompanying them through interactions with their family, peers, and others. In order for these lessons to be significant to the child as an individual, that is, in order for the learning to be fully and correctly integrated, the child must develop a concept of her uniqueness and a confidence that she has mastery over her desires, boundaries, preferences, values, and feelings toward others. She must understand that she is a person, complete and whole.

Therefore, it is desirable that children develop the ability to function within a peer group, as leaders and as followers. They must learn to cooperate and to compete, but also to know when to secede from a group and be independent.

We believe that one of the important tools in the development of children's ability to function within a group is **awareness** — awareness of their own characteristics, those of others, and of interpersonal processes. This kind of awareness leads to a child's ability to choose functional interpersonal behavior patterns through the full awareness of his individual potential and the rights and uniqueness of the others with whom he interacts socially.

One of the characteristics of modern society is its heterogeneous nature. Children live in different kinds of families with different ways of life.

In order to learn to live with others, children must develop tolerance, which is the ability to respect what is different through the judging of the other's behavior, *but not according to just one criterion.* The child's increasing sensitivity to the fact that everyone is unique and different is likely to increase his tolerance and will enrich his social interactions. The web of relationships in a family and in the greater society raise problems and tension. Not every interaction with a person is enjoyable or satisfying — sometimes it includes disappointment, anger, sadness, or fear.

One of the ways to help children learn how to cope with these emotional states is to emphasize and express emotionally laden interpersonal situations through the legitimizing of tense interactions between family members while stressing that the solution to the tension lies in keeping channels of communication free and open. A child's development within the family is an incremental process of developing independence and responsibility.

In order to function as a responsible and independent person, a child must learn to take responsibility for his actions, desires, and feelings from a very young age. At this age, responsibility is expressed by making choices and being able to stick with them to a certain degree, the ability to accomplish tasks, and the ability to look out for others and care for them.

In summary:

The chapter, "The Child within the Family and Society," focuses on strengthening the child's self-concept and the child's interpersonal relationships within and outside of the family through the support of abilities such as independence, responsibility, tolerance, the ability to make choices, and cooperation with others.

Sub-goals under the heading: The child within the family and society

1. Who am I?
- Height
- Hair color
- Eye color
- Weight (fat/thin/in between)
- Special things connected to my physical

characteristics: near or far sightedness/glasses (sight), sharp hearing or hearing difficulties/ hearing aid (hearing), clumsy or agile (athleticism)
- Gender
- Age
- Preferences (What do I like and what do I not like?): Types of food/games/clothing items
- My place in the family: parents, siblings, grandparents, cousins
- My place in society: in kindergarten, in my building, in the neighborhood
- What is mine: toys/objects/animals/books
- What can I do by myself and what can I not yet do by myself: at home/sports

2. Self-confidence:
- Children will develop the ability to verbally express pride and self-appreciation for the activities that they can carry out within their peer group.
- They will also develop the ability to verbally express pride and self-appreciation for their place within the family.

3. Coping with failure
- Children will identify their feelings of frustration in situations of failure.
- Children will identify other people's reaction of disappointment in situations of failure.
- Children will understand that failure in a particular area does not lessen the love or

appreciation of the people in their immediate surroundings.

- Children will learn effective ways of dealing with failure: trying again, trying something different, identifying the source of the problem, asking for help, or understanding that the goal is impossible to achieve.
- Children will realize that some people do things better than others, and some worse.
- Children will understand that people older than they, and even adults, can't do everything.

4. Initiative

- Children will understand that by taking initiative, they can influence things connected to them and their environment.
- Children will understand that taking initiative is usually positive and will be supported by their environment.

5. Taking responsibility

- Children will learn that taking responsibility is part of growing up (and that doing so is usually accompanied by feelings of pleasure and independence) and that the older they get, the more responsibility they can take on.
- Children will learn to choose different alternatives in taking responsibility.

6. Feelings

- Children will be able to identify and name their basic emotions and those of others: happiness /

anger / sadness / surprise / pride / missing something or someone / fear / pleasure

- Children will learn that they are allowed to experience negative emotions such as anger or fear.
- Children will learn to categorize emotions as pleasant and unpleasant.
- Children will be able to identify the feelings of other people and to take them into account.

7. Family

- Children will understand their family structure, who makes up their family, what typical are activities in their families, and family connections and relationships.
- Family events.
- The family as a place of safety and the supplying of basic needs: love, food, clothing, sleep, hygiene, and care in the case of sickness or unhappiness.
- The family as a supportive framework.
- The family as a given fact. (You can't change your family.)
- Tension within the family (discipline, borders, jealousy, sibling rivalry, and ways to cope with this).

8. Cooperation

- Children will recognize that doing things together is pleasant and efficient.
- Task allocation as a way to cooperate. (Advantages of planning and sharing work.)

- Combining talents and skills. It will be proven that goals are easier to attain when each member of a group contributes his or her unique skills to the task.
- Mutual help: Children will learn to identify situations in which they need help or can help others.
- Integrating into a group: Children will learn different strategies for integrating into a group.
- Children will learn to identify another person's needs and help integrate that person into a group.
- Children will learn to identify difficulties in integration and functioning in a group.

9. The neighborhood

- Children will learn the neighborhood in which they live (the street, shops, kindergarten, school, public parks, clinics).
- Children will learn to identify relationships between neighbors and to decipher their meanings (cooperation within an apartment building, joint responsibility for the building — cleaning, gardening, guarding privacy, noise).

10. Same and different

- Children will learn what is the same and what is different among all people (behavior patterns, external appearance, language, taste).
- Children will learn what is the same and what is different among groups of people.
- Children will learn that different people can

have similar feelings and skills, and different ones.

- Children will learn that with a tolerant attitude and respect for others, they can live together and learn to like and love one another.
- Children will learn that they have a right to be different from others.

● ● ●

The first chapter of the curriculum, presented here as an example, deals with one subject among ten others that are all treated with the same amount of detail. A scriptwriter who plans to write a script around the idea of "The child within the family and society," will take a look at the curriculum, at the relevant chapter, and identify a sub-category which speaks to her, such as "same and different." The first section of this category suggests that the writer help children learn what is the same and what is different among people (behavior patterns, external appearance, language, and taste). To the best of my memory, a scriptwriter who decided to tackle this subject invented a plot in which the hero of the series arrived, panting, at his friend's house. He tells his friend that on the way to the house, he met a real witch with a big black hat, a big nose, a black cloak, and a witch's staff. The witch almost enchanted him, but luckily, he knew immediately that she was a dangerous witch so he managed to run away in time. The two friends keep discussing the witch animatedly until there is a knock on the door, and the host's grandmother walks in. She has come to babysit while his parents go see a movie. The grandmother is wearing a big, black hat and a black cloak-like coat, and she walks with the help of a black and silver walking stick. The grandmother, amused, tells her grandson that a boy on the street called her a witch.

Everyone understands what happened, including, of course, the boy who made the mistake. He gets to know the grandmother and learns that she is not frightening at all — in fact, she is quite playful, not to mention the delicious *secret cookies* she baked (as no one else knows how) and brought along with her.

In the category of *window to science*, for example, other goals are presented, such as learning about: the water cycle, the shape of the globe, identifying climate phenomena, identifying common materials in the world around the child, and science tools that children use every day, such as a magnifying glass, a wheelbarrow, scales, measuring tape, and more. In the chapter presented below, the scriptwriter decided to deal with one of these subcategories, that of planet Earth.

PLANET EARTH

<u>Target subject:</u> Science

<u>Particular goal:</u> **Children will learn to recognize the shape of the globe; the shape of the seas and the continents; and the connection between the shape of the globe and the cycle of daytime, nighttime, the stars, and planets.**

<u>Characters:</u>
Pistachio — A quaint and clown-like eccentric. The character is not clearly a child or an adult. Pistachio usually evinces great confidence in his pronouncements, but the viewers know that he is usually wrong and knows less than they do.

Hangon — a young boy who serves as the character with whom viewers can identify. Hangon is their cohort on the screen.

Scene 1. Daytime; morning; Pistachio's house — Hangon is waiting impatiently for his friend. Pistachio walks in looking like he has just come back from a hike, with a backpack, a water bottle, and a walking stick.

Hangon:
Hey! You've finally come. I've been waiting here for you for... maybe... at least... a long time.

Pistachio:
Hangon, listen. You wouldn't believe where I just came from.

Hangon:
Where?

Pistachio:
(enjoying the secret)
From somewhere very, very far away.

Hangon:
You went to the playground?

Pistachio:
Farther than that.

Hangon:
You went all the way to the new neighborhood they're building at the end of the street?

Pistachio:
Even farther than that.

Hangon:
You went to the wood?

Pistachio:
Even farther than the wood.

Hangon:
So I don't know. Tell me.

Pistachio:
Guess.

Hangon:
Hang on, hang on, hang on... **(worried)** *Don't tell me you went all the way to the main road?*

Pistachio:
Farther than that.

Hangon:
There is no farther than that.

Pistachio:
There is.

Hangon:
There isn't.

Pistachio:
There is.

Hangon:
So where did you go?

Pistachio:
You won't believe it. I went to the end of the world.

Hangon:
To the end of the world?

Pistachio:
Yes, all the way to the very end, to where the world ends. That's where I was.

Hangon: (astonished)
Are you sure?

Pistachio:
Sure I'm sure! **(He puts down his backpack, his water bottle, and his walking stick.)**

Hangon:
And how do you get there?

Pistachio:
With shoes. Walking shoes like these are the best. **(He shows them to Hangon)**

Hangon:
When I asked, "How do you get there," I didn't mean "in what," I wanted to know how to get there.

Pistachio:
(bringing Hangon to the window and pointing)
Do you know the playground?

Hangon:
I know it.

Pistachio:
You pass the playground, keep going to the new neighborhood, pass the wood, keep going to the main road, cross carefully at the light, and keep going and keep going and keep going... until you get there.

Hangon:
To where?

Pistachio:
To the end of the world.

Hangon:
(who has understood something)
Hang on, let me think about this. You're saying that behind the playground, after you pass the new neighborhood, after you pass the wood, after you cross the main road, you get to the end of the world?

Pistachio:
Um... yes... That is, not exactly there, but a little after that.

Hangon:
I get it. And how does it look? I mean, the end of the world.

Pistachio:
It's really pretty. There is a lot of sand there. A lot of sand, and water. A lot, a lot of water. And there is even someone there selling popsicles. But when you take a really good look to see what comes after the water, you see that nothing comes after the water. Just nothing.

Hangon: **(suspicious)**
Hang on, hang on, hang on! I think I know what place you're talking about. **(In the tone of a detective)** *Tell me something, Pistachio. Did you happen to see comfortable deck chairs there?*

Pistachio:
Pine chairs? **(amazed by Hangon's knowledge)** *Yes, there really were comfortable deck chairs there. Many. How did you know?*

Hangon:
Okay, I get it. I think you made a little mistake. That place you went to, with the comfortable deck chairs and the popsicle seller and the water, it's not the end of the world.

Pistachio:
It isn't?

Hangon:
No! The place you went to is called the beach.

Pistachio:
The beach! No way! You can't even know what you're talking about because I've been there and you haven't.

Hangon:
Of course I have. Sometimes I go bathing with Uncle Buddy, right?

Pistachio:
Right.

Hangon:
So that's just where we always go.

Pistachio:
I don't think so.

Hangon:
Hang on... how long did it take you to get there?

Pistachio: (calculating)
Hmm... a long... almost an hour.

Hangon: (giggling)
And you think you can get to the end of the world in an hour?
If you could get to the end of the world in an hour... the world would be tiny!

Pistachio:
And it isn't?

Hangon:
No.

Pistachio:
How do you know?

Hangon: (with pride)
My uncle, who is a ship's captain, told me once.

Pistachio: (in a tone of acceptance)
Okay. So if the place I went to wasn't the end of the world,
(curiously) *where is the end of the world?*

Hangon:

Ah... I... um... don't know. But Uncle Danny does. I can ask him if you really want.

Pistachio:

Of course I want.

Hangon:

Okay, I'll ask him tomorrow.

Pistachio:

Why not now?

Hangon:

You want me to ask him now?

Pistachio:

Yes. I want you to ask him now, and you'll see that I'm right.

Hangon: (turning toward the door)

Okay, I'll go ask him now.

Pistachio:

Go ask him.

Hangon: (going out)

I'm going to ask. **(He goes out.)**

Pistachio: (half to himself)

You'll see that I was right. I did get to the end of the world.

*** Time Passes ***

Scene 2. Daytime; morning; Pistachio's house. After some time, Hangon comes in holding a big globe.

Hangon:

Hi Pistachio, look what I brought. **(He gives him the globe)**

Pistachio: **(in wonder)**

Wow! What a beautiful ball. Nice colors! Catch! **(He throws the ball to Hangon)**

Hangon:
(catches the globe, appalled)

No! You don't play with this. It's a globe.

Pistachio:
A globe? What's a globe?

Hangon:
A globe is the world.

Pistachio: (amazed)
The world is this small?

Hangon:
No, it's like the world. Just small.

Pistachio:
(examining the globe)
What are these blue and brown things?

Hangon:
Those are all the continents and oceans in the world.

Pistachio:
What are continents and oceans?

Hangon:
You see all this brown and this green and this yellow? Those are continents. That means land you can walk on. And all the blue, all around here... and here... and here... that's the sea.

Pistachio:
Sea that you can swim in?

Hangon:
Yes. And sail in, like my Uncle Danny sails in his ship. **(Pointing to the division between land and sea)** *And this place is the beach.*

Pistachio:
(giggling. Laughing at himself)
What? So I went here and thought I had reached the end of the world?

Hangon:
Exactly.

Pistachio:
(continuing to examine the globe)
Wow! Look how much blue there is. What? The world has so much sea and so little land?

Hangon:
(interested in Pistachio's observation)
I guess so.

Pistachio:
So where are we in the world?

Hangon:
Uncle Danny showed me that. Here. We're right... here.

Pistachio:
So why can't we see our house and our street here?

Hangon:
Because if we had to draw our house and street here, then we'd have to draw all the houses and all the streets in the world on the globe and you can't draw so many, many drawings on such a small globe.

Pistachio:
(nodding with understanding and examining the globe interestedly)
I wonder where the end of the world is.

Hangon:
(remembering why he brought the globe in the first place)
Oh... that's it... Uncle Danny explained to me that there is no such thing as the end of the world.

Pistachio:
What? How can that be?

Hangon:
Here. Look. **("walking" his fingers on the globe along one of the latitude lines)** *Let's imagine that we're here. And now we're walking and walking and walking and walking...*

(He "walks" his fingers all around until he returns to his starting point.) *In the end, we get to the same place that we were when we started.*

Pistachio: (amazed)
That's amazing. And Danny explained that all to you?

Hangon:
Yes. **(He remembers something enthusiastically)** *And he showed me other things. Do you want to know why we have light in the day and darkness at night?*

Pistachio:
Yes.

Hangon:
Bring me a flashlight, quickly.

Pistachio:
(suspiciously brings a flashlight to Hangon)
Here you go. A flashlight. Just be careful with it.

Hangon:
Excellent. Let's say that this is the sun.

Pistachio: (amazed)
What? The sun is a flashlight?

Hangon:
Don't be silly. I said, "Let's say." So when the sun lights the world, wherever there is light has daytime. And everywhere the light doesn't reach is dark, so they have nighttime. **(spins the globe)** *But when the world spins...*

Pistachio: (even more amazed)
The world spins?

Hangon:
Yes. **(he keeps explaining)** *You see? Now this side has light, so it's daytime, and this side is dark, so it's night.*

Pistachio looks at the dark side of the globe and is appalled. He gets up and leaves, coming back with a long rope.

Hangon:
Why did you bring a rope?

Pistachio:
So I won't fall.

Hangon:
Fall? From what?

Pistachio:
(takes a little person doll and puts it onto the globe as an example)
You explained to me yourself that in the daytime we're here, right? **(The doll stands erect on the globe.)**

Hangon:
Right.

Pistachio:
(Puts the doll's feet on the bottom of the globe and then lets go. The doll falls to the floor. Pistachio says to Hangon with horror) *You see?!* **(He runs to the window**

and comes back) *We have to hurry. Soon it will be evening. If we don't tie ourselves down very well, we'll also fall, just like that, off the world!* **(He ties himself and Hangon to the bed as he speaks)**

Hangon:
(who has caught Pistachio's horror)
Hang on, but how does it help us to be tied to the bed? The bed isn't tied to anything. We can fall off the world together with the bed!

Pistachio:
You're right. So let's tie the bed to something. **(He ties the end of the rope to the dresser.)**

Hangon:
(frees himself from the rope, goes to the window, and then comes back)
Listen Pistachio, I think you're making a mistake.

Pistachio:
I'm not making a mistake. I'm completely sure. Come and tie yourself down quickly or you'll fall off the world!

Hangon:
Hang on and think, Pistachio. The world has been spinning for a long time. It was spinning yesterday and the day before yesterday, too. And up until today, you and I have never fallen off the world.

Pistachio:
So what? Just because we didn't fall yesterday or the day before, doesn't mean we can't fall today.

Hangon: (approaching the window)
Pistachio, come quickly!

Pistachio:
What happened?

Hangon:
Come see. Outside, it's already nighttime.

Pistachio: (suspicious)
Nighttime? **(He frees himself from the rope and joins Hangon at the window. They both examine the star-strewn sky.)** *What a beautiful night. And look at all those stars.*

Hangon:
Danny told me that each of those stars is a whole world, just like ours.

Pistachio:
Really?

Hangon:
Yes.. And do you know what could be?

Pistachio:
What?

Hangon:
It could be that right now, in a different house, on a different planet, two friends exactly like us are looking at the sky full of stars.

Pistachio:
Two like us? Like Pistachio and Hangon? It can't be.

Hangon:
Why?

Pistachio:
Because there can only be one Hangon.

Hangon:
Yes... and there can only be one Pistachio.

Through this example, we can see how Hanan Feld, the writer, chose to deal with the curricular assignment: *learning to recognize the shape of the globe; the shape of the seas and the continents; the connection between the shape of the globe and the cycles of daytime, nighttime, stars, and planets.* He created a plot around two beloved characters with whom children identify. Pistachio, the series' protagonist, the ultimate mistake-maker goes to the beach for the first time. He believes that he has reached the end of the world. Hangon, who *has* been to the beach (as have most of the program's viewers) is convinced that Pistachio is mistaken, and their argument, including their trial and error experiments, helps them and their viewers to absorb basic information about the shape of the world.

Tackling curricular assignments like this one is, of course, the daily bread of content writers for children. Children's television series usually include tens, if not hundreds, of episodes, and the writers are mainly required to create plots that take on the list of educational subjects and goals that were predefined as the series' objectives.

The writer's process of choosing a curricular subject is

not fixed, and it depends on the different channels' accepted work models. Or it can depend on the work model of the content editors or main writers of the various production companies. In some systems, the writers choose their curricular subjects according to their personal tastes and report their choice to the head editor or head writer in order to get the go-ahead. The editor makes sure that no other writer chose the same curricular subject on which to focus in order to avoid repetition. In other production systems, in which content is very carefully constructed, the subject is defined ahead of time for every writer and every episode. I imagine that there are many more ways in which things can be handled and this depends, of course, on local work models and methods.

Nevertheless, despite everything I have written here, quite a few networks and channels that create children's content exist without demanding that their writers stick to any curricular demands or educational content. Even in these contexts, there is a general understanding that content should have some kind of educational value. The creators and editors of these series are careful to preserve the content and plot character of the series, and they leave the choice of whether to include educational content in a particular episode to the writer. As someone who has been used to working with curricula for years, I have discovered that relying on a specified educational objective makes the process of writing simpler and more focused. As such, even when I have been asked to create content for a series without particular curricular demands, I know that a brief look at one of my curricula will help me to identify an "educational objective" which will help me in turn to create a clever and fascinating plot. There will be times in which your writing process will begin with a story you wish to tell and only afterwards, in the process of writing, will you discover that taking a look at any list of goals will help improve the advancement and focusing of the plot.

In most of the television channels and production companies who do reliable work, professional advisors accompany the writing process on a daily basis. These advisors include didactic professionals, psychologists, and science experts where appropriate. Therefore, when writing for children, the writer can find herself in constant dialogue with two or three experts (whose comments may not always be compatible with the dramatic structure of the developing screenplay). Most times, though, only one didactic expert — perhaps an education professional who understands better than the writer the needs and skills of viewers of a particular age — will accompany you as you write. This didactic expert is supposed to help you match the level of your content to the needs of your viewers. When working with a curriculum, a didactic advisor will usually be the one to help you deeply understand the implications of your chosen educational goal. He will also make sure that the denouement of your plot actually serves the stated educational goal.

In addition to didactic advisors, western television channels sometimes employ child psychologists in the scriptwriting process. The psychologist makes sure that none of the broadcast content includes any situation that can harm the viewing child in any way. These channels take the fact that children often watch television without their parents into account and that there are quite a few subjects which could disturb them or raise difficulties. Therefore, it is important to be careful when dealing with subjects such as death or loss and to understand how to address them without hurting the viewing child. Another expert whom you will no doubt meet in the course of your writing is the academic. If you are working on a children's program whose aim is to teach math, language, science, or even crafts, it is almost certain that an academic expert will be part of the process. This expert's area of expertise will parallel the targeted goal of your screenplay. This advisor's job is to make sure that the information you impart in your screenplays is accurate and that you have matched your method of presenting the information to that of the developmental level of your viewers.

We can understand the involvement of various educational advisors in the writing process and the way in which advisors help to refine and upgrade the educational messages of screenplays by reviewing the process of criticism and rewriting that a screenplay undergoes on its way from the draft level to the final version.

I have chosen the screenplay, "Boys Can't," which was written for the *Sesame Street* series, as an example of this process (2007 season, Hop channel, Israel). Below, I present the first draft of a screenplay written according to a curriculum specifying the following educational goal: **Children will learn that boys and girls can aspire to a career in any field and that there are no fields barred to them as a result of their gender.**

It is important to remember that the screenplay is in initial draft form; it didn't make the cut. I am only including it here in order to demonstrate the process of writing in conformity to particular goals and to show the didactic input from which the screenplay benefitted in its development.

"BOY OR GIRL?"

Target subject: Gender

Particular goal: Children will learn that boys and girls can aspire to a career in any field and that there are no fields barred to them as a result of their gender.

Characters:

Piney — A furry, orange muppet, designed in the best tradition of friendly, Sesame Street monster muppets. He loves cleanliness and order, hates getting dirty, and is very organized. He hates spontaneity and likes to understand things on a deep level.

Noah — Also a furry muppet (red) designed in the best tradition of friendly, Sesame Street monster muppets. The character of Noah represents a joyful and active boy of about five years old. In his character description, Noah is defined as even-tempered and good-hearted. Everyone loves him, and he loves everyone.

Abigail — Plays the part of all the neighborhood kids' ultimate little sister. She is very naive and sees things as they are, which often gives her an advantage over the other characters and their world views.

1. EXT. A table in the park — daytime.

Piney is building a model airplane with the help of an instruction sheet. Abigail arrives at the table on her bike and watches him.

<u>Abigail:</u>
Hey, Piney, what are you doing?

<u>Piney:</u>
Building a model airplane.

<u>Abigail:</u>
A model airplane? That's great... I want to help.

<u>Piney:</u>
(mumbling while he cuts something out)
I'd be happy to have you help me — it's just that I don't really think you can do it.

<u>Abigail:</u>
Why not?

Piney:

Because it's complicated. There are a lot of tiny pieces, and you have to know each piece, and it's very delicate.

Abigail: (offended)

So what? I also want to do it.

Piney gets confused, and he cuts the piece he is working on wrong. He gets up.

Piney:

Oh no. Look what happened here because of you. **(In an angry tone)** *Listen, Abigail. Don't be offended, but there are some things that, in my opinion, you can't do.*

Abigail:

What things?

Piney:

Things that... **(he has difficulty getting the words out)**

Abigail:

Things that what?

Piney:

Things that... that only boys can do.

Abigail: (amazed)

What? What kind of things can only boys do?

Piney:

All kinds of things. Like... like... playing soccer, or basketball, or building model airplanes like this one, for example.

<u>Abigail:</u> **(Defiant)**
I can do all those things. And I can build a model airplane like this one.

<u>Piney:</u>
You can't.

<u>Abigail:</u>
I can.

<u>Piney:</u>
You can't.

<u>Abigail:</u>
Phooey!!! **(She turns to leave)**

<u>Piney:</u>
(something doesn't work again in his model building)
Yeah, phooey is right!

Abigail leaves, angry.

2. EXT. Irwin's nursery — daytime

Noah is in the nursery watering plants with a watering can. Abigail arrives.

<u>Abigail:</u>
Noah!! Tell him!

<u>Noah:</u>
Tell who what?

Abigail:
Tell Piney. Tell Piney to let me help him build his model airplane. He won't let me.

Noah: (stopping his work)
Why?

Abigail:
Because he says I'm a girl. And girls don't know how to do some kinds of things.

Noah:
**(puts down his work tools.
They both move to the foreground)**
But it's his model. He's the only one who gets to decide who can help him build it. And anyway, it really is a complicated one to build. Even I don't know how to help him.

Abigail:
But I do know. I even have pictures of airplanes at school.

Piney's voice is heard from far away.

Piney: (out of frame)
Noah!! Noah, can you come here for a second?

Noah:
Hang on a sec, Piney. I'm busy.

Piney: (out of frame)
Please, Noah. I need you.

Noah:
Okay, Piney. I'll finish watering and then come right away.

3. EXT. A table in the park — daytime.

Piney is still building his model. Noah arrives.

<u>**Noah:**</u>
Yes, Piney?

<u>**Piney:**</u>
Listen Noah, I need someone to help me build this model.

<u>**Noah:**</u>
No problem. I'll be happy to do it, Piney. Just tell me what to do.

<u>**Piney:**</u>
My fingers are sticky, so I need someone to pick up the right pieces and give them to me.
I'll tell you which piece to give me, and you'll give it to me. Okay?

<u>**Noah:**</u>
Sure, Piney.

Abigail arrives while this is happening and watches the other two.

<u>**Piney:**</u>
Great. So give me the back wing, please.

<u>**Noah:**</u> **(he has no clue)**
The back wing... the back wing... **(Abigail points to the wing.)** *Oh! Thanks, Abigail. Here you go, Piney, the back wing.*

Piney:

Thanks, Noah.

Piney:

Now give me the cockpit, please.

Noah:

The cockpit? What does the cockpit look like?

Piney:

Oh come on, Noah.. Don't you know what a cockpit looks like?

Abigail points to the cockpit for Noah.

Noah:

Oh! Thanks, Abigail. Here you go, Piney, the cockpit.

Piney:

Thanks, Noah. Now give me the front wheels, please.

Noah:

The front wheels. Coming right up, Piney.

Piney:

Thanks, Noah.

Noah suddenly notices Abigail, who has left and is getting farther away.

Noah:

*Hey, Abigail, where are you going? You can't leave now...
we need you! You have to help us.*

Abigail:

I'd be happy to help you; it's just that Piney is right. It looks like there are things that only boys can do.

The screenplay, "Boy or Girl," was disqualified at the outset for a number of artistic and moral reasons. The action was too predictable and uninteresting. The characters' behavior was stereotypical and offensive. Additionally, their behavior in the script did not match their given character traits at all and veered from the consistent behavior patterns they showed throughout the rest of the series. The screenplay was handed over to a didactic advisor in the hope that her comments would help the writer with his next draft. Indeed, her comments identified the value-based problems with the script and helped the writer with the next version of the screenplay.

"BOY OR GIRL" / ADVISOR COMMENTS:

I have read the screenplay and find that it does not meet the expectations of the curricular goals.

The plot includes negative behavior around gender. Noah and Piney's objection to including Abigail in the building of the airplane model just because she is a girl is a negative behavior model. We have no way of knowing what the viewing child will choose to learn as a result of this segment and we should therefore avoid showing any negative behaviors at all in the segment.

It is preferable to deal with the subject in a way that models positive behaviors around gender from the outset. When dealing with other screenplays, for example, in screenplays which tackle the subject of children wearing glasses, we approached the problem from two angles. In some of the screenplays, we simply used a positive modeling approach, in that we showed children wearing glasses taking part in the action in some way without making a particular issue of glasses-wearing. In other screenplays, we called a spade a spade and chose to develop plots in which glasses-wearing was made the center of the action. For example, the screenplay in which a boy showed up one day without glasses and his friends couldn't figure out what had happened to him and what was different about his face. Some of them thought that he had gotten a haircut, others thought he was angry all of a sudden, and only at the end did they notice that he looked different that day because he wasn't wearing glasses. This was the way in which we drew the viewer's attention to glasses as the central focus of the story. Here too, we avoided including negative behaviors in the plot. In my opinion, we should take the same approach when tackling the subject of gender.

I would be happy if you wrote another version of the screenplay in which you avoid negative behaviors around gender as a basis for the story.

● ● ●

The screenplay written in response to the expert's advice follows.

"BOYS CAN'T"

Target subject: Gender

Particular goal: Children will learn that boys and girls can aspire to a career in any field and that there are no fields barred to them as a result of their gender.

Characters:

Piney — A furry, orange muppet, designed in the best tradition of friendly, Sesame Street monster muppets. He loves cleanliness and order, hates getting dirty, and is very organized. He hates spontaneity and likes to understand things on a deep level.

Noah — Also a furry muppet (red) designed in the best tradition of friendly, Sesame Street monster muppets. The character of Noah represents a joyful and active boy of about five years old. In his character description, Noah is defined as even-tempered and good-hearted. Everyone loves him, and he loves everyone.

Irena — Owner of the Magic and Surprises Store on the street. She has emigrated from Russia and speaks with a Russian accent.

Irwin — Owner of the local mini-market. The ultimate grandfather of the neighborhood. He offers warmth, patience, and unconditional love to everyone.

1. INT. Irena's store — daytime

Irena is talking on the phone, surprised, happy, exhilarated

<u>Irena:</u> **(in Russian)**
What?!! Say that again!?? **(Noah walks into the store and watches Irena curiously)** *I'm so happy for you!! So I'm going to be an aunt!! Woah! I'm so excited!! I'm so ha-ppy!! Bye bye, sweety-pie!*

Irena puts down the phone and dances toward Noah. She hugs him and kisses him with great happiness.

<u>Irena:</u>
I'm going to be an aunt!

<u>Noah:</u>
Whose aunt are you going to be?

<u>Irena:</u>
My sister's son's or daughter's. My sister's pregnant and soon she'll be a mommy!

<u>Noah:</u> **(surprised)**
And that's so exciting?

<u>Irena:</u>
Of course! The fact that she's going to have a baby is the most wonderful thing in the world!

<u>Noah:</u>
(leaves the store while he thinks about this)
Hmmmm...

2. EXT. Park bench — daytime

<u>Piney:</u> (enthusiastic)
Noah! Come and see how cool it is to fly. **(He shows him a picture of the sky from a pilot's point of view.)** *I think flying must be the most wonderful thing in the world.*

<u>Noah:</u>
(deep in thought. Asks in a philosophical tone)
More wonderful than having a baby?

<u>Piney:</u> (astonished)
What?

<u>Noah:</u>
Irena says that having a baby is the most wonderful thing in the world.

<u>Piney:</u>
Having a baby? That could be wonderful. But I think the most interesting thing is being a pilot!

<u>Noah:</u> (unsure)
I don't know.. I think that maybe when I grow up I want to have a baby like Irena's sister.

Piney:

But... but Noah... you can't have a baby, because you're a boy. Only girls can have babies.

Noah:

*Yes... I know... but (**pause**) are you sure?*

Piney:

Of course I'm sure. Only mothers have babies! That's the difference between boys and girls.

Noah:

Hang on. So I can't have a baby just because I'm a boy?

Piney: (thinking)

Hmm... you can't... you can't... hmmm... I think that's it. Just that.

Noah:

And are there things that boys can do that girls can't?

Piney:

Hmm... things that girls can't... hmm... I think girls can do everything.

Noah: (gets up; angry)
*Then that's not fair!! (**He leaves**)*

Piney (yelling after him)
But Noah!! You can be a pilot.

3. INT. Irwin's mini-market — daytime

Irwin's on the phone when Noah comes in. Noah is disconsolate.

<u>Irwin:</u> (to the receiver)
Well, congratulations. Yes, I was very happy to hear the news, Irena, and send my regards to your sister!

He replaces the receiver, turns to Noah, and immediately notes that he is disconsolate.

<u>Irwin:</u>
What happened, Noah? Why are you sad?

<u>Noah:</u>
It's just... Piney told me that only girls can have babies and that's not fair at all!

<u>Irwin:</u> (thinking for a moment)
Hmm... I understand. That's true, **(wants to mollify Noah)** *but other than that, girls and boys can do everything just as well as the other.*

<u>Noah:</u>
But I like children!

<u>Irwin:</u>

You don't have to be able to have babies in order to have children. You can be a daddy.

<u>Noah:</u> (starting to feel better)
That's true.

Irwin:

You can be a kindergarten teacher.

Noah:

A kindergarten teacher? But a kindergarten teacher... a kindergarten teacher is a girl!

Irwin:

Not necessarily. You can open a kindergarten and call it Noah's Kindergarten, and a kindergarten teacher who is a man will take care of the children!

Noah:

Hmm... That's an idea! **(he starts to leave)** *Thank you, Irwin!!* **(He stops)** *Hang on Irwin, can I be a kindergarten teacher and a daddy and a pilot?*

Irwin:

Of course.

Noah:

Great!

Noah leaves.

Irwin (to the camera, astonished)
Hang on, a pilot? What's that got to do with anything?

The revised screenplay that I presented here was inspired by the comments written about the failed version, and this time, the screenplay achieved its objectives. No one disagrees that the fact that girls can give birth and boys cannot is the most fundamental difference between them.

Understanding this allowed the writer to write a script dealing with this fundamental difference without using negative behaviors to move the plot forward. Later, this screenplay received a few more comments in which the writer was asked to emphasize the point that though Noah understood that he couldn't ever be a mother, he *could* be a father. Additionally, the writer was asked to minimize the stereotype of the macho pilot that Piney presented in the screenplay. Nevertheless, all in all, the new version was received with applause by all the program's advisors. It was especially interesting to see children's reactions to the screening of the segment. They were greatly amused when Noah discovered, for the first time in his life, that fact known to all the viewers, including them, of course — that only girls can have babies. The idea that in all other fields there are no significant differences between girls and boys was understood as natural by the children. By talking to them after the screening, we discovered that that was exactly how the children saw things too.

Usually, working with advisors on content is very frustrating for writers. This is because often, advisors are not aware of the story-building process and only see plot development through the narrow prism of its messages or the conclusions the child will probably draw from the action.

As someone who has worked most of his years with advisors, I have to admit that the more I engage in dialogue about this, the more I understand and appreciate the great benefit there is to be had in this process — including benefits beyond the educational message.

It is true that the comments of advisors focus us primarily on the way in which children will grasp the content we have written, but if we involve them at an early enough stage, advisors can also help us on the plot development level. A perfect example of this is the "Boy or Girl?" screenplay where the advisor got involved when the plot itself was problematic. Her intelligent comments allowed the writers to free themselves of their narrow thinking and to tackle the subject in a new and refreshing way. In my experience, the great advantage of involving advisors lies in their angle of reference which helps me to understand that, from the point of view of a child, sometimes the heart of the plot isn't where we thought it was. It turns out that sometimes the question, "Where is the treasure?" is much less important than the relationships of the characters who seek the treasure or the question of who gets to hold the telescope on the way to finding the treasure.

FAIRIES, MONSTERS, KNIGHTS AND MORE...

CHILDREN'S FAVORITE CONTENT REPERTOIRE

It could be said that, to a certain extent, the chapters I have presented so far have served as an introduction to this upcoming chapter, which truly deals — finally —with the talents necessary for writing for children, according to my approach. The serious and dreary name of the chapter, *Content Repertoire,* hides all of the worlds of fantasy from which content that is truly designed for children emerges: industrious dwarves who wear red caps and live underground; fearsome giants; flying horses; fairies; goblins; princesses; geese that lay golden eggs; beanstalks that grow to the heavens; Puss in Boots; dragons; monsters; brave knights; heroes; and more. The real requirement of those who write for children (authors or screenwriters), therefore, is the ability to create wondrous worlds such as these, worlds that capture the imagination of children and make it possible for them to take part in fantastic adventures just like their heroes do.

Perhaps it is not incidental that most of the people I know who write content for children still preserve a little of the child within themselves. They tend to get excited about all the fantastic characters that star in these stories, and they greatly enjoy their ability to create wondrous worlds and enchanting characters themselves.

At one of the first seminars where I spoke on the topic of "Writing Scripts for Children," I opened with a marathon screening of select television programs and movies for children. I showed the student audience a selection of my favorite movies and television programs, and I hoped that they would enjoy (as I do) these series that star, for example, a bunch of plump wild chicks, two friends, Ernie and Bert, and their assortment of arguments, an ultimate grandfather who lives with a group of stuffed animals, or an odd character who confuses tomorrow with yesterday, near with far, fast with slow, and so on. I thought that watching these colorful programs would help me gracefully convey a children's fantasy world to these serious students of screenwriting, who were currently focused on writing dramas.

In contrast to my expectations, it became clear to me that the young students were unable to shed their years of "growing-up," and the content that caused me and my young friends (ages four to five) to break into giggles and collapse from laughter, did not elicit even a smile from the students. It would seem that they were a little embarrassed by me and the "inferior" material with which I forced them to engage.

After a short program of failed experiments, I understood that it fell to me to change my approach. At the next seminar on writing for children that I presented, I opened in a different way. Instead of screening children's television programming, I brought a pile of socks in different colors. I attached button eyes and a button nose to each sock, and the students chose sock puppets in their favorite colors. Students were then asked to prepare, in pairs, short home videos of dialogue between the sock puppets.

The result was wondrous. The students operated the puppets with great skill, and the dialogues that they put in the mouths of the puppets were steeped in humor, innocence, and charm. It would seem that something in this totally childish exercise helped to free them of the weight of their years and made it possible for them to connect with the creative starting point that is critical to writing for children: namely, *to connect to the child within.* I saw the ultimate proof of this connection during the break, when some of the students took their puppets with them and continued to "speak" to their classmates through them, in their free time.

As someone who has worked with many children's authors over the years, I find that the greatest danger in the process of writing for young children generally lies in the author's effort to "come down" to the eye-level of the child and the author's experience in writing something at the "low level," as it were, of the target audience. Many children's authors tend to think — in error — that writing for children means writing for someone inferior to themselves. They tend to create situations that run from simplistic to boring. They use basic, impoverished language and unsophisticated humor, and all from the sense that a higher level of writing or more sophisticated humor would fundamentally result in the child's lack of understanding and enjoyment. I am far from agreeing with this claim. The best children's authors I know do not make every effort to come down to the eye-level of the child — on the contrary! They are barely aware of the age of the reader. They write first and foremost for themselves, or, more precisely, they connect to the child within without any concern for their own biological age.

Writers who have difficulty connecting to the child within may, as needed, connect with actual children, those who are the appropriate chronological age, children who will help them learn to extract all the fun from exciting games with toy cars on the carpet, from the building of muddy sand castles at the beach, the magical tour of shelves packed with toys at the toy store, the watching of an emotion-laded film like *Bambi,* or delving into the world of children's books, such as: *Peter Pan, When We Were Young,* or *Alice in Wonderland.* Children's worlds include many enjoyable and quality experiences that do not require us to regress in our maturity at all in order to join in the fun.

Avraham Shlonsky, among the great children's authors, once said, "What is a good children's book? A book in which adults repeatedly find meaning and pleasure." Shlonsky adds, "An author must not write 'specially' for children, to descend to the lowest level of a child's understanding, to crouch before the child and disguise himself as an infant." So said author and illustrator Nachum Gutman as well: "I do not think that one must target one's writing to children. I maintain that one can speak about any topic with a child..." In addition to these great authors, C.S. Lewis, author of the *Narnia* series, is quoted as having said similar things. Specifically, "A children's book that only children will enjoy is a bad children's book." (*The Notion of Childhood*, Zohar Shavit, 1996)

The masterpiece that provides the paradigm of writing for children without compromise is, of course, *Alice in Wonderland*, written by Charles Lutwidge Dodgson, better known by his pseudonym, Lewis Carroll. One day, Charles took his nieces, ten-year-old Alice and her sisters Lorena, aged 13, and Edith, aged 8, on a cruise on one of the Thames River tributaries. Over the course of the outing, Alice turned to Charles and asked him to write a story for her that described events in which she herself took part, as it were. The story that Charles Lutwidge Dodgson wrote for Alice on that same cruise is one with which we are all familiar. One of the important elements of this example is specifically the process. Charles Lutwidge did what most parents do when their children ask them to tell a story in which the child stars as the hero. He put himself in Alice's place and invented a variety of experiences that, to the best of his understanding, Alice would greatly enjoy experiencing. The story that Charles wrote on that outing was designed for a ten-year-old girl; however, I have no doubt that he himself enjoyed the creation of it. Indeed, the wonderful story is enjoyed by people of all ages to this very day. The fantastic characters of the story — the Mad Hatter, the Queen of Hearts, the White Rabbit, the Cheshire Cat — together with the fantastic tale that blends reality with the absurd, yielded a mix that captured the hearts of millions of readers throughout the world.

If we carefully examine the creation of other masterpieces for children, in the realm of cinema, drama, and television, such as: *Once Upon a Time... Man, The Smurfs, The Brady Bunch, Mr. Rogers' Neighborhood,* and *The Wonderful Adventures of Nils*, or the creation of important

children's movies like Walt Disney's *Mickey Mouse, Bambi, Fantasia, Dumbo, Pinocchio* and *Mary Poppins*, or Albert Broccoli's *Chitty Chitty Bang Bang*, and of course the important literary creations of Hans Christian Andersen, Theodore Seuss Geisel (a.k.a. Dr. Seuss), Mark Twain and others, we are able to establish with certainty that not one of them worked to come down to the eye-level of the child. I have no doubt that most, if not all, of them created worlds that are *also* appropriate for children, but first and foremost, they wrote for themselves.

As an attempt to catalogue this range of worlds of content for myself, and inspired by the writing of this book, I decided to do a little experiment on the topic.

I surfed the Internet to find a site specializing in selling children's books. I defined my target audience as between ages three and seven, and the site retrieved 1,457 titles as age-appropriate. I checked out the summaries of these books and tried to sort them according to content type. I categorized books like *Peter Pan* and *Pippy Longstocking* with child heroes or children with superpowers. I categorized fables and stories like *Goldilocks and the Three Bears, Puss in Boots*, and others like them as stories based on a world with anthropomorphic animals, and the like.

As a result of my superficial, unscientific survey, it turns out that the collection of 1,400 books on the site could be condensed into 25 different worlds of content alone. The list includes:

- **Worlds of animals** (that is, animals that speak and function like human beings)
- **Worlds of dragons**
- **Worlds of dinosaurs**
- **Witches and wizards**
- **Fairy tales**
- **Tales of castles, kings, princesses, and knights**
- **Tales of family and family events** (I have a new sibling, I'm growing up, bedtime stories, It's my birthday, etc.)
- **Circus tales**
- **Children with superpowers** (child heroes)
- **Smart children** — tales of children who are smarter or more skilled than the adults around them
- **Tales of adults who fail** (Grandpa goes to first grade, Dad is confused, and the like)
- **Children's pranks and tricks** (Dennis the Menace and the like)
- **Absurd worlds**
- **Tall tales**
- **Etiological** stories (providing narrative explanations for natural phenomena, such as: why the elephant has a trunk, or why the rabbit's tail is short, or why a bat is a rodent and not a bird)
- **Stories of empowering the weak, in which the little, weak character always saves the great, strong one in the end**

- **Detective stories for children**
- **Treasure hunts**
- **Stories of travel to exotic or undiscovered lands**
- **Heroes**
- **The world of little people** (dwarves, elves, fairies, pixies, etc.)
- **Stories that occur under the sea**
- **Stories that occur between the celestial bodies or between the clouds**
- **Stories that occur in the school yard, in kindergarten, or among children** (without adult involvement)
- **Stories of monsters**

This list is, of course, superficial, and does not take the place of systematic research. It is clear that the 1,457 titles are not divided in equal measure among these 25 categories. If we divide 1,457 by 25, we should have 58 titles per category. The distribution of content around topics, however, shows that where one given topic boasts 200 titles, another has fewer than 20. Nevertheless, this list delineates 25 clear directions in the world of content beloved by children, and more importantly, it indicates the wonderful freedom that exists specifically and particularly in creating worlds for children.

The great strengths of reliability, logic, and reality that generally function as the core of artistry for adults are not part of the toolbox for creating these worlds.

If, for example, you have a pair of worn slippers that you really love, and you want to create a story about them, this is the place to breathe life into them. The world of children will be happy to share a plot which includes all the scuffed shoes that should have been discarded long ago, but in which you, and only you, see magic powers. Indeed, the wearers of these slippers, from the moment they are put on, anywhere in the world, can close their eyes, count to three, and (Pop!) find themselves back at home, safe and sound. I assume that anyone who has ever created any content that was beloved by children knows the wonderful creative freedom of doing so. Anything goes; all is possible. An old plastic pacifier can become a hero; a pocket flashlight can become a magic torch that, with one flash, can shrink a fearsome lion, reducing it to the size of a tiny ant. Then it is possible, without any difficulty, to put the lion into a small matchbox, and continue on your way.

Those who stand at the top of this pyramid of content are the **protagonists, the heroes**: a cowardly lion, a courageous scarecrow, a dandy cat, a lost chick, an all-powerful king, an evil sorcerer and others like these heroes that excite our imagination, and that of children, and makes possible the spinning of fascinating plots around unique traits, enabling children to watch them and admire them, to laugh and to identify with them.

Avi Becker, an excellent child psychologist who has worked with me for many years in children's programming, once brought my attention to an issue of great interest, that of small children watching soap operas, programs that should not, as it were, capture their interest at all. Avi believes that the reason young children enjoy watching soap operas so much lies in the level of superficiality and simplicity of the characters on the shows. They can usually be described in a sentence or two, as is illustrated in the table defining personalities below, taken from the official website of one of the recent, popular soap operas.

The model — betrayed, seeking revenge

The TV producer — a liar, conniving and **unscrupulous**

The mobster — tough and mean-spirited

The actress — trying to make a come-back, despite a **checkered past**

The soldier — a combat officer, tough and hiding his **homosexuality**

These characters are clear, distinct, and one-dimensional, striving ceaselessly to accomplish one goal.

The soap opera's characters' lack of depth is very similar, of course, to the one-dimensional nature of characters in children's stories. There too, characters are stereotypes, with minimal personal details. Characters in the world of children are often caricatures: the *wicked* witch, the *good* dwarves, the *wise* old man, etc. Or the characters come from the world of the professions: *the police officer, the bus driver, the pilot, the firefighter,* and the like. Generally speaking, they have one desire only, and that drives the plot.

Analysis of a well-known character like *Winnie-the-Pooh,* for example, yields that he loves honey, is slow-witted ("maybe because I have cotton wool for brains"), and likes to make up songs. Analysis of the characters surrounding Pooh confirms the assessment that the characters possess few personality traits:

Eeyore the Donkey — depressed, certain that nobody likes him, does not like doing anything.

Tigger the Tiger — happy, likes to play.

Owl — wise and likes to use complicated words.

Rabbit — neat, organized, and likes to feel important.

Piglet — brave and likes to help his friends.

Roo —likes milk and wants things to be good for him.

Kanga, his mother — a worrier, worries about her son all the time.

If we continue to analyze other well-known characters from children's literature or television programs whom we remember from our own childhoods, we discover that regardless of the honored place they hold in our minds, the list of their personal character traits is virtually unknown. All that is known, for example, about *Mrs. Pepperpot* is that she is an old woman who lives on a farm with her husband, and that her peaceful life is disrupted every time the magic spoon she possesses shrinks her to miniature size.

Analyzing the traits of the *Smurfs* also allows one to learn more than a little about the restricting of personalities in the world of children's content.

Papa Smurf — *ancient: 542 years old; wise (reads a lot); knows magic.*

Smurfette — *the only female in the village, until Sassette arrived; loved by everyone in the village, including Papa Smurf.*

Hefty Smurf — *the strongest Smurf in the village.*

Brainy Smurf — *knowledgeable and arrogant; likes to preach.*

Jokey Smurf — *an amateur prankster (especially exploding gifts).*

Grouchy Smurf — *cranky and grumpy; a constant complainer, accustomed to saying "I hate" for everything he can think of.*

Dreamy Smurf — *the Smurf who loves sleep; able to sleep anywhere, at all times; daydreams, especially about other worlds and aliens.*

Clumsy Smurf — *clumsy and unlucky.*

Greedy Smurf — *chubby; he knows many recipes; he likes to eat, cook, and especially bake.*
Vanity Smurf — *a dandy, who wears a flower on his hat; looks at himself in the mirror and enjoys the view.*
Handy Smurf — *does maintenance; an inventor; very diligent, of course.*
Scaredy Smurf — *a coward; startled by everything; trembles with fear most of the time.*
Tracker Smurf — *has an excellent sense of smell and a talent for predicting things with this sense.*
Sloppy Smurf — *loves dirt, garbage, and rotten fruit; has a pet fly.*
Harmony Smurf — *a musician; likes to fake-play a trumpet, and gets on everyone's nerves.*
Painter Smurf — *an artist; active in most areas of the visual arts.*
Poet Smurf — *a poet; likes to wander in nature and to improvise songs about nature.*
Baby Smurf — *a baby.*
Gargamel — *an unsuccessful evil sorcerer; known by his proclamation, "I hate Smurfs."*
Azrael — *Gargamel's aide, and no less evil.*

As we continue to examine the personalities of the heroes of children's series, be they Teletubbies or Dora; Steve and Blue the puppy; Clifford the Big Red Dog; Bob the Builder; Sam the Fireman; or Noddy; we discover that defining their personalities does not take two lines, as opposed to the personalities in screenplays for adults. In adult screenplays, every character has a known biography and a mystery too — an internal and external identity, desires, attitudes, patterns of behavior, motivations, blocks, and personality traits with internal contradictions. It is perfectly possible to go on and on in describing their personalities and characteristics.

The unidimensionality of the characters written specifically for children is not the result of superficiality but a response to a need. In contrast to complex characters, the conduct of one-dimensional characters is usually predictable, and characters with predictable behavior allow children to anticipate their processes. We have already noted, in the chapter that addresses principles of writing for young children, that the ability to predict and decipher plot lines successfully strengthens children's confidence in themselves and in their knowledge, granting them a sense of control, and increasing their enjoyment.

Unidimensionality is given expression primarily when defining a character's personality traits. However, anyone who ever presented a personality in a children's program knows that they have to be very precise. Indeed, over the course of the personality's design, endless subtleties are manufactured, like a type of law, where it is clear to everyone that the character would never say certain things that would be peculiar to her, and that a particular style of speech and mannerism is unique to the character as well. The children who watch are incredibly aware of these subtleties and would not tolerate the slightest departure from the known behaviors of their beloved characters.

In my eyes, the process of inventing and developing a world of content is the inner heart of creating for children.

It is difficult to see what comes first: the world or the characters. At times, it seems that the world determines the characters, and at times, the personalities write the world. It is this process, surely, that is particular to each author and creation, especially as, in the process of the specific development of a program, there may be dynamic movement between the two. A given creator may think of a world that is established within a pinball machine as an interesting starting point for a series. From there on, it is clear that the personalities created will be of that world. They will have to answer to the laws of the pinball world that surrounds them. That is, they will have to be a type of ball, or some other creation which logic dictates could exist in a pinball world. Alternatively, in a different process of development, a character can be the starting point. It is well known that children the world over show great interest in garbage trucks. (My own children, for example, were accustomed to rising early every other day to run to the balcony and wait with eyes wide open for the exciting morning encounter between the giant green garbage truck and the house dumpster in the courtyard, overflowing with trash. They were fascinated by the way the large amount of garbage would disappear into the belly of the truck, together with all of the unique hydraulic sounds it made.) As a young parent, I thought about developing a show starring four urban garbage trucks: mother and father in the role of large garbage trucks, and two children, in the role of smaller trash-collecting vehicles. At the time, I thought that the Garbage Truck Family could provide me with wonderful, foundational characters for a series. It was understood, in that case, that the characters had to be the driving force, writing the world. Where would they live? What would the laws of the world of garbage trucks be? With whom would they be in contact? What do garbage trucks do when they are sick? Who are their friends? And so on.

In most cases, therefore, creating content for children is based on the creation of broad worlds, populated by magical creatures, in which the endless expanse makes it possible for us to break down barriers in every direction imaginable.

Moreover, the more that we challenge the boundaries of the watching child's imagination, the better. In these worlds, one might meet a family of penguins leading their petit bourgeois lives; a group of steam engines that struggle with the same social problems that affect kindergarten children; a giant friendly red dog as large as a four-story building; adventurous piglets; duck detectives; a group of mushrooms that go to school; a talking steamship; cubes that want to become bouncing balls; and more.

These fantastic characters carry on their backs the stories that we want to tell and live in worlds where even the sky is not the limit — for the heavens can become a world of wondrous content, fascinating in and of itself.

CHARACTER TYPES

The process of inventing "magical characters" for fantastic worlds of content is fundamentally different from the process of developing characters for a regular dramatic script. A dramatic personality in a movie or on TV is examined on two main fronts: parameters of identity and parameters of character. The *parameters of identity* include all the external details of the character: physical givens, style of dress, age, profession, manner of speech, comportment, socio-economic standing, and so on.

The *parameters of character* include all of the details that are hidden from view but that come to expression through the character's conduct, that is, values and traits such as uprightness, falsehood, courage, cowardice, generosity, miserliness, and more. The caveat is, however, that the toolbox of parameters of identity and of character include only human traits, or traits that are anthropomorphically ascribed to animals. In the process of inventing fantasy characters, the importance of these parameters becomes secondary. The uniqueness of the character and the magic the character reveals become paramount. If we take a look at a lineup of magical creatures, such as the cat with the magic violin that caused all who heard it to go out and dance; the wooden seahorse that toured the world to find himself a true friend; the arrogant toy car that did not care to play with little boys; or the locomotive that helped children find the Land of Nod every night; we understand that the raw magic is not expressed in the parameters of identity and character, but first and foremost in the invention of the character's form. The invention is intended to enchant and captivate the hearts of children for the long term, and the parameters of character stick to the extent that they were intended to help the magic character integrate into the plot in the best, most fascinating way.

The invention of magical characters appears to be a release from the gravitational laws of believability, and a look to the endless regions of imagination, capped only by the author's own imagination. But this is not the case. Together with the limits of one's imagination and one's talent for invention is another limitation: budget. In the chapter that deals with the fundamentals of writing, we already discussed budgetary limitations, and how the production rests on the shoulders of television screenwriters. They have a different job from that of writing children's books or scripts for animation, as they enjoy far less creative freedom, given that writing for television must conform at all times to production parameters: on the set of the studio, or on location, or in the time limit for the filming of every episode.

In order to understand how magical characters fit into the budgetary vise, it is worth knowing the various character types that generally appear in children's television programming. If we analyze personalities that usually star in these programs, or in home movies for children (not including animated film!), we discover that the personalities in these programs may be divided, at long last, into several categories:

A. HUMAN CHARACTERS

There are two kinds of human characters:

1. **Realistic human characters** (that exist in worlds that tend to be a little less realistic). This includes human actors who play regular roles, such as the program's presenter, in a program where there is direct appeal to the child watching at home. Humans also play dramatic roles: the parent, the neighbor, the confused uncle, and so on.

2. **Figurative, unrealistic human characters** that could only possibly exist on screen and may fill a broad range of unrealistic roles. They can be superheroes such as Superman, Batman, and others like them — humans with superhuman characteristics. Or, they could be Why Man, who is found only when the question "why?" is asked, or Danger Man, who is adorned with red lights that light up in times of danger.

What usually distinguishes these characters, as well as other figurative characters that belong in this category, is appearance. Every one of these personalities has a unique, figurative appearance that characterizes that character and only that character, whether it is a vampire's suit, a propeller on the head, a garment made of musical instruments, a pair of clock hands on his back, or a small child's costume. Sometimes, these figurative characters have unique names as well: the Music Man, Mr. Time, Batman, Iceman, Mr. Confused, and others.

Another thing that characterizes these personalities are the "laws" that govern their behavior. The program relies on the fact that their patterns of behavior, which are nearly mechanical, and their reactions to the events of the movie or show, are usually completely expected. Heroes activate their special strengths in reaction to whatever problem they have stumbled across. Other figurative characters, who are not heroes, act in a mechanical, defined and predictable fashion too, though their characters are usually more clownish. Mister Noodle, a clown personality who is part of Elmo's World on Sesame Street, makes a good example. Mister Noodle is the type of clown that does not speak. He always comes up with a plan to demonstrate a simple activity for Elmo and the viewers, familiar to them from daily life, like putting on shoes or catching a ball, but for Mister Noodle, these activities are always completely new. He has never encountered them in the past, leading him to unsuccessfully struggle with them in an amusingly clownish and idiosyncratic manner until eventually... he succeeds in accomplishing the task.

Figurative characters like these and others make up a large portion of children's programming, and they generally act like a kind of grown-up child.

B. PUPPET CHARACTERS

There are several subcategories of puppet characters.

1. **Puppets that have the appearance of human beings**. That is, a puppet that looks like a boy, girl, grown-up man, and so on.

2. **Puppets that represent animals**: dog, cat, duck, or any other animal.

3. **Puppets that represent undefined creations** (for example on Sesame Street, where they are generally called "monsters"). This category includes all the puppets whose form does not link them to any population group.

4. Puppets representing definite objects or plants that can move or speak.

As I mentioned, puppet characters are divided into types, according to their external appearance. But they are also divided according to their "operating techniques." The three widely accepted operating techniques in television or cinema puppets are:

1. **Body puppets** — the actor wears some kind of character shape over her whole body and head (bear, giant roll, alarm clock).

2. **Glove puppets** — a puppet that has a head and hands. The actor/operator sits or stands behind some object which serves as a screen, blocking what would be the lower part of the character. These puppets are called glove puppets because the actor who operates them puts her hands into the palms of the puppet, and in this way, operates it.

3. **Rod puppets** — Rod puppets also have a head and hands, and here too, the operating actor sits or stands

behind a screening object and is hidden fully. These puppets are called rod puppets because of the thin rods that are attached to the limbs of the puppet, by which the actor controls the hands of the puppet.

Of course, there are several other forms, such as marionettes, finger puppets, black theater, shadow theater, and any other technique that uses puppets, objects, or accessories which are brought to life by the puppeteer who operates them. Still, use of these techniques in the world of television and cinema is far rarer.

Nearly every single studio-filmed children's television program in the world includes at least one puppet. Sometimes, a puppet character stars alongside a human character, and sometimes, completely independently. A survey of current broadcast programming by the BBC teaches us that 9 out of 56 shows that are aired by the BBC children's channels star puppets. As for the rest of the shows, they are animated shows of different types. Also, on the American P.B.S. Kids channel, 6 of the 22 shows star puppets (and here too, the rest of the shows are animated). It is understood that nearly every show geared for children will be based on puppets or at least on a partnership between human beings and a puppet or two. Slightly closer examination of the kinds of puppets used reveals that puppets of different kinds star in the various television programs. The difference between the puppets is found in the materials from which they are made, in their operating technique, and — fundamental to the definition — the *type* of puppet. That is, puppets are usually divided into four basic types of puppets:

A. PUPPETS THAT LOOK LIKE HUMAN BEINGS

These puppets generally have a human face structure and nearly always wear clothing. They usually portray a caricature of some human trait, in some way, depending on their dominant characteristic (e.g., shyness, mischievousness, innocence). This characteristic is emphasized in the puppet's basic facial expression and is reflected in its design. The decision to give a puppet a human appearance stems from the fact that there are usually several animal puppets starring in that same program, and there is a need to distinguish between the puppets, as in between a boy and his dog or between a farmer and his cow. As a rule, the explanation for the puppet's appearance lies in the series' content. That is, something in the material of the show justifies the use of puppets with a human appearance. For example, when a puppet plays the role of a police officer, a firefighter, or some other familiar professional role, there is good reason to think that too abstract of a look (in other words, something unlike a standard human) will miss the mark for the child who watches the show.

That said, in addition to all the "scholarly" reasons brought here, the decision to use puppets often emerges from a gut-level instinct in more than a few instances. A show's creators give the initial plans to a puppet designer (or to a design company), and through a collaborative process, accompanied by more than a few sketches, the cast of puppet actors in the show are designed.

Human-looking puppets

B. PUPPETS THAT LOOK LIKE ANIMALS

This refers to puppets that look like a dog, a bear, a rabbit, a frog, a chicken, a crocodile, a butterfly, a parrot, and so on. This category includes (perhaps most importantly) unrealistic-looking puppets, like the Checkered Raccoon, a unique raccoon with checkered fur; a puppy made from fabric patches; a combination of two kinds of animals, and more. At times, animal puppets do indeed represent the animals they resemble, but the animal puppets are not necessarily affected by the living animals themselves. For example, Kermit the Frog functions as a sportswriter, Fozzy Bear is a failed stand-up comedian, and Miss Piggy is a melodramatic actress with an inflated ego. None of the three are perceived as an animal straight out of nature. Often, the specific animal is chosen in order to emphasize the character traits which that animal and the character share. For example, a peddler puppet may be presented as a fox to help the audience discern his cunning and trickery easily. Similar cases include a baby chick puppet which heightens the sense of the character's innocence, or an owl puppet, underlying the character's propensity for knowledge, or a peacock puppet, highlighting the fussiness associated with that

In other instances, one might choose an animal puppet because of its physical appearance, like the penguins that epitomize waiters, or a Dalmatian that represents a firefighter. The creation of a gang of animals including a giraffe, a leopard, a monkey, and a parrot is also a good option, for the differences between the animals draws out the character differences that exist between the four friends and strengthen the individuality of each of the separate characters.

That said, in many cases, puppets are designed without any intent to connect the animal figure to traits or characteristics of any kind. The choice can emerge directly from the thought that a classroom full of playful squirrels or young monkeys would simply be entertaining to the audience.

Puppets that look like animals

C. CREATURES

With reference to puppets, *creatures* tend to mean something with eyes, a nose, and a mouth, and therefore, a generally human appearance, without connecting them to any particular population or specific biological family. The *creatures* may appear to be human, to be animals, or to be a geometric shape: spherical, elliptical, pear-shaped, or any other shape. They have no clearly defined conduct, and one can invent the laws that govern their existence. Using puppets shaped like creatures is convenient, because for puppets such as these, one is likely to invent the logic that allows them to serve the needs of the television show or movie completely.

Creatures (Also known as Monsters)

If you want to invent *The Family That Says "No"!, The Nappers, The Laughers, The Confused Bunch*, or a group of friends who only exist within a toy box, it is reasonable to assume that the characters will be creatures.

When we design a lion, a mouse, or a cat, we are always obligated to consider all of the lions, mice, and cats that have been designed in endless plans over the many years. The creature is not based on a clear personality that was already designed in the past, meaning that the designing of creatures entails far more creative freedom.

D. OBJECTS OR PLANTS THAT HAVE BEEN HUMANIZED

This category of puppets is generally geared to answering a defined and local script demand. That is, the series' regulars encounter specific plots where a cookie speaks, or a banana sings, or a television puppet expresses its own opinions. The object or plant puppets are usually personalities that appear in the plot just once, or they are secondary characters who appear infrequently, such as a talking road sign, consulted in order to correct one's travel route. Other examples are the Wise Compass and the Talking Lunchbox, which knows better than anyone what foods are healthful and which to avoid. Just as every rule has its exception, there are exceptions to this rule too. It is therefore reasonable to assume that you will come across certain programs where the object or plant puppet will have a starring role. I myself set out to develop a puppet with personality in the form of a telephone and one in the form of a book of legends that enjoyed recounting legends to children. I have encountered a talking post office box, a microphone puppet that commands other people, a talking pineapple, a dancing doughnut, and a spoiled tree that no longer likes standing in the rain… and more.

Despite these examples, to the best of my experience, in most cases, these puppets are very limited, providing their writers and creators with the answer to a need for specific content — usually in exchange for reduced freedom. In my eyes, the central task for object puppets and plants is to strengthen the world of fantasy in which the programs are usually found. There is no doubt that in a street where both regular people and various furry, colorful creatures live, or where animals speak, logic allows for a talking mailbox as well, or a traffic light that proclaims the merits of caution in crossing the streets, or a puppet in the shape of a loaf of bread, master of many human traits.

Puppets in the form of objects or humanized plants

Operational Techniques

We have already identified that puppet types can be grouped according to external appearances, as well as according to their operational techniques. The accepted operational techniques include operating the complete body of a *body puppet,* hand puppets, operated like gloves, and called *glove puppets,* and hand puppets operated with rods, called *rod puppets.* These operational techniques naturally impact the forms of expression of the various puppets.

Body Puppets

Body puppets have a capacity for expression that is lacking in other puppets. They can articulate themselves with unique gestures, such as standing defiant, curling up, or developing a unique walk. These puppets also have the privilege of walking alongside human actors on the set, without needing to resort to finding a hiding place for the puppet's operator.

Body Puppet

Glove Puppets and Rod Puppets

Glove puppets and rod puppets have specific advantages over body puppets. For example, they have the ability to change their facial expression. The puppeteer's hand fills a hole in the puppet's face, and she can therefore manipulate the face of the puppet to express a variety of emotions.

If we compare glove puppets and rod puppets with body puppets and the like, we discover a broad range of advantages and disadvantages in their abilities to express emotion. The differences in range of expressive abilities will affect your decisions as a creator regarding the kind of puppet you choose to take on the task of embodying the characteristics of your creation.

Understanding the connection between a puppet's operating technique and the content which suits the puppet would require me to enter into the minutiae of puppetry, and a deep understanding of this topic requires practical experience and direct contact with the full range of puppets available.

Glove Puppet & Rod Puppet

The technical details that are relevant to puppeteering technique, together with the various considerations for choosing the most suitable puppet for the given material, are delineated below, in a chapter dedicated solely to puppets. At this point, therefore, we limit ourselves to identifying the techniques and knowledge for operating puppets that are the dominant factors in the planning stage of matching puppet form to content, for the starring puppet characters.

CHOOSING CONTENT

The meaning of the expression *content repertoire* in simple words is: *the invention of worlds, characters, and plots that children really, really love.* As with any successful learning process, the best way to understand the process of developing worlds and the accompanying content is by reconstructing the creative process from the stage of identifying the demand through the final results, which should include the following:

A magical world that will excite the imagination of a child.

Original, playful characters.

An exciting plot.

For educational series which attempt to convey specific educational messages to the children who watch the show, it is necessary to add another fundamental condition to these three, namely:

Curricular topics that form the foundation of a show must be *existentially necessary* to the fascinating characters and the world in which they exist.

The starting point of most of children's television programming is the identification of a need. Children's television channels identify a new need expressed in the target audience. Sometimes, such a need is simply a question of fashion, in that it comes to address a new social trend. For example, a new game that conquers the hearts of children is suddenly found on the shelves of stores. Analyzing the daily schedule of the viewing audience helps the channel to identify a topic like this one, which has not yet been addressed. Sometimes, a channel identifies a social need and sometimes, it identifies the need for a set of values to underlie what will become their flagship product. And sometimes, a simple idea is sent as a suggestion and it somehow rolls over to the content development department. Either way, generally speaking, the first step is defining the need. At the next step, the need is converted into a brief (a working paper). Large entities that include several content departments handle the brief through the research department, or through the head editor or writer, both of whom are helped in turn by their team of writers.

Here is an example of a need that has been translated into a brief: Children's television channels identified a new need, based on the outcome of a recent study that determined that children begin to learn to read at a younger age than they had in the past. On the basis of this given, the television channel decided to develop a program for children that would focus on reading preparedness for early childhood. The television channel wanted to develop a program that would both entertain and also provide children with their first tools for grappling with written language.

Below, I have included the brief produced by the channel and passed on to the creators.

BRIEF FOR A SERIES DEALING WITH READING READINESS

Target audience: pre-reading children, ages four to seven
Length of each episode: six to eight minutes

Goals of the Series:

The series has four fundamental goals:

- To arouse the viewers' curiosity about language and to convey to them the pleasure and love of engaging with language.
- To enrich the viewers with literacy know-how.
- To encourage viewers to take up more literacy activities outside the screen, based on the subjects dealt with in the chapters.
- To encourage viewers to think about language, for the purpose of developing awareness for language patterns and forms.

Short Background:

Children are exposed to the sounds of language from a very early age. Later on, deciphering the graphic symbols of a language (which is, in fact, reading) joins hearing-based deciphering. The series' viewing audience is wide and covers the entire range from language deciphering based solely on auditory data to the development of initial reading skills. At this stage, hearing plays a very important role as a basis for acquiring reading and writing skills. Therefore, it is important that screenwriters pay special attention to how the words and language sound, and this attention should serve as a point of departure for their writing. One of the central goals of the series is to present language as intriguing and worth listening to.

Many of the topics included in the curriculum are topics that are familiar to viewers from their intimate familiarity with the language, since most of them talk, compose comprehensible sentences, use verbs and nouns, adjust verb usage according to the appropriate tenses, use singular and plural, etc. However, despite their intuitive use of language, in preparation for learning to read and write, it is important to develop awareness of different aspects of language and the ability to consciously manipulate language rather than to make do only with intuitive usage.

Topics such as identification of letters, syllables, and sounds (open, closed, mid-word) are new for some of the viewers, while others are partially familiar with them. Topics dealing with the meaning of words, expanding vocabulary, and enriching forms of expression are familiar or unknown to viewers depending on the social environment in which they live. The fact that the Hop! channel is watched by children from all social levels, and that many of its viewers live in a poor linguistic environment, should be taken into account.

● ● ●

The above brief was sent to me and a group of writers I headed when we began to develop the series. In addition to the brief, we also received a curriculum booklet that included sixty curriculum goals in the various fields of preparation for reading, including:

- **Dividing words into syllables**
- **Distinguishing between singular and plural**
- **Synonyms**
- **Ambiguous words**
- **Prepositions**
- **Expressions**
- **Adjectives**

Because the motivating force of a television series is first and foremost the captivating leading characters, the development team tried to come up with ideas for leading characters for which reading preparedness was the center of their world, just like a carrot is the center of a rabbit's world or honey is the center of Winnie-the-Pooh's world. In this case, subjects such as dividing words into syllables, distinguishing between singular and plural, or synonyms should be at the very center of the characters' world.

The first character proposed was that of a *word technician*, or in other words, a character that has a workshop for repairing damaged words. A person to whom people bring broken-down words or defective sentences, who tries to repair them. The team of writers was excited by the idea and tried to write experimental scripts based on the concept. The scripts written based on the word technician idea proved that the technician was a bad idea. The situations were repetitive, the technician's character wasn't exciting, the plots didn't take off, and it was clear that a new leading character was urgently needed. Another failed attempt was based on a parrot puppet. The parrot, that typically repeats what other people say, served as a message deliverer in the home of a family. Members of the family used to leave each other messages via the parrot, who inadvertently mixed them up and caused very amusing situations between the family members, who had to decipher the parrot's garbled messages, and these situations were used to focus on the topics in the series' curriculum. The parrot idea did indeed result in several amusing scripts but did not provide a long-term solution. The concept of the mix-ups as a plot turning point worked quite well in the first four scripts, but it didn't seem feasible to use it for the forty episodes of the series. A leading character must have freedom of plotline, and basing all the scripts in the series on a message mix-up situation with the parrot was too restrictive and fettered the writers' creative freedom, leaving the scripts empty of content.

Later in the development process a new idea was raised, about a grandfatherly character who tells stories to two creatures that haven't really mastered language. The two were a grouchy goldfish living in an aquarium and a pampered flower living in a flowerpot.

The fish found it hard to hear the stories because it is difficult to hear what is being said when you're underwater. His hearing problem provides a logical basis for his grouchiness and gave him quite a lot of reasons to be cross. The flower was an egocentric type, living in a pot, and wanting all the stories to be about him.

Based on the scripts written for the storyteller version, it seemed that the series was on the right path because, between the three of them (storyteller, fish, and flower), a family-like relationship began to develop that finally succeeded in nurturing and contributing to the plots. Since the flower and fish were not human, it was only natural that they did not understand some of the words or expressions, and their misunderstandings were a great vehicle for conveying the messages included in the series' curriculum.

Sometimes they didn't understand a word; other times they misunderstood the meaning of an expression, and the dialogue of misunderstanding between them was definitely amusing. The grouchy fish, that had real hearing problems, quickly turned into the hero of the series. All the plots developed from the fish's mix-ups, and the misunderstandings contributed to the creation of more and more amusing, as well as educational, situations. It appeared that the storyteller version was about to put the series on the road to success.

And indeed, a magical home was created, a world in which the storyteller lived and shared his life with the grouchy fish and pampered flower.

Everyone loved the supporting cast of the fish and flower, who were genuinely amusing and original, but something about the storyteller character felt old-fashioned, used, and not exciting enough to meet the expectations of his role as the hero of the series.

The storyteller character seemed to weigh down the plots and prevent them from developing in truly fascinating directions. From reading the test scripts and analysis of the problems that bothered the writers during the writing process, it appeared that the main problem of the series was a lack of horizon. Something about the static situation of telling stories to puppet characters and viewing children did not enable the writers to add energy into the plotlines. We then decided to stay with the current concept, but try to find a different character to replace the storyteller.

At this point, we had an idea that got everyone excited: a superhero who is actually an antihero — a hero without superhuman powers! A character that is actually incapable of really resolving problems. Every time that this hero faces a problem, he can put on his superhero cape, take his special toolbox, and reach the scene in an instant. But here the real problems begin, since his special powers only enable him to reach the problem site but not to truly resolve the problem.

The type of problems that the superhero will face will always have to do with language: a misunderstood word, an incorrect sentence, etc., so that language will be at the center of our hero's existence.

The idea of the loser superhero seemed like a winning concept. The scripts began to come to life. Each script began with an amusing problem or mystery, and our superhero's limitations provided excellent material for numerous comic situations.

Alan the All Powerful - The Antihero

But at this stage a new question arose. Are the grouchy fish and pampered flower from the earlier versions the two most suitable characters to accompany the adventures of our new anti-superhero?

The answer was soon to come. The pampered flower appeared to be an excellent partner, while the grouchy fish did not find his place in the new version. But since the fish's grouchy character was found to be a great comic driving force, and since we also remembered the message mix-up skills of the parrot (from the first versions) as a wonderful tool for creating plot twists and turns, we decided to try to combine the traits of these two (parrot and fish) and implant them in a third, new character. The character we chose was a confused and grouchy telephone puppet.

This was a telephone that shunned its official role as a communications pipeline between humans. The grouchy telephone disliked people touching him or speaking through him. He preferred to answer all the incoming calls himself and only take messages for the other residents of the house.

Another screenwriting decision we made was to let viewers actively participate in various episodes by contacting them directly. Although this was a purely technical decision, since we knew that contacting viewers directly was an excellent method to involve children, we decided to try adopting it in our series.

The attached episode, which was part of the series that was produced at the end of the development process, deals with the curriculum topic of expressions. This episode represents the results of the process.

From left to right: Victor the Angry Telephone, Alan the Schlemiel superhero, and Holly the Pampered Flower

"MAKING A MOUNTAIN OUT OF A MOLEHILL"

Goal of the episode: Common expressions — enriching the viewers' vocabulary in two contexts;

Particular goals: 1. Learning the term *expression* - a common pairing of words with a special meaning that is different from the meaning of each one of the words separately; **2.** Getting to know expressions. It is important to use concrete expressions and expressions based on simple and not complex symbolization. For example: big heart, heart of gold, golden hands, keeping an open mind, ants in his pants, and making a mountain out of a molehill.

1.   **Interior, Al's home, Daytime.**

Al (the unsuccessful superhero) is taking care of Holly the Flower. He is weeding the soil and watering it with a gentle mist sprayer.

Al:
(**to camera**) *Hi there kids. How are you?*

Children:
(**Off***) Fine.*

Holly / Flower:
(**Drawing all the attention to her**) *And what about me? Why doesn't anyone everyone ask how I am?*

Al gestures to the viewers to respond to Holly's request.

Children:
(**Off**) *How are you, Holly?*

Holly / Flower:
Fine, thank you.

Al:

(**To Holly**) *See? They are interested in how you are.*

Holly / Flower:
Well... that's true, but only sometimes.

Al:
(**To viewers**) *You're just in time. I have something very exciting to tell you! My friend Sally, who hasn't visited me in a long time, called half an hour ago and left me a message that she's coming to visit!*
(**Looks at the clock**) *And I'm so excited!*

Victor / Telephone:
(**Wakes up**) *Drring... Drring... Al!*
Why aren't you answering?
Can't you hear that you have a phone call?

Al runs to answer the phone.

Victor / Telephone:
Leave it... don't touch me. I'll answer. Hello? Sally?!
(**To Al**) *Who's Sally?*

Al:
(**Excited**) *Sally is a friend of mine from Rally Creek.*

Victor / Telephone:
Al!!!

Al:
(Impatient, moving close to Victor) *Well? Is she on
her way?
When is she coming? What did she say?*

Victor / Telephone:
*Wait… I can't hear her this way. It's very hard to
concentrate when everyone is sticking their noses in.*

Al looks around.

Al:
(Does not understand) *Everyone is sticking their noses
in? What does that mean? How can you stick a nose in?*

Victor / Telephone:
(To Al) *Quiet!* **(To Sally)** *Yes, Sally. I didn't understand.
Can you repeat the message? Ah… Aha…
Now I understand. Okay, I'll tell him… bye.*

Holly / Flower:
(Laughing) *Al, you're so funny. When someone says
"stick your nose in," he doesn't mean to really stick
a nose, it's an expression that means don't interfere
in other people's business.*

Al:
Really? So… **(suddenly understanding)** *wait,
but Sally is my business!*
(To Victor the Telephone) *So it's you who's sticking his*

nose into my business!

Victor / Telephone:
I'm allowed cause I'm a telephone.

Al:
Okay, what was Sally's message? When is she coming?

Victor / Telephone:
Well, she isn't coming. Sally said that she is sorry she's been delayed because *she 'lost her way'.*

Al:
(Upset) *Oh no. Lost her way? I can't believe it. Poor Sally. How did it happen?*

Holly / Flower:
Did what happen?

Al:
(To the flower) *Sally lost her way. I wonder where she put it?* **(To the telephone)** *Did you tell her to try to remember where she put it last time?*

Holly / Flower:
No, Al, she meant that…

Al:
(Speaking in a superhero tone) *If Sally "lost her way", that's a big problem. We've got to help her find the way that she lost, and quickly! This seems like a perfect mission for…* **(to the viewers)** *who?*

Children:
(Off) *Al the All-Powerful!*

Al:
Exactly!

Electronic sound effect / music; Al whirls around and appears to the viewers in superhero costume.

Al:
Come on! Let's find the way that Sally lost!

Holly / Flower:
Al, wait a minute!

Another sound effect — Al disappears before he hears Holly's warning.

Holly / Flower:
Oh silly Al, you can't lose a way. It's just an expression.

Victor / Telephone:
What do you mean just an expression?

Holly / Flower:
It's an expression that means that she got mixed up on the way and doesn't remember how to get here!

Victor / Telephone:
(Justifying himself) *Well, but that's not what she said.*

2. **An intersection of paths in the forest. Daytime.**

Al appears in the clearing with a circular effect. After he recovers from the twirling, he looks around in wonderment.

Al:

Hey, this is amazing. Here's the way. I found it. The way is where it has always been! Right here! I found Sally's way easily. Now I only have to let her know that her way has been found.
Wait a minute… to be on the safe side I'll leave her a note on the tree: **(writes a note and draws a tree)** *Hi, Sally. Here is the way you lost!* **(Puts up the note.)**

Effect — Al twirls in place and disappears.

3. Kitchen. Daytime.

Effect — Al appears back in his kitchen.

Al:

Victor, Holly! The mission was completed successfully. Everything's all right. I found the way that Sally lost. Now we just need to call and tell her that it was found!

Victor / Telephone:

(Drowsy) *It's okay. Sally called and said she bought a road map and will use it to find her way so she'll know how to reach us.*

Al:

(Frightened) *A road map? What for? Victor, call Sally and tell her that I already found her way, the one she lost. The way is exactly where it always was. There's no need for a map.*

Holly / Flower:

(Laughing) *Al, Al… you're confused. Sally didn't mean that she lost her way like you lose a pen or pencil. It's just an expression.*

Al:

What?! Are you sure?

Holly / Flower:

*Of course. When Sally said that "she lost her way,"
she meant that she got confused and doesn't remember
the route!*

Al:

*Ah, so there was no need to search for the way.
I should have looked for Sally who was lost?*

Victor / Telephone:

*Drring... Drring... Yes? Who is this? Sally?... Okay,
Okay, Okay... thank you.*
(Hangs up) *Sally said that she found the intersection of
the paths using the map, and she'll be here soon.*

Al:

*Great! So Sally found the lost way. Everything's okay
now?*

Holly / Flower:

Yes... **(laughing)** *it was just a case of making a
mountain out of a molehill.*

Al:

(Jumps up on the stool, frightened) *A molehill?*

Holly / Flower:

What are you scared of?

Al:

I don't know anything about any mountain or mole hill! A hill with a mole the size of a mountain? It doesn't even make sense. How can a mountain fit in a hill? **(Looks at Holly the Flower who is laughing)** *Ah! You were joking. You're laughing at me? Kids, is she making fun of me?*

Children:

(Off) *No!*

Al:

(Surprised) *No?*

Holly / Flower:

No, silly Al, it's just an expression. When people say "make a mountain out of a molehill," they mean that something that you thought was very big and complicated turns out to be small and simple.

Al:

Oh, so it's an expression.

Victor / Telephone:

Drinng... Drinng...

Al:

(Doesn't hear) *What?*

Victor / Telephone:

(Shouting) *I said Drinng... Drinng... and that means there's a phone call... forget it. I'll answer. Hello? Yes? Who? Sally? Sally who?*

Al:
Sally! Sally from Spring Creek! Well, is she coming?

Victor / Telephone:
All right, I'll tell him.

Al:
Well?

Victor / Telephone:
It was Sally again. She's on her way. She asked if you're still waiting for her or have you 'lost your patience'?

Al:
"Lost my patience"? **(searches in his pockets)**
I didn't notice that I'd lost it.
Why, did she find my patience on the way?

Holly / Flower:
No, Al, it's just…

Al:
I know, I know, this time I was making fun. It's just an…

Children:
Expression!!!

Laughter

The series, *Alan the All Powerful*, eventually reached 80 episodes, written and filmed. The development of this program therefore succeeded in creating a long-term vision for the show's writers, and the series had the great fortune of becoming very successful.

One of the conclusions that emerged from the analysis of the process of development of *Alan the All Powerful* (and additional development processes as well) was that at the idea stage, it is very difficult to determine the true raw potential of a show's concept. Sometimes, the very concept that seems to be a shining star, amusing and full of excellent potential, may turn out to be a dead end. It may not open new horizons for its writers but instead lead the writers to tread water, as it were, while another, less exciting concept might come to embody an endless writing horizon. The only way of checking for the ongoing potential of a concept is to write experimental screenplays. From the process of writing these experimental screenplays, it is possible to learn first what level of pleasure the writers take from the placement of the idea into the concept (a vital parameter), and to what extent does the concept lend itself to the writing of a wide variety of possible plot lines?

With *Alan the All Powerful*, it became clear, when all was said and done, that only the idea of a superhero could be successful in producing a show that allowed the writing of many wide and varied plots. Essentially, this was thanks to the fact that reading comprehension became the very existence of *Alan the All Powerful*. In each episode, he set out to accomplish some kind of redundant heroic act, whereby the problem of *reading incomprehension* always stood in his way, propelling the plot, and feeding the show's message for its audience.

The program presented below is geared to older viewers. It was originally described as a series for eight- to twelve-year-olds — that is, children in their later childhood years (or early adolescence). At this age, children are nearing the capacity to understand the adult world. Therefore, creators who write for children of this age are released from the cognitive limitations of younger children. The viewers are not limited in their abilities to comprehend, and are already accustomed to watching programs for grownups: sitcoms, soap operas, dramas, and more.

The repertoire of content that interests children at this age consists of adventure stories, enigmas, mysteries, secret societies, brave bands of friends, programs taking place in educational institutions, family dramas that focus on the problems of youth, and so on. Of course, for writers, it is far easier to connect to this population and to this kind of content. In one case, however, the development team faced a problem: a very long list of educational messages designed to be included in the series, which was supposed to be broadcast by a new children's science channel. The channel's goal was "to produce an engaging drama around a list of **scientific content** for the audience to understand and internalize." That is, the program's developers were required to produce a world of content that would fascinate children and adolescents and that would deal with a new scientific concept in each episode, all wrapped up in a new and dramatic plot. In order to be exact, below is the brief that was attached to the Children's Science Channel, to create the show.

BRIEF: PROPOSAL FOR THE DEVELOPMENT OF A TELEVISION SERIES FOR THE CHILDREN'S SCIENCE CHANNEL

Series purpose: To awaken intellectual curiosity in the different branches of science for the younger viewing audience and to present different science topics in a variety of fields:

- Natural sciences (botany/zoology/physics)
- Geography (physical, political, ecological, geological)
- History (watershed events; people)
- Culture (cultural turning points, famous works, skilled artists)

Type of show: comedy/drama

Target audience: youth, ages 8 – 12

Series length: 26 episodes of 24 minutes each

Complexity: Studio drama, including up to six actors (not necessarily famous), at a level of complexity that allows for the filming of a large number of scenes in one day.

The series is geared to be the flagship program of the channel.

Artists are invited to offer ideas in every possible genre: sketches, sitcoms, mockumentaries, or any other genre, with the condition that the program's content will provide the viewers with nuggets of quality information from four different areas of the sciences, listed at the beginning of the brief.

Below is the list of specific topics, as an example:

Radio waves / Electric fields / Gravity / The Solar System / Lightning / Democracy / Theories of governance / Basic rights / The Food Chain / Impressionism / Surrealism / Confucius / Archimedes / The Principle of Leverage / Leonardo da Vinci / Picasso/ etc.

The complete list of goals will be detailed separately.

The list will include approximately 20 values to be clarified by each one of the four desired areas (Nature, Geography, History, and Culture).

● ● ●

The pamphlet detailing the series' goals was fast in coming and the development team launched its work.

And again, as with the previous series, the primary goal was to develop a format where a list of topics of trivia in the sciences would form the basis of the show; indeed, they would be *existentially* necessary to the plot from the perspective of the main figures, and the world in which they exist. Because of the clear need that this be a studio drama, the possibly of filming on location was nixed, as were ideas such as creating a team of laboratory investigators or a group cruising in a time machine, and their encounters with scientists or important artists from the past. These ideas were excluded as possibilities because they did not cross the threshold of originality required or were unable to overcome the limits of a simple production. Thus, in the process of suggesting ideas, we were left with few feasible ones. The first of them was a mock science contest, by name of The Forensic Lab, a contest that would address the rules of drama, and involve the viewers as partners in what happened before and behind the scenes of the contest. Underlying the idea of the contest was a concept that forms the basis of many contests — that of identifying the correct of two answers.

In accord with this concept, the studio established two "forensic laboratories," each lab staffed by three actors, all playing forensic scientists. A contestant was presented with a work of art, a law of physical science, or significant historical information. Two forensic teams analyzed the contestant's data in their laboratories and took turns using scientific arguments to try to convince the contestant that the information was accurate — or inaccurate, as the case may have been. Contestants then had to decide whether they accepted the theory put forth by one of the forensic teams or the other. Another innovation suggested by the initiators of this idea was that the contest would be presented by a police robot, as it were. This idea was rejected out of hand (even though several screenplays were written along these lines, and they were not bad). The main reason for knocking out the idea emerged from the difference in what it cost to produce and the results on screen, since this was meant to be a series that absolutely conformed to the rules of producing drama: precise text written for all actors, including the contestants — unlike a real contest. The participants would be required to take part in rehearsals, and the production required special effects. In short, there was no balance between the complex production and the end results that would be seen on the screen by viewers as "just another contest." Audiences tend to view game shows and contests as a relatively low type of entertainment, and given that the channel included in its brief that this series was meant to be "a flagship series for the new channel," the idea for the contest was deemed unsuitable.

The second concept raised was called *The Courtroom*. It was presented as a situation comedy based in the court of a small, far-flung town. The idea that formed the basis of the concept sounded fantastic. By its very nature, a court deals with an infinite number of questions to which it must then find the answers: forged paintings that must be compared to the originals; someone who claims to be a history professor but his lectures are shown by the prosecutor to be full of historical mistakes; or a land ownership dispute through which it is possible to teach concepts of measurement and scale. Through the use of the courtroom device, it was relatively easy to produce fascinating plots in all the areas upon which the channel wanted us to focus: nature, geography, history, and culture. In order to ensure that this sitcom would also be funny, a group of amusing characters was built for it:

An elderly judge — who had lost interest long ago in plaintiffs and defendants and was just waiting for the moment he could retire, buy a small yacht, and sail the seven seas (a model of his yacht always standing on his desk).

An assertive prosecutor — an ambitious young woman who dreams of getting the judge's job but meanwhile contents herself with providing the local newspaper with small scoops in order to glorify her name.

The public defender — a young man with little self-confidence, straight as an arrow, stutters when under pressure, and head-over-heels in love with the assertive prosecutor.

The court clerk — a single mother of three children who works part-time and often needs to absent herself from work such that the judge (who feels attached to her) takes her place, when the need arises. The clerk also runs the court's café franchise, but since she rarely makes it to the café, the coffee and sandwiches are usually sold in "do it yourself" style.

About three other actors participate in each episode, in diverse roles. These roles usually include: **the plaintiff, the defendant,** and in some episodes, an **expert witness**.

The Courtroom proved itself in the process of development. The list of scientific content that was passed on to the writers gave fruit to excellent stories, such as the story of someone accused of selling plots of land on the moon at exorbitant prices, including flights there and back, such that, in the context of the story, the viewer learns the concepts of the *speed of light,* the *solar system,* and *galaxies.* Or, in another case, a farmer sues an advertising company that convinced him to buy expensive vitamin pills. The farmer contends that the company "sold" him on the sensational names of the vitamins, such as *Biotin* and *Folic Acid* and *Ascorbic Acid* and other things that turn out to exist in the fruit and vegetables that he raises on his farm and eats on a regular basis — except that he didn't know it, and as a result, spent large amounts of money on vitamins that he didn't need. In yet another case, a man sues a pet store that sold him a pet fox and a pet rabbit, except that, according to his accusation, the rabbit ate all of the carrots in his vegetable garden before being eaten in turn by the fox. The defendant claims in his defense that if the plaintiff wants to find a culprit, he should go ahead and sue nature, and in his defense he cites (and teaches) the concept of the *food chain.*

The experimental screenwriting stage proved that the concept provided a good answer to the content demands. However, when the content was run by children aged between eight and twelve, it turned out that the world of a courtroom, its figures and conflicts, did not speak to the soul of this audience and was far from riveting to them. Thus the courtroom sitcom was put aside and the development team set out in search of a new idea where the goal was to find a new concept — as successful as the courtroom concept — whose central tenet would revolve around scientific and cultural information and which would be amusing, fascinating, and funny to the target audience. The problem was that the search had already lost its innocence. The development team was convinced that the courtroom situation provided the perfect answer to the stated demands of the series. This made things difficult, because every idea raised was compared to the courtroom idea and then rejected immediately.

Given this difficulty, it was decided that we would not search for a whole new concept at this stage and that instead, we would try to identify exciting worlds of content. And then, one evening, as I happened to be watching one of the episodes of the second series of Black Adder (an extremely funny BBC series from the '80s, starring Rowan Atkinson), it occurred to me that I had stumbled across an exciting, riveting world of content: a royal palace full of plots and intrigue and a cast of kings, dukes, and duchesses who ceaselessly tried to assassinate one another with neither reason nor success.

The next morning, I showed the episode to the development team and, wonders of wonders, all the puzzle pieces of the series fell into place. It happened when one of the writers proposed a brilliant idea that managed to combine the courtroom concept with that of a royal palace and all its colorful characters. The idea was a sitcom based in the courtroom of King Solomon's palace.

King Solomon judged his people, allowing us to place his courtroom in the center of the action. This made it possible to present scientific content in much funnier ways than the previous courtroom situation allowed, since most of the concepts we needed to present had not even been discovered in the time of King Solomon. Since King Solomon was "the wisest of men," though, he could know (as it were) concepts that would not be known by the rest of humankind for thousands of years.

We added a cast of plotting characters to the heart of King Solomon's courtroom and the concept began to take shape. In this new concept, King Solomon received a particularly awful advisor. This advisor had originally been the advisor to King David (Solomon's father) and King Solomon had inherited him along with the kingdom. The advisor does not think that King Solomon is an appropriate ruler, and so he tries, without success, to assassinate King Solomon throughout the series. Every time he tries to poison the king, or push him off a cliff, etc., the plot fails and the advisor himself falls victim to the plan. The advisor has a good friend who runs the restaurant outside in the palace grounds.

The café owner is a criminal character. He occasionally deals in weapons, selling swords, bows, and arrows from King Solomon's stores to whomever pays the most.

A beautiful, young, honest, feminist who is in love with King Solomon works for the café owner.

A string of experimental screenplays proved that the new concept lived up to all the expectations of the channel and was appropriate to the content world of the target audience.

Below is the series proposal which was presented to content managers of the science channel and approved for production.

KING SOLO MAN - SERIES PROPOSAL

Characters:

King Solomon: Very young — age 30–35. Handsome, wise, royally dressed in exaggerated splendor, and possessed of patterns of behavior appropriate to a rock star. In his soul, he is a rock musician and he loves to appear in front of crowds. He relates to his court cases as if they were stage appearances before the masses. After every successful court case, he writes and composes the verdict in song form and performs it as a solo, like a rock star, as he accompanies himself on a harp.

His throne is placed on a royal podium upon which tens of lamps are trained, giving the effect of a lighted stage. The lamps create era-appropriate lighting for a rock star. (Spotlights are created with specially colored candles.) Nevertheless, Solomon is naïve. This naïveté originates in a certain childishness: he is not suspicious; he is not involved in palace conflicts; he does not understand, nor is he interested in, politics at all; and he is not interested in creating political coalitions, whether at home or abroad. He is not made for those things. The thing that saves him from the traitors and plotters who surround him in his everyday life is... luck. King Solomon has amazing luck. If he were to take a walk in front of a class of archers, his luck would lead him to walk between the rain of arrows and not a hair of his head would be harmed. This is how he is always saved from his enemies, usually without noticing that they were out to get him in the first place.

Sir Brobottom: He is the king's rotten personal advisor, similar to the biblical King David's advisor. Sir Brobottom advises the king on every subject, but when all is said and done, he is pretty stupid and no one has a clue how he got to his lofty station in life, and why King David, on his deathbed, commanded Solomon to keep using this troublesome and stupid advisor, whose advice is near to worthless. Sir Brobottom is neurotic and nervous. He is always greatly afraid of something or other. He causes conflict everywhere and is the ultimate traitor who is constantly trying to figure out how to assassinate the king. On the other hand, when he stands before the king, he turns into a nauseating flatterer. Sir Brobottom believes that King Solomon's rise to the throne is a historical mistake. A mistake which falls to him to correct — that is, to have himself crowned king instead.

Sir Brobottom is head over heels in love with Dahlia (the waitress in The Garden Café. The difference in their ages does not concern him. He will do anything to get her or to prevent someone else from getting her.

Buzi: proprietor of The Garden Café, the café-bar outside, in the palace plaza. Buzi is an "inside trader" who is always willing to make deals with those in power. He is a Mafioso without a conscience who is willing to organize any crime or injustice for the right amount of cash. He deals in weapons (and other equipment which he gets from the palace) or stolen land, has a protection scheme, rents vehicles (horses and carriages) and "contracts" breaking and entering jobs, "eliminations" — everything for a price and all in flashy Sicilian style.

Sir Brobottom is Buzi's inside man in the palace. The two are dependent on each other. Sir Brobottom gets Buzi everything he needs from the palace (certificates of approval, weapons, big work contracts, land, and more). In turn, Buzi does whatever Sir Brobottom needs him to do, including "eliminations" as necessary. It is never clear which is more dependent on the other and there is a sort of hidden competition between them on that front.

Dahlia: Waits tables for Buzi in The Garden. Dahlia is young, beautiful, lively, knowledgeable, and adrenalin filled. She is a modern feminist in her outlook toward men. She waits tables but dreams of being a singer. A burgeoning romance lies between her and King Solomon, but it can never become real because Dahlia will never agree to become King Solomon's thousandth wife and would only marry him on the condition that he divorces the other 999.

In addition to these four regular characters, two guest characters appear in every episode — the plaintiff and the defendant who come to the palace or to the king. In other cases, witnesses for the prosecution or the defense or expert witnesses may also appear.

Progression and spirit of the episodes

From the very first episode, Sir Brobottom tries to assassinate the king and take his place. Sir Brobottom is always trying to make important connections, to instigate revolts and conflicts and manipulate events so as to kill the king and take over the kingdom. He believes that the moment he becomes king, Dahlia will fall for him like a ripe fruit falling from a tree.

Chapter by chapter, his plots to eliminate the king become more and more sophisticated, but the king is always saved by his own astonishing luck and, more often, by Sir Brobottom's own stupidity. So it happens that Sir Brobottom falls victim to the very intrigues and traps that he has set for the king in the same way that Wile E. Coyote always falls victim to the intricate traps that he prepares for Road Runner.

An additional source of magic in the series is King Solomon's ability to talk to animals. King Solomon gets classified information from birds, ants, worms, snails, and any other creature who is in the area and can give him information about Buzi and Sir Brobottom's plans or those of the plaintiff and the defendant.

There is no conceptual problem with Sir Brobottom's fall at the end of every episode because the series relates to this character as one does to an animated character. And so, at the end of every episode, he falls into the trap that he set for the king (not to worry) only to be back again, safe and sound, at the beginning of the next episode.

Sets

1. INT — King Solomon's Hall of Justice

From here, several swing doors open, as it were, into the rest of the palace. In the center of the hall is a raised platform on which the throne rests and around which period-appropriate lamps are theatrically situated.

2. EXT The Garden Café in the palace plaza

The Garden Café is situated right outside the gate of King Solomon's palace. The series' plaintiffs and defendants sit there before they enter the palace for their cases. All the dodgy plots that keep the series moving are schemed here.

3. INT Barred window of the palace jail cell

This window is carved into the wall of the palace and looks out at Buzi's café. Defendants who are found guilty are locked in this cell as are the ones who have not yet been tried.

4. INT The king's office — King Solomon's bedroom and workroom.

This is a palace room which serves as King Solomon's bedroom and workroom. King Solomon sleeps here and dreams dreams that help him judge his people with wisdom. The palace safe, which plays an important part in the plot of many episodes, is also in this room since both Sir Brobottom and Buzi pine for its contents.

Technique for introducing scientific content

The series' targeted subjects will be introduced primarily through King Solomon's court cases. In this context too, it is possible to introduce a shrewd, period-appropriate real estate agent, who sells land on the moon to innocent clients and promises to catapult them to Mars... Here too, it will be possible to learn, through King Solomon's wisdom, the concepts of *the speed of light, galaxies,* or *the solar system.* That is, given that King Solomon is "the wisest of all people," he understands concepts that the rest of humanity will have to wait thousands of years to learn. Additionally, it will be possible to plant much information in the body of the plots themselves.

The episode titled *The Identikit* provides an excellent example of the series' style. The original episode is written for a 24-minute broadcasting slot (about 30 pages), so a summary will be sufficient here.

THE IDENTIKIT
FROM THE SERIES KING SOLO MAN

The chapter deals with the two following topics in science:

1. Lightning

2. The principle of leverage

A. EXT. Daytime. The Garden Café

The episode opens with a meeting between Sir Brobottom, the king's advisor, and Buzi, the local Mafioso and proprietor of The Garden Café, a café in the plaza at the entrance of the palace. The table is crawling with ants, and

Sir Brobottom sees this as a sign of neglect and an indication of the low level of hygiene in the café. Buzi apologizes and calls Joshua, the new dishwasher, to rid the table of the ants. Joshua arrives, and Buzi introduces him to Sir Brobottom. Joshua, whose hair and face are a little singed, shakes Sir Brobottom's hand and explains that he was singed while conducting a recent fascinating scientific experiment. Buzi explains to Sir Brobottom with amusement that Joshua is an intellectual who is forced to wash dishes because he insists on focusing his interest on a new and unknown field named "science." According to Buzi, scientists are people who are interested in all sorts of ideas and who conduct all sorts of experiments in the belief that sometime in the future, this will become profitable. For the moment, Joshua is poor and is therefore forced to wash dishes in The Garden Café. Sir Brobottom, who has never met a scientist before, wants to know more about this interesting profession. Joshua complies with happiness. He enthusiastically tells Sir Brobottom all about his new invention, the *lightning rod*. Joshua shows Sir Brobottom an iron rod that he has fixed to the roof of Buzi's café. He explains with enthusiasm that according to his findings, the lightning we all know is in fact a burst of powerful static electricity charge that is found in the clouds. Joshua continues speaking about this natural phenomenon which brings about the flow of electric charges from cloud to cloud or from clouds to the ground. He explains further that his new invention, the lightning rod, attracts electric energy and leads it through the rod right into the ground, thus preventing damage to people or property and protecting them from bursting into flames. Joshua expands on his explanation of the phenomenon of lightning and ends with a warning: The electric charge that passes through the lightning rod is very dangerous and that, to his great fortune, he was only singed in the course of his last experiment and not electrocuted. The word *electrocuted* immediately fascinates Sir Brobottom, who tries to understand what could happen, for example, if one were to attach a lightning rod to something like a throne ... of someone like... King Solomon? Joshua is repelled by the idea and explains that in a case like that, there is no doubt that the nation's dear, beloved King Solomon, would most likely, God forbid ... be electrocuted! Sir Brobottom is taken with the idea of this new and scientific *electric charge*. He asks the scientific dishwasher for a sketch that would explain how to build a lightning rod and how to attach it to a chair or a bed. Joshua begins to sketch with enthusiasm. Buzi gets annoyed and reminds him that he is being paid to rid the table of ants and not to sketch diagrams.

B. INT. Daytime. King Solomon's Palace

Sir Brobottom, who has managed to acquire an iron rod and copper cable, is attaching the lightning rod he has fabricated to King Solomon's throne, prior to attaching it to the palace roof. In the middle of his tinkering, King Solomon storms into the Hall of Judgment. Sir Brobottom hides the offending equipment and listens to the king. The king is shaken and upset. It turns out that a diligent ant has come to the king, the wisest of all people, speaker of the languages of the beasts, to tell him that that at very morning, as she was taking a walk on a table at Buzi's café, she witnessed a plot to dispatch the king with the aid of a lightning rod. Sir Brobottom, panicked, tries to find out immediately if the tattletale ant has told the king who, exactly, plotted to kill him. It turns out that she has no idea and that she is therefore in the king's private office, putting together an identikit that will help him identify the culprit.

C. EXT. Daytime. The Garden Café.

A panicked Sir Brobottom goes to Buzi, the Mafioso, at the same time that Joshua the scientific dishwasher is explaining a new principle to Buzi — that of the *principle of leverage.* Joshua shows Buzi that it is possible to use a small pulley to lift a huge boulder. Similarly, he shows Buzi how he can lift another boulder with the aid of a long rod and a fulcrum. Joshua shows Buzi diagrams he has sketched and explains that "the farther from the fulcrum the force is applied, the easier it is to lift the object," etc. Sir Brobottom observes this scientific demonstration with impatience, since he absolutely must speak to Buzi. Finally, Buzi becomes available, and Sir Brobottom waits for Joshua to return to the kitchen before whispering to Buzi that he must take care of an "elimination" without delay. Buzi asks to know who the target is, and Sir Brobottom points to a little ant on the ground. **"The ant!"** he says. "We have to eliminate the ant, and fast!" Buzi does not understand and Sir Brobottom explains about the tattletale ant who at this very moment is in the act of dragging grains of sand around a big board in order to create a sketch of the man who is plotting to harm the king — that is, himself. Buzi listens patiently and understands that Sir Brobottom will now be willing to pay any sum to get rid of the ant. Buzi refuses the job. He explains to Sir Brobottom that eliminating ants is very complicated. It is an expert's job. He would have to bring in a professional tattletale ant eliminator, which would cost a lot of money. Sir Brobottom, of course, is willing to pay any price, and he runs to get the money.

Buzi waits for Sir Brobottom to get far away, calls Joshua the dishwasher, and tells him to drop everything because the next job his boss has for him is... the elimination of an ant!

D. INT. Daytime. The Hall of Justice.

Meanwhile, a sweating Sir Brobottom reaches the palace. As is well known, his job is to bring accused citizens in before the king. Sir Brobottom apologizes, takes his usual place, examines the list of accused and, to his astonishment, sees that the next name on his list is... his own. He is accused of plotting to harm King Solomon. Sir Brobottom cannot believe it. He comes up with all sorts of alibis and excuses, but the king is not willing to hear any of it. Sir Brobottom asks for evidence of this perverse accusation and the king invites him to the king's office to show him the identikit picture which the ant has created. The identikit identifies him as the culprit who plotted to harm the king through the agency of a lightning rod.

E. INT. Daytime. Hallway in the Palace at the Entrance to the King's Office

The king's retinue, Sir Brobottom, and the palace guards arrive at the king's office just as Joshua, the scientific dishwasher, gets to the entrance of the office to execute the "elimination." Joshua is holding a colorful slipper — the weapon meant to eliminate the tattletale ant. Sir Brobottom indicates to Joshua that he should hide and wait for the king's retinue to enter the office first. Then Sir Brobottom asks the king to wait for a moment in his office as, he claims, he needs to go to the bathroom. Sir Brobottom promises to return immediately to view the identikit picture. The king agrees. Sir Brobottom starts off in the direction of the bathroom but then makes an about turn and approaches Joshua, who is hiding behind a large statue at the entrance of the office. Sir Brobottom whispers to Joshua that he should now forget all about the tattletale ant. "It's too late," he says. Then he asks the dishwasher if he still has the pulley with which he had explained the principle of leverage that morning. Joshua pulls the pulley from his pocket. Sir Brobottom asks Joshua to carefully attach the pulley to the ceiling and with it, hoist up the large statue behind which Joshua is hiding. Joshua doesn't understand why, but Sir Brobottom tells him not to worry. "Trust me. I have to go into the king's office now, but in a few minutes, when the door of the office opens and someone walks out, you have to immediately let go of the pulley so that the statue goes crashing to the ground and squashes whoever walks out of the office!" Joshua is ambivalent, but Sir Brobottom convinces him that everything is kosher and this is an act of importance undertaken with the full permission of the king.

F. INT. Daytime. The King's Office

Sir Brobottom enters the king's office, and the king shows him the conclusive proof of the identikit. The identikit picture has been carefully constructed in sand and clearly shows the face of Sir Brobottom. Sir Brobottom is speechless. He searches for an explanation and then bursts out laughing. "Wait! That? That's not me at all. It's... my twin brother, Sir Bottom!" he says. "Why do you think that they call me Sir Brobottom? It's because my twin brother is called Sir Bottom. And I'm his bro. So I'm Sir Brobottom! And if you want to see him, your majesty, I invite you to step outside because he happens to be right here as we speak. Right on the other side of this door. And you can just step out to see him."

"I would be delighted to meet your brother, Sir Bottom," answers the king. "Let's both go out together to meet him. I suggest that you go out first, so that you can introduce him to me..."

Sir Brobottom, miserable, understands what is about to

happen, but he steps into the hallway because he has no choice. The tremendous crash of the statue falling to the ground is heard in the king's office, and then a cloud of dust makes clear what has just happened to Sir Brobottom in the hallway.

In addition to the summary above, which shows the spirit of the series, below is a two-page taster from the third scene of the screenplay *The Identikit*.

THE IDENTIKIT
A SCREENPLAY FROM THE SERIES *KING SOLO MAN*

Scene 3. EXT. Daytime. The Garden Café Plaza

Sir Brobottom storms into The Garden Café. Two pulleys are attached to the roof of the shade-giving pergola in the café's garden. Joshua, the dishwashing scientist, is using the pulleys to demonstrate the principle of leverage to Buzi, the proprietor, by lifting a huge boulder off the ground. Sir Brobottom turns to the astonished Buzi.

Sir Brobottom:
Buzi, listen...

Buzi:
(fascinated by the demonstration)
Shhh! Not now, Sir Brobottom.

Joshua:

*So, as I already explained, the more pulleys you add to the
contraption, the less force you need to exert
in order to lift the boulder.*

Buzi:

Wow! Whadayasay? It's an amazing idea.

**Joshua leaves the rock hanging in the air and turns to an
even bigger boulder which has a long rod beneath it,
resting on a fulcrum.**

Joshua:
(continuing with enthusiasm)

*And how does this rock look to you? Even bigger, right? But
let it be known that I can lift this one with just as much ease
as I lifted the other, by using my next great idea: a lever or
long rod which is shoved under one side of the rock and
rests on this **fulcrum**. Now, all I have to do in order to lift
this boulder is to push down on the other side of the rod.*
(The boulder lifts easily.) *And the rock rises! Amazing, huh?
The longer the lever is and the farther the handle from the
fulcrum, the less force is needed to lift the object. That's a
principle... I discovered it by myself. I call it*
The Principle of Leverage.

Buzi:

Amazing, amazing, amazing...

Sir Brobottom:
(whimpering angrily)

Buzi! Buzi! Buzi, I'm talking to you!

Buzi:
Hang on, Sir Brobottom!

Sir Brobottom:
(dragging him away from Joshua)
It's urgent; I'm finished. This is it. I'm a goner!
The king is about to discover that I plotted to kill him!

Buzi:
What happened? Did someone squeal?

Sir Brobottom:
Yes, as it turns out. Unbelievable. An ant! An ant told on me!
(He claps his hand to his mouth.) *Shhhh! We have to*
speak quietly! **(He looks around suspiciously at a few**
butterflies and flies.) *Who knows what kind of creature is*
listening to us now. **(Whispering)** *The ant is in the king's*
office at this very minute making an identikit picture of me!

Buzi:
Hoo Weeh! You are a goner.

Sir Brobottom:
We have to eliminate the ant!

Buzi:
But how can an ant make a picture?

Sir Brobottom:
The same way it makes a nest! Solomon brought her some
sand and she's arranging the grains in the shape of my face.
I tried to get into the office, so I could squash her myself, but
there are guards guarding the place. I need one of your
professional assassins!

Buzi:

Shhh! Hello? What do you think you're talking about? (**In a loud voice**) *Who's an assassin? What's an assassin? No one around here's assassinating anything!*
(**In a soft voice**) *That is, not for free.*

This episode explains two concepts about the physical world: the phenomenon of lightning and the principle of leverage.

In general, the series' concept provided an excellent basis for the writing of funny and unexpected plots. They were full of high quality nonsense, combined with nuggets of information which answered the program's demand for scientific content. The world of content that this series developed conquered the hearts of its young viewers, who greatly enjoyed the idea of a scientific sitcom which takes place in biblical times.

In another episode, for example, a newlywed couple comes to the Hall of Justice. They are suing the biblical photographer who photographed their wedding. They claim that, contrary to his promise, he had not yet provided them with the photographs from their wedding. The photographer claims that he could not possibly have made such a promise because cameras and film had not yet been invented. King Solomon wonders, if that is the case, "Why does he present himself as a photographer, and isn't that a kind of deception?" The photographer explains that he goes to events "...and every picture is engraved in my memory because of my photographic memory. I stand here in this witness box and promise that justice is on my side! Any time this couple wants to see their wedding pictures, they have but to come to me and I will describe their wedding to them in great detail."

In this episode, the brain's capacity for memory is

explained. That is, **the method of encoding and retrieving memory in the human brain.** In another episode, the king decides to disguise himself in order to find out from one of his simple citizens what the citizenry thinks of him. The king does not know that Sir Brobottom is plotting to take the opportunity to prevent the king's return to the palace and to take over the kingdom himself. Sir Brobottom's plot fails, of course, through a series of events that teaches him, and the viewers, **Murphy's Law.** In yet another episode, the king falls ill, and the viewers learn about the importance of **vitamins**, and in a further episode, dealing with the building of a new residence for the king's one thousand wives, the viewers learn what happens when one tampers with **nature's ecological balance**. These are just examples of the variety of science and engineering topics with which the series deals.

THE PROCESS OF CONTENT DEVELOPMENT

The most fascinating aspect of the content development of a series is usually the winding path taken by the *primary demand*, from the moment it is defined and according to which the production sets its sights, to the final product. The process of content development is more interesting than the screenwriting stage and even more interesting than the production process. It is a sort of quest, including snaking paths and wonderful ideas, which may first appear as dead ends or mistakes that stray from the path.

Most of the development processes I have led have included about ten development meetings, on average. Between meetings, experimental screenplays are written and infinite ideas are generated. Sometimes, the development team gathers for a fifth or sixth meeting with no idea of the guiding theme or any idea as to the final look of the series.

Up to that point, the screenplays look like they are not worth the paper they are written on, and despite this, somehow, when all is said and done, some fine day-magic happens. In expected and unexpected ways, something falls into place and engenders more and more correct decisions. And then, all the *mistakes* that were made on the way become logical and even critical to the process. Everyone understands how it turned out to be important to make mistakes in that direction, and the most astonishing thing is that, despite the regularity with which this phenomenon occurs, there is no other way to describe it than *magic*.

What distinguishes this magic from others — such as the pulling of a rabbit out of a hat or the changing of a green handkerchief into a red one — is that the moment of magic usually remains unrecognized. Sometimes, 24 hours are needed before the magic becomes apparent. The development team is expecting failure, after tons of ideas causing people to applaud enthusiastically subsequently prove to have been false starts, and therefore, when the magic occurs, it remains unnoticed or unappreciated as the true turning point. Only afterwards, slowly, after everyone has gone home, does the consciousness dawn that the last idea is really different and more correct than all the others. This one could really work. At this stage, people begin to feel each other out. Each member of the development team gingerly inquires if the others also feel that the magic has happened, or if this is yet another mirage.

And thus, only at the next meeting does it become apparent that everyone feels the magic. Everyone has thought deeply about the concept and realizes that the idea, which was first viewed as "not bad" is, in fact, terrific.

It does happen that some series are developed in a shorter amount of time, but there is no doubt that the feeling of satisfaction at the end of the development process is much smaller in these cases.

In this chapter, which focuses, as you remember, on content repertoire, three processes of content development are presented. These three processes relate to three different age levels. *Alan the All-Powerful*, a preschool series, is targeted to preschoolers, of course — the age for which most children's television programs are written, according to my experience. *King Solo Man* is a television series targeted at adolescents, the most advanced age in the world of children's television. The third series, presented below, is targeted to toddlers, children from one-and-a-half to three years of age.

This series, like others, began with a brief detailing its primary content demands.

SMALL WORLD

BRIEF FOR TODDLERS' TELEVISION SERIES, TARGETED AT CHILDREN AGED ONE-AND-A-HALF TO THREE YEARS.

Introduction:

The development of children begins with the connection to their environment. Babies' first meeting with the world comes from direct touch with their mothers. A mother is responsible for her baby's scope of movement. Later on in the life of children, society and environment permit them to define their identities and creative abilities through familiarity with their surroundings. The series, *Small World,* is directed at supporting the baby's process of getting to know the environment.

The Demand:

The development of the concept of a television series for children aged one-and-a-half to three years. A series that is aware of the processes of development which children of this age undergo. A series that answers the motor, sensory, cognitive, emotional, social, and verbal demands of these children.

Structure of the Program:

The series must conform to two broadcasting formats.

A. 13 episodes of about 15 minutes each (which are divided into 4 equal subsections).

B. 52 independent, short broadcast segments of about 4 minutes each that are appropriate for broadcast at different times throughout the day. This is the origin of the need for

each full episode to be divisible into four equal sub-
episodes that are suitable for independent broadcast or for
broadcast as a unified episode.

Areas of Content Focus

The Recommended Areas of Content Focus Constitute:

A. Prepositions: The understanding of the words: on,
under, in(side), out(side), next (to), between, far, near

B. Identifying Musical Sounds and how they are
produced: tapping, piping, scraping

C. Identifying Shapes: identifying shapes and materials
from the child's close environment

D. Problem Solving: improvement of the child's ability
to solve simple problems, at the child's age level

E. Useful Information: gaining familiarity with objects
and their uses from the child's daily world

F. Coping with Challenges: encouraging toddlers in
their grappling with daily tasks. For example: "I wash by
myself." "I get dressed by myself."

● ● ●

The process of developing series for toddlers is
significantly different from the process of developing series
for children aged three to four and up, and much more
difficult. This difficulty rises from the fact that at this stage
of their lives, everything, even the most trivial, is perceived
as magical: water flowing from a faucet is magical, a balloon
in the process of inflating is magical, and even the turning on
or off of lights is magical. Imaginary magical worlds of the
sort that their four-year-old counterparts would enjoy do not
yet speak to their souls. A family of elves who live in a
pumpkin, winged ponies who fly among the stars, or a band
of monkeys who take off for the moon in a hot air balloon is
not different, in their eyes, from a group of friends playing in

a room.

This is the reason that the *Teletubbies* series is such a work of genius. The creators of the series created a magical world which requires absolutely no previous knowledge. In order to enjoy winged ponies, the child must know that, usually, ponies do not fly. The *Teletubbies* creators focus on the child of this age's primary interests — colors, shapes, and sounds. They created a magical world of spectacular shapes and colors, pleasant sounds, and simple creatures and situations that speak straight to the soul of the series' diminutive viewers. As such, the fundamental questions that we directed to ourselves in the course of developing our new series were: This time, what comes first? That is, should we start, as we usually do, with the creation of the characters and only afterwards create their world? Or would it be better, this time, to work in the opposite direction? Should we create a magical world with which toddlers could identify, and only then think about what kind of characters would be best suited to populate this world?

Series targeted to toddlers usually depend on a warm, mother-like presenter who connects to her audience with the help of a puppet or several mobile puppets, all soft, cute, and colorful. However, given that one of the demands of the series' commissioners was "that it be easy to dub into different languages," we dropped the idea of using a human presenter at all.

In the first stage, we tried to operate along familiar work patterns. That is, before anything, we tried to create our characters, and only then to create a suitable world for them. But since the need for easy dubbing removed the option of a human presenter, we had to focus on the world of puppets. We wondered which kind of puppet would be most suited to our target audience. A human puppet? A puppet creature?

An animal puppet? Or maybe a talking object? We decided that in this case, the most appropriate choice was that of puppet creatures. They would be of a colorful and relatively abstract shape that required no previous familiarity on the part of the child, but nevertheless, their shape would be vaguely familiar so as not to be completely foreign to the child. Our second option was to design more realistic characters. That is, to develop characters that came straight from the child's world — ones that resembled a familiar toy or common fruit, like a banana or an apple, or maybe a familiar animal, such as a puppy or kitten. It quickly became clear that trying to come up with our characters as a starting point was not going to represent the route to success. No exciting ideas for the series gelled in the process of designing our characters, and so we recalibrated and began to think about the world we wanted to create.

It turned out that this change of direction did not make our lives easier, since the creation of a world on the basis of colors, shapes, and sounds brought us in the direction of something that looked a lot like the *Teletubbies*. Most of our development meetings were very frustrating. We found ourselves trying to see the world from the point of view of a one-and-a-half-year-old child, but this didn't help either. The breakthrough came from an unexpected direction. In the course of my search, I walked into a baby daycare center in my neighborhood. I had decided to stay there for a few hours in an attempt to get to know the world from the point of view of its clients.

I watched the babies play with their toys inside the building and in the yard, crawl on the carpet in the playroom, stare at the television screen, or nap in their little cribs. After a while, I set up a camera from several points of view — on the carpet, in the sand pit and in the cribs — in a mildly amusing attempt to show my writing team the world from the point of view of a baby. When I showed the pictures to the development team, we suddenly discovered that they held the key to the series' concept. In the various pictures that I had photographed was one that I had taken from inside a crib. The picture was taken from the point of view of the baby who spent time there. From this angle, the world suddenly looked warm, safe, comforting, colorful and interesting to us.

We tried to figure out what concept for development arose from this point of view. We defined the *inside of the crib* space as the center of our world, and we checked if this world could be reproduced in a studio. That is, we tried to reconstruct the *inside of the crib* space in our set. The floor would be constructed from a soft material resembling a mattress.

This space would be defined by bars resembling the bars of a crib. Beyond the bars, the rest of the room — the bedside table, window, door and wallpaper — would be visible but muted. From the audience's point of view, the center of this magical whole wide world would be *inside the crib*. Inside the bed, there would be a cozy patchwork quilt whose folds would provide the exit and entry point for our main characters, just like the mouth of a cave or a door. Above the crib would hang a huge mobile, suspending a sun, clouds, stars, and other heavenly bodies and defining the film space as a complete and independent world.

From that moment on, the process of development became very simple.

inside the crib – illustration

The development of the world flowed almost by itself, and the translation of educational directives into content and plot became a piece of cake. Below is a description of the characters and the structure of the series in the version that was presented and accepted by the client broadcast channel.

SMALL WORLD

A TELEVISION SERIES FOR VERY YOUNG CHILDREN

The Goal:

The development of the concept of a television series for children one-and-a-half to three years of age.

A series that is aware of developmental processes which children of this young age experience at this stage of their lives.

The series responds to these children's motor, sensory, cognitive, emotional, social and verbal needs.

The Characters:

Two characters, **Jilly** (female) and **Boom** (male) live in a *Crib World.*

Jilly and Boom are soft and cuddly stuffed puppets. They are made from very soft materials (an acrylic textile or sponge interior), covered in toweling material or other fuzzy cloth from which such puppets are usually made.

The puppets have a soft but defined shape. They move freely within the entire set. The puppets can speak, sing, move, and pick up and put down objects.

Jilly, the older of the two characters, has the characteristics of a three-and-a-half-year-old child. She is very curious, daring (willing to try new and unknown things), and a bit more knowledgeable about the world than Boom. She remembers being Boom's age, and this helps her to understand his difficulties. She loves funny things (at a basic humor level which amuses very young children, of course), and she loves laughing out loud.

Boom, the younger of the two characters, has the characteristics of a one-and-a-half-year-old child. Everything is new to him: objects, words, and situations. He is a little hesitant but he loves to learn new words, to encounter new objects, and to accomplish complicated tasks, among other things. Boom is dependent on Jilly. He imitates her movements and behaviors and needs her to always be at his side. He derives great enjoyment from succeeding in new things and needs Jilly's encouragement, or the audience's.

The Introduction and the Conclusion of Each Episode:

The goal of the introduction and the conclusion is to widen the studio bound *Crib World* of the series and to tie this world into the real, everyday world of the child. This requires a focus on all possible areas of interaction between the viewing children and the program they watch.

Method

In order to open up the *Crib World* and to widen it, the introduction relates to the other side of the crib — that is, the side in which the children (the viewers) sit.

Detail

The introduction and conclusions are filmed in white limbo [iv] in which elements from the *Crib World* set (in smaller size, of course,) are strewn, in order to create continuity between the studio and the viewing children's real world.

Opening Shot Example:

Boom and Jilly drag a big block and then push it toward the camera.

Against a limbo background, a (real) one-and-a-half-year-old baby picks up the same block (but smaller, of course) and plays with it.

The puppets, Boom and Jilly, applaud the baby.

A second child laughs and also applauds the baby.

Boom and Jilly dance and move (like babies).

Two (different) children dance and move in the same way, as if they are imitating the pair of puppets.

Varying Content

The introduction is accompanied by a song which introduces the characters and invites the viewers to take part in the program's activities today and every day.

During the last part of the song, Boom and Jilly wish the viewers a "nice day" and try to figure out what day it is today.

Seven versions of this segment are filmed and slotted in as appropriate.

Concluding Shot

Boom and Jilly wave goodbye, taking their leave of the audience.

A baby waves back.

Boom and Jilly play peek-a-boo from behind a piled-up blanket.

Children play peek-a-boo from behind their own blankets…

The series can be broadcast in full episodes of 15 minutes each, or each episode can be divided into four separate segments. In the latter case, each segment focuses on a separate developmental challenge. The developmental challenges on which this series chose to focus are the understanding of prepositions, the building of new vocabulary, the trying and mastery of new motor skills, and music.

Broadcast Segments:

1) Preposition segment — This is designed as a daily game of peek-a-boo. Each time, the two characters choose a clue which will help them find an object or help one of them find the other. In one episode, for example, one of them hides himself or herself, or hides an object *inside something.* The next day, the clue will be *under something,* etc. Every episode focuses on a different preposition: *over, under, inside, next to, near,* etc. The added benefit of the amusing peek-a-boo segment is the learning of prepositions. The seeker seeks the hidden object or person while involving the viewer in his or her search and dilemmas.

2) Information Segment — In every episode, our characters discover a different familiar object but do not know exactly what it is for and how to use it (a comb, for example). They begin to exchange ideas and guesses as to its use ("Maybe it's for back scratching?" or "Maybe it's a kind of paintbrush?") until they figure out the correct answer.

3) The *I Can* Segment — This is set up in circus style. Jilly, the ringmaster, announces throughout the episode that a character will do an "unbelievable" act. ("Your attention please! Boom is about to brush his teeth all by himself!" "Today, Boom is going to put his shoes on all by himself!") As the episode progresses, the viewers see Boom and Jilly struggle with the announced impossible task *"against all odds..."* and, of course, they succeed in accomplishing the task, to the roaring cheers of the large virtual audience.

4) Music Segment — Each of these episode segments opens with a sound made by a certain object (a pot on which one can bang, pot lid cymbals, a box full of beads, a honking toy). A simple melody begins to play and then Jilly and Boom incorporate their sounds into the melody with a suitable rhythm and beat. The melody slowly develops into a simple daily dance and song.

The Daily Connection between Segments

Despite the seemingly separate educational content of each segment, the four separate episode segments have a common denominator in the shape of an object, which provides an unbroken thread throughout the program. For example, the four screenplays below revolve around a spoon. Similarly, other sets of segments revolve around a hat, a comb, a bell, etc.

THE SPOON

FIRST SEGMENT (PREPOSITION SEGMENT):

Jilly and Boom are on the crib. A few disorganized objects are around them. They jump on the mattress and wave to the camera.

Jilly:
Hi! I'm Jilly!

Boom:
Right! And I'm... Boom!

Jilly and Boom:
Hello everyone! Hello!

Children (OS):
Hello! Hi!

Jilly bumps into a toy and slips onto her bottom.

Jilly:
Oooops!

Boom:
Jilly, did you fall? Does it hurt?

Jilly:
No. I'm fine, but we have to clean the crib up a little, or we won't be able to jump on it!

Boom:
Hooray! I have a great idea! Let's clean up!

<u>Jilly:</u>
(picking up the toy)
*Okay. Look, Boom, there are pockets hanging on the crib,
and we can put things into them .So put this toy
into one of those pockets.*

**Boom takes the toy and runs to the other side of the crib
where a set of cloth pockets hang from the bars. He puts
the toy into one of the pockets but discovers a spoon
inside the pocket. He takes out the spoon.**

<u>Boom:</u>
Hey, Jilly, look what I found!

<u>Jilly:</u>
Cool!

<u>Boom:</u>
What is it?

<u>Jilly:</u>
Uh... um... hmm... I don't know... **(She examines the spoon)**
It's something that... **(She turns to the viewing children)**
*Hmm... I wonder what we do with this? Children, do you
know what this thing is? Do you know what to do with it?*

<u>Children (OS):</u>
Yes! We know!

<u>Jilly:</u>
*Shhhh! Shhhh! Don't tell us. Boom and I like
figuring it out ourselves, right Boom?*

Boom:
Right. Boom likes to figure it out himself. But you try first.

Jilly takes the spoon, examines it, and puts it on her head.

Jilly:
Maybe it's a little hat with a sunshade?

Children: (laughing OS)
No! It's not a cap with a sunshade!

Boom takes the spoon off Jilly's head and examines it.

Boom:
Hi! Here's Boom! I see myself! Maybe it's a mirror?

Jilly:
(looking at the spoon)
But it's a little too small to be a mirror! **(To the camera)**
It's not a mirror, right?

Children: (laughing OS)
No! It's not a mirror!

Jilly:
How strange. So what is this thing? What can we do with it?

Boom takes the spoon and puts it against his chest.

Boom:
I know! It's a decoration. It's a very pretty decoration!

Jilly takes it and tries it on her chest.

Jilly:

No. It's not such a pretty decoration... **(To the camera)**
What do you think of this decoration?

Children (O.S.):

It's not a decoration at all!

Jilly: (pensive)

No? Hmm... It's not a hat, and it's not a mirror, and it's also
not a decoration. It's something else that we don't know yet...
so... **(turning to the children)** *maybe it's a back scratcher?*
(She scratches her back.)

Children: (laughing OS)

No way...

Jilly:

Hang on. It has a handle... so that part must be for holding,
and... **(she brings the spoon to her mouth)** *I know!*
You eat with this!

Boom:

Oh! I know! I know! You eat with it! You eat with it, right?

Children (O.S.):

Right! It's a spoon!

Jilly:

Right! It's a spoon! We eat with a spoon!

Boom:

A spoon? How do we eat with a spoon?

Jilly:
(modeling eating with a spoon)
Like this! You pick up the food with this part, and you put it in your mouth!

Boom:
Cool! You eat with a spoon!

They both start jumping on the mattress as they had been at the beginning of the segment. They sing:

Boom:
We eat with a spoon...
We eat with a spoon...

Boom:
Hey Jilly, you know what? Because of the spoon we found... I've gotten hungry.

Jilly:
Right... I'm also hungry now.

Both:
We want to eat with a spoon...
We want to eat with a spoon...

Second Segment (Information Segment):
INT. Crib. Daytime
Jilly and Boom jump (on a soft surface and a mattress) and wave at the camera.

Jilly:
Hi!

Boom:

Hi! **(pointing at Jilly)** *That's Jilly!*

Jilly:

(pointing at Boom)

And that's Boom! **(She stops jumping and holds her belly)**
Hey, Boom, I'm hungry. Are you also hungry?
Do you want to eat?

Boom:

Hmm... yum yum! Boom is very hungry! Boom wants to eat!

Jilly:

So Jilly will get food and Boom will bring a spoon.

Boom:

Ok. We eat with a spoon, right?

Jilly:

That's right, we eat with a spoon.

Boom:

Hang on. But... where's our spoon?

Jilly:

(trying to remember)

Yes... where is our spoon? I think that we put it somewhere.
*I think we put it **on** something.*

Boom:

*Maybe it's **on** the block.* **(He checks)** *No!*
The spoon is not on the block.

Jilly:
*So maybe it's **next to** something... no no,*
*I remember we put the spoon **in** something.*

Boom:
*"**In**" something???*

Jilly:
*Yes, **in** is when one thing is **in** another thing.*
*But **in** what is the spoon?*

Boom:
*I know! We put the spoon **in** the... the bottle!*

He runs again to the bottle and checks inside of it. Jilly comes too.

Jilly:
*No, we didn't put the spoon in the bottle! There's water in the bottle. A bottle's not the right place for a spoon! But maybe we put the spoon back **in** one of the pockets that are hanging over there!*

She points at the other side of the crib where a set of cloth pockets are hanging on the bars.

Boom:
*Right! **In** the pockets... That's the right place for the spoon.*

Boom hurries toward the pockets, checks their contents, and doesn't find the spoon.

Boom: (disappointed)
*No... the spoon isn't **in** any of the pockets.*

Jilly:

No? (**Turning backward. Boom has disappeared**) *So in what did we put the spoon?* (**She notices the blanket**) *I know! We put it* **in** *the blanket!* (**She crawls into the blanket and then comes out**) *No. The spoon is not in the blanket!*

Boom:

Ugh... so where is the spoon? (**He looks around**) *Spoon? Spoon? Where is our little spoon?*

Jilly:
(**searching**)
In what are you hiding, little spoon?

Boom sighs. While Jilly says the next line, he sits down.

Jilly:

Try to remember, Boom. You held the spoon **in** *your hand, and then...*

Boom suddenly gets up.

Boom:

Hey! What's stopping me from sitting here? What's in the way?

He puts his hand into the big pocket on the front of his body and searches inside of it.

Boom:
Hey! Here you are!

He takes out the spoon and waves it.

Boom:
*The spoon was **in** my pocket!*

Jilly:
Hooray! We found the spoon. Boom, you put it ***in*** *your pocket, and you forgot!*

Boom:
Right... So now can we go eat at last?

Jilly:
Of course! Let's go!

Third Segment (I Can Do It By Myself):
INT. Crib. Daytime

Boom and Jilly jump (on a soft surface and a mattress) and wave at the camera. A bowl of whole grain cereal is next to them.

Boom:
Hi! Hello...

Jilly:
(To the camera) *Hello...* **(pointing at Boom)** *That's Boom!*

Boom:
(pointing to Jilly)
That's Jilly! And this is the spoon I found today. And now we will eat this cereal with this spoon.

Jilly: (stops jumping)
Come on! We're eating cereal! **(To Boom)** *Boom, you start eating, and I'll go get myself a spoon, too.*

Jilly goes and meanwhile, Boom sits near the bowl, puts his spoon inside of it, and gathers up some cereal. On the way to his mouth, the cereal falls from the spoon.

<u>Boom:</u>
Ugh. It's not working.

He tries again. He fills the spoon with cereal but on the way to his mouth, the cereal falls from the spoon and the spoon is empty by the time it gets to his mouth.

<u>Boom:</u> (frustrated)
Ugh! I've had enough! I don't want cereal. I don't want it!

<u>Jilly:</u> (coming back)
What's happening, Boom?

<u>Boom:</u>
This spoon doesn't work. I can't eat with it.

<u>Jilly:</u>
The spoon looks fine to me.

<u>Boom:</u>
So... Jilly. Can you feed me with the spoon?

<u>Jilly:</u>
But Boom, you can eat with a spoon all by yourself!

<u>Boom:</u>
No, Boom can't.

<u>Jilly:</u>
Yes, you can!

Boom:
No, I can't!

Jilly:
Of course you can. **(She enters into her ringmaster role)**
*And now you're going to show everyone that you can eat
cereal with a spoon — all by yourself!*

Boom:
What? But...

**Appropriate music — drumroll, circus style music in the
background. The background light dims and a spotlight
shines on Jilly, who is holding her spoon like a
microphone. Boom stands next to her, astonished.**

Jilly:
*Ladies and Gentleman, girls and boys — your attention
please, your attention please. Boom is about to eat cereal
with a spoon — all by himself and with no help at all!*

Boom:
(whispering to Jilly)
But I told you that I can't do it myself!

Jilly: **(whispering back)**
Of course you can! Go on! **(In a big voice, to the viewers)**
*Pay attention. Boom is putting his spoon into
the bowl of cereal!*

**Boom hurriedly puts his spoon into the bowl and fills it
with cereal.**

Jilly:

And there you have it! The spoon is now full of cereal!

Sounds of cheering come from outside the frame. Boom bows.

Jilly:

Pay attention. In just another moment, Boom will use this spoon (**Boom shows the spoon**) *to pick up this cereal* (**Boom points to the bowl**) *and then put the cereal into his mouth* (**Boom points to his mouth**)*. And now... all Boom has to do is... hold the spoon very straight, because if you hold a spoon slanted, the cereal can fall out* (**Boom spills some cereal into the bowl on purpose in order to show the audience what Jilly is talking about**) *exactly like that. Ladies and gentlemen, pay attention. Boom is now filling his spoon with cereal,* (**she begins to whisper**) *and he is now slowly bringing the cereal to his mouth. And he is doing all of this without allowing the cereal to fall from the spoon! Yes, yes, ladies and gentlemen!* (**Boom brings the spoon to his mouth with great concentration**) *This isn't easy, believe me, it's not simple at all, but Boom can do it!*

Boom:
I can do it?

Jilly:
Yes, Boom, you can do it.

Boom slowly brings the spoon to his mouth. There is a drumroll.

Jilly:
Will he succeed? Will he succeed?

Boom opens his mouth and puts the cereal-filled spoon into it.

Jilly:
Yes! Yes! He has succeeded!

Cheers from the crowd. Boom gets excited, raises his arms, gives a victory wave. The virtual crowd roars; Boom is wild with excitement. He jumps, skips, rolls around...

Jilly:
Yes! He succeeded! Ladies and Gentlemen, girls and boys, Boom ate his cereal with a spoon all by himself. Woo hoo! He did it!

Boom and Jilly bow to the camera.

FOURTH SEGMENT (MUSIC SEGMENT):
Jilly and Boom sit on the mattress. An empty bowl is between them.

Jilly:
(playing with a spoon)
Can you hear? My spoon goes click-click.

Boom bangs his spoon gently on Jilly's spoon.

Boom:
And mine goes clack-clack.

Jilly:
(banging on the bowl)
Click-click

Boom:
(taking another spoon and banging two spoons together)
Clack-clack

Jilly:
(banging)
Click.

Boom: (banging)
Clack.

They begin to bang spoons in rhythm.

Jilly and Boom:
Click click click
Clack!
Click click click
Clack!
Click
Clack-clack
click
Clack-clack!

Jilly:
(clicking and beginning to sing)
Click click click, what a funny trick.

Boom:
(clicking and singing)
Clack clack clack, give your spoon a whack.

Jilly and Boom get up. They keep singing, and they add a simple dance.

Jilly and Boom:
Click clack, click clack
Put yourself right on the track
Clack click, clack click
Move your body strong and quick
Hands up, click click click
Hands down, clack clack clack
Now you've got the knack!

Jilly and Boom laugh and give each other a high five with their spoons.

Boom:
Again! Boom wants to do it again!

Jilly:
Yes, yes, yes, again!

They repeat the song and dance.

Jilly and Boom:
Click clack, click clack
Put yourself right on the track
Clack click, clack click
Move your body strong and quick
Hands up, click click click
Hands down, clack clack clack
Now you've got the knack!!

The End

PUPPETS IN CHILDREN'S PROGRAMMING

(INFORMATION ABOUT PUPPETRY THAT SCREENWRITERS SHOULD KNOW)

From a technical perspective, the writing, direction, and production of drama for children should not be different from that of adults except that some of the characters in the drama... **are puppets!** Writing or directing a screenplay which includes puppets is dependent on a familiarity with the subject since the involvement of puppets has many implications for the production. The use of puppets requires knowledge of the technical abilities and limits of the different dolls, the different methods of hiding the puppeteers, and all the other special technical and electronic requirements the puppeteers have and which need to be in place at the film site. This world of knowledge is worth acquiring for anyone involved in a production with puppets.

For writers — in order to facilitate the writing of scenes that can be handled by the kind of puppets involved in the series.

For producers — in order to understand the technical complexities of the different kinds of puppets involved in the production. This will ensure that they can accurately estimate the resources required for filming scenes with puppets.

For the artistic team — in order to facilitate the building of puppet-compatible sets, taking the kind of puppets involved into account, in addition to the means of hiding the puppeteers.

For the props team — in order to understand the difference between props meant to be used by puppets and those meant to be used by human actors.

For the technical team (camera operators, sound technicians, light technicians, other technicians) — in order to help them construct the illusion which allows the viewer to view the screen and believe in what is happening there. They must enable the viewer to forget that under the colorful strips of foam which walk and talk on screen, a group of people, who enable this magic to take place, is hiding.

And for directors (of course) — who are supposed to have understood and mastered all the jobs listed above and to conduct this puppet concert.

The director has the final vision of the creation and makes most of the production's artistic decisions. In order to realize her vision, she must have an in-depth understanding of all the artistic and technical fields involved,. that is, design, acting, filming and lighting, among other things. In scenarios where puppets star, she must also acquire a kind of knowledge that is not usually taught in academic programs for film or television directing — knowledge of the art of puppeteering.

In the context of practical education workshops that I have facilitated over the years for many young writers and directors interested in joining the children's programming industry, I have needed to dedicate quite a lot of time to this subject.

The frequently asked questions that came up in these workshops almost always related to the integration of puppets into programs and films for children:

- Is it always necessary to use puppets in children's programs?
- Why use a puppet rather than an actor?
- How does a puppet affect the real world around it?
- Why is there a need for so many different kinds of puppets?
- How do you decide what kind of puppet to use for a particular situation?

It is important to emphasize that the *world of puppets* presented in this chapter and in others is just the tip of the iceberg of this wide and complex world; the subject could easily fill many books. This chapter is meant to be an introduction to the field and its goal is to throw a little bit of light onto this world and to answer the basic questions presented above, among others.

A. WHY PUPPETS?

I am not sure that the real reason to use puppets as characters in television programs or movies can be expressed in words, but I'll try anyway. *Cinematic truth* is credible to the extent that a movie manages to induce the belief in a viewer that what he sees on the screen, at a certain moment, is actually happening there as he watches. Despite the fact that the viewer knows, for example, that aliens do not actually exist or that there is no such thing as ghosts, during those moments of observing the silver screen, he enjoys believing in the existence of these beings in the moment.

The goal in working with puppets is to reach this same *cinematic truth*. A raging argument between a frog puppet and a movie usher, happening on the screen right before our eyes, can create this kind of cinematic truth, bringing the indescribable pleasure of watching a situation which can be completely preposterous. Despite our absolute knowledge that there is no real sense in a rip-roaring argument between a frog puppet who wants a discount, just for being a frog, and the movie usher stationed at the entrance of the theater, we enjoy believing in this unrealistic event, which, in fact, is happening as we watch on the screen in front of us.

I well remember the moment in which I fell in love with puppetry as a medium. It was love at first sight. It could be that a dissection of this moment would reveal part of the rhyme and reason that leads creative people to use puppet characters in movies and television programs, though I'm not sure about that at all. My moment of falling in love occurred in 1982, in the context of a workshop led by Sesame Street, New York staff for directors and producers who had been selected to produce the series in their home countries. In the context of that morning, I watched an acting rehearsal in the studio between the two glove puppets, Telly and Elmo.

The set for the segment was a public library in which both puppets wanted to look at a particular picture book. Little Elmo needed the bigger Telly's help in reaching the book, which was on a high shelf, but Telly was paralyzed by anxiety. He couldn't stop worrying. He worried that if he were to get up from his place at the reading table, someone else would take it; he worried that the book that they were looking for would not be on the shelf because someone else had already borrowed it; he worried that if the book were actually to be there, someone would come and take it at the very moment that he reached it. He worried that the book might be on such a high shelf that he wouldn't be able to reach it at all, etc., etc.

Telly was therefore characterized as the *ultimate worrier*, and I was amazed by the ability of the puppet to broadcast such deep anxiety. His anxiety was expressed in every part of his being — in his worried look, in his timid voice, and mostly in what was expressed in the brilliant operation of his puppeteer, who got Telly to express an infinite number of tentative and amusing gestures: Telly gets up to go and hurries to sit down again without knowing exactly what he wants. He fidgets incessantly with his fingers, he glances anxiously in all directions, his whole body trembles at the height of his anxiety. He scratches his head, the back of his neck and his chin; he wipes sweat from his brow with a handkerchief; bites his nails; embarrassedly mumbles the ends of his sentences and so on. Between rehearsals, the puppeteer put down the furry purple blanket (that's how the puppet looked to me when it was not being operated) and went for a quick rest, or to drink a cup of coffee. I was utterly thrilled every time he picked up the furry purple blanket again and, before my eyes, magically infused it with the breath of life. This puppeteer managed to create within me a deep and complete identification and empathy with the distress and uncertainty of what was, when all was said and done, a swatch of purple fabric. And that is how, during that rehearsal, Telly and his puppet-kind conquered my heart forever.

As someone who was already involved in children's programming, I discovered the unrealized potential of puppet characters and their extraordinary abilities. This was the first time that I saw a character with just one trait as a basis for building a personality, succeed in producing such a wide range of behaviors. Eventually, I learned to understand the ability of puppets to turn one personality trait into a stirring, fascinating, and fully realized character.

If we take five random characteristics, for example: anxiety, laziness, suspicion, fear, and timidity, and we decide to create puppets around these characteristics, it is almost certain that the action will not be difficult to imagine. Take a plot which is centered on the friendship of Warren Worry, Maisy Lazy, Scout Doubt, Aidy Fraidy, and Timmy Timid, who decide to go on a trip to the African jungle in order to find their good friend, Maudy Muddled — sounds promising, doesn't it?

In the previous chapter, we defined the heroes of children's plots as "characters with only one trait designed to move the plot forward and/or establish the character's role in the story." Since we have already understood that puppets have no competition when it comes to the portrayal of one-dimensional characters, there is no doubt that when we need to portray the one-dimensional personality of, say, the bad guy; the angry guy; the forgetful guy; or any other one-dimensional individual, the option of using a puppet becomes obvious. (Not to mention that human actors have a much more difficult time portraying one-dimensional characters — something which risks being interpreted as bad acting.) Another advantage of using puppets over human actors can be found in the very phrase, *human actors*. It's clear that when portraying non-human characters, like animals, creatures, monsters, etc., puppets, given their technical superiority, are the clear winners.

On the visual front, one can make a puppet of any desired shape and color. The gravitational pull of logic means nothing to a puppet. Human characters, who can also be picturesque and unrealistic in a given scenario, are still expected to toe a certain realistic line of appearance, as opposed to puppets, who can look like anything — a talking shoe; a ballet-dancing elephant; a space creature who looks like Swiss cheese; or a gentle, glasses-wearing punching bag.

In addition to all these rational claims, as I have already pointed out, puppets have a kind of magic, a collection of bits of sponge and colored cloth that come to life when the lights are turned on and the cameras begin to roll.

B. PUPPET TYPES

In chapter eight, we divided puppets into four basic types. We classified them as:
- Puppets that look human
- Puppets that look like an animal
- Puppets that belong to the *family of creatures*
- Puppets that look like plants or objects

In addition to these categories, we pointed out that it is common to distinguish among puppet types according to how they are operated. The three most common operation methods in film and television are:
- Glove puppets
- Rod puppets
- Body puppets

In this chapter, we will try to understand how the different puppet types work, what the advantages and disadvantages of the three types of puppets are, and how to choose the right type of puppets for our needs.

BODY PUPPETS

A. Large body puppet operation

B. Medium body puppet operation

In essence, body puppets are full-body costumes worn by the actor. They are usually built in two parts — the head and the body. In the first stage, the actor wears the body of the puppet and later on, he puts on the head.

Some puppets that require more significant neck and mouth movement are worn with the actor's extended arm operating the head portion (see the sketch below), which renders one of the puppet's arms immobile. An inoperative arm may be a disadvantage, but in many ways, it can also be advantageous. The advantage lies in the operating of the face of the puppet by hand; this allows the face and the neck of the puppet to be much more expressive. The mouth area of the puppet is usually made from soft materials allowing the puppeteer to evince a range of expressions. Additionally, in some puppets, the puppeteer has an eye or eyebrow control device attached to one of his fingers. By moving the control device, he can bestow a wider range of expressions to the puppet. In certain puppets, the eyes and eyebrows are controlled by a second puppeteer who is external to the puppet, and controls the eyes and eyebrows with a remote control device. However, regular body puppets which allow their operators to move both arms are the most common type. This is because these puppets are easier to design, create, and operate, and they cost less to produce.

Large body puppet operation

Wearing a full-body puppet costume is not easy, and a puppeteer needs breaks every five to ten minutes. In addition to this, it is hard for the puppeteer to see his acting environment. In the vast majority of cases, the puppeteer sees through the mouth of the puppet. Black, one-way netting stretches from one side of the mouth to the other, hiding the puppeteer from the camera. In this way, he can see without being seen. He can also breathe more comfortably through the puppet's mouth. In some puppets, in which the height of the mouth is not parallel to the height of the puppeteer's eyes, there are ventilation slits or peep-holes in other parts of the body, depending on the particular construction of the puppet in question. In some cases, a small video camera plus receiver is fitted into the body of the puppet upon which the puppeteer can see himself in relation to the other characters on set.

Large body puppet operation

This is a very complicated system, necessitating the building of a special transmitter just for the puppeteer. A system like this increases the difficulties of handling the puppet as well as the costs of its operation. The puppeteer is also usually the one to give the puppet its voice. He speaks as he acts and his voice is heard through a tiny wireless transmitter mounted either on the puppeteer or to the inside of the puppet costume itself. The transmitter receives signals from a microphone mounted inside the puppet, near the puppeteer's mouth.

In general, regular body puppets have a narrow range of possible expressions compared to rod puppets and glove puppets. This narrow range of expressions is the natural consequence of the great number of technical tasks its puppeteer must accomplish. A body puppet must be able to move around a set freely, and at the same time, to accomplish a host of physical tasks, according to the demands of the screenplay (walking, climbing, dancing, taking objects from point A to point B, etc.) while rod puppets and glove puppets remain in one place by their very nature. They don't move around the set and are built in a way that allows their operators to focus on their hand movements and facial expressions. This, of course, allows them a much greater range of expressions.

On the other hand, a clear advantage of body puppets is that their inclusion in a scenario does not demand any special modifications of the set and they can *act* with or without human actors on almost any set.

GLOVE PUPPETS

The second kind of puppet is the glove puppet. In its basic configuration, the glove puppet is operated by two puppeteers: the head puppeteer and an assistant. The two puppeteers insert their hands into the hands of the puppet such that the hands of the puppet actually function like large gloves (see sketch).

The operation of a glove puppet by two puppeteers

The fact that the puppeteers' hands are in the puppet's allows the puppet a large range of movements. Glove puppets can hold objects, move their fingers over a keyboard as if they are playing the piano, point to things, and count things on their fingers. In short, they can accomplish a particularly wide range of tasks requiring fine motor control.

A video screen mounted opposite the puppeteer's eyes allows him to operate his puppet. The screen is connected to a camera which films the scene. The screen shows the puppeteer his puppet and the facial expressions he is creating as well as its movement in relation to the other characters on the set. This allows him to fully assess his puppet's operation and to provide a nuanced performance. The video screen allows the puppeteer to fashion astonishingly accurate expressions such as wonder, disappointment, boredom, anger, sadness, and other expressions that would be much more difficult for a body puppet to express.

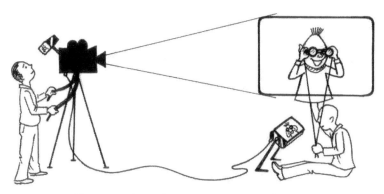

*The use of a video screen as an aid to
the operation of a puppet*

The decision as to whether a glove puppet should be operated by one puppeteer or two depends on the demands of the screenplay — that is, on the actions that the puppet-character is supposed to do. If the puppet is supposed to clap hands or build a block tower, it is clear that a second puppeteer is critical. On the other hand, if the puppet just needs to speak or to hold a phone receiver or a balloon, only one puppeteer will be needed.

Just like with body puppet puppeteers, glove puppet puppeteers provide the voice of their characters as they operate the puppets. A tiny wireless microphone mounted near the mouth of the puppeteer transmits his voice as he speaks through the puppet's neck region.

ROD PUPPETS

Operating rod puppets greatly resembles the operation of glove puppets. The only significant difference is the way in which the arms are moved. As opposed to glove puppets, whose hands are essentially the hands of the puppeteer, rod puppet's arms are operated by narrow rods that are attached to the puppet's hands at one end and held in the hands of the puppeteer at the other. The puppeteer uses the rods to create the character's arm and hand movements (see sketch).

The operation of a rod puppet by one puppeteer

Rod puppets cannot be operated without a video screen mounted opposite the puppeteer's eyes, either. Here too, the video screen shows the feed from a camera, allowing the puppeteer to watch the functioning of the puppet he is operating and its movements in relation to the other characters on set.

The biggest restriction in the use of rod puppets is the method used for moving their arms. As opposed to a glove puppet, a rod puppet cannot clasp something, move its hands, or wave its fingers. It can, though, hold various objects such as an umbrella, an apple, and the like, but only on condition that the object was attached to its hands before filming. It can also wave goodbye, and the like, but it cannot accomplish all the fine motor movements of a glove puppet. Nevertheless, rod puppets have two great advantages over glove puppets:

1. Both hands can be operated by just one puppeteer (see sketch).
2. Their hands are proportional to their bodies, as opposed to those of glove puppets, whose hands are big in proportion to their bodies given that they have to be big enough to encase the hands of their operators.

The choice of method of operation of a puppet depends on various factors. The first factor going into the decision is usually that of design. What kind of arms suit the character better? It is clear, for example, that the character of a little mouse would look strange with big paws that would look out of proportion with the rest of its body. Sometimes, however, the choice is made on technical grounds. For example, when the space for the puppeteer on the set is very small and it is clear that a puppet requiring operation by two puppeteers is out of the question, or when the actions that the puppet is supposed to do are more suited to one type of arm than another.

BASIC PUPPET OPERATION METHODS FOR FILMING

It is much easier and more comfortable to operate glove and rod puppets while standing. Nevertheless, they often have to be operated from a sitting position or in a crouch position while the puppeteer hides behind a counter or table. Operating the puppet from a standing position allows the puppeteer to move freely in all directions and to create the illusion that the puppet is actually walking from place to place.

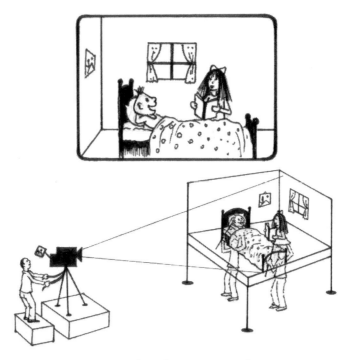

Raised set for puppets only

There is no doubt that the illusion of the puppet as a living creature is more concrete when the puppeteer can move freely within the entire set. Sets meant for the operation of puppets from a standing position are built with the floor of the set raised about a meter and a half above the studio floor. The raised set allows puppeteers to move freely, upright, on the studio floor while they operate their puppets.

The scenery on sets built for puppets usually includes objects that *happen to* hide the bottom half of the puppets. In this way, the puppet can "walk" from the writing desk to the kitchen counter, for example, while creating the illusion that the puppet's legs are actually stepping from place to place and that the only reason we cannot see this is that the table or counter *happen* to hide its legs.

It is clear that raised sets are appropriate for programs designed primarily for puppet characters and not for human actors. The raised set is designed as a kind of giant stage under which the puppeteers move and work. In a case where the screenplay calls for a human actor to act alongside the puppets on a raised set, the actor would be required to work on a ladder or on stilts in order to reach the height of the puppets. Of course, this is impossible, so instead, an additional raised platform is built alongside the raised floor of the set in order to allow the human to stand or sit next to the puppets, thus maintaining the illusion that the human actor and the puppets coexist on the same plane.

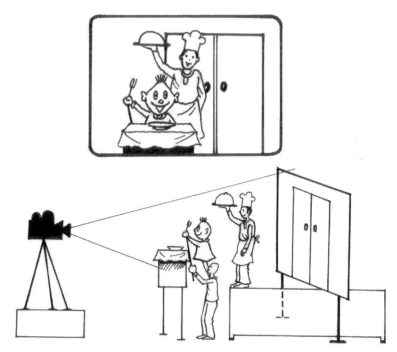

Raised set for both puppets and human actors

Clearly, in cases like these, the puppeteer's movement and acting range will be severely curtailed. His motions will be restricted to the raised platform built for the puppeteer and he will not be able to move freely on the entire set.

For this reason, this kind of set is not appropriate for programs in which human actors and puppets act alongside each other as a rule, and therefore, in these programs, the set is designed to be compatible with the free movement of human actors. These sets resemble regular sets built for regular programs. With that as a given, they are designed for the interaction of humans and puppets and as such include many niches in which puppeteers can hide and scenery can be created with this purpose in mind. The objects in the scenery that hide the puppeteers must be integral to the set and cannot stand out. There must be a logical reason for their presence on the set and that is why most of the situations in which puppets and human actors appear together on screen occur behind a big table, at a store counter, by a tree trunk, behind the backrest of a bench or alongside any other physical object whose presence on the set can be rationally justified. These objects must be sufficiently wide to allow the puppeteer, his assistants and his technical aides (camera, screen, props, etc.) to remain hidden in a natural way.

Puppet operation in scenes such as these must always be done in a sitting or crouching position because the puppeteer must work behind an object whose height is also suited to the presence of human characters. Clearly, it is much more comfortable for a puppeteer to hide behind a 90 centimeter high table (and not a 70 centimeter high table, which is the standard height), though if a human actor must stand next to or sit at the table, the unusual height of the table would interfere with the believability of the set.

Puppet operation on a realistic set

Therefore, the table, the bannister, the backrest of the bench, or any other object behind which the puppeteer is meant to hide, has to look normal in relation to the human actors situated next to it, and as such, has to be built to a more or less standard height.

Incidentally, sometimes props are built on a small stand intended to raise them slightly in order to ease the situation for the puppeteer who may be required to sit for hours with back rounded and head bent. When appropriate, it is possible to remove the stand and return the object to its regular height.

THE OPERATION OF GLOVE OR ROD PUPPETS ON A REGULAR SET

Puppeteers who handle different kinds of glove puppets, and who must work behind tables or counters, are restricted to their one place of operation and cannot move freely on the set. Any sideways movement puts them at risk of being seen by the cameras and thus ruining the magic of moving, talking puppets for the viewer. Of course, it is possible to create the illusion of movement when a puppet "leaves" one closed frame and "enters" another in a different part of the set. In this way, the viewer gets the impression that the puppet got up and moved from one place to another (especially if the viewer hears "footsteps" during the time that the puppet is supposed to be moving.) This operation requires the cameras to stop rolling while the puppet is moved but the end result is effective.

In addition to the moving of the puppet from one place to another, it is possible to actually show glove puppets "walking" on set. Though this requires extended filming time, the walking puppet illusion created is definitely satisfying. Special wheeled platforms are usually used in order to "walk" glove or rod puppets. These padded platforms (which look like car mechanics' creepers) allow the puppeteer to operate the puppet while lying down while an assistant pulls or pushes the platform in the desired direction while the cameras roll. The camera shows only the puppet, of course, and avoids the puppeteer below, allowing the puppeteer to move from place to place on set, creating the believable illusion of a moving character.

*Moving Platform Allowing the Movement of
a Glove or Rod Puppet*

Video screens stationed along the wagon's path show the puppeteer the puppet's progress and help him to assess his performance. Sometimes, when the puppet must move its arms in time to its "walking," two platforms are joined together to allow an assistant to move the puppet's second hand alongside the head puppeteer.

In addition to the one described above, many other types of wheeled contraptions exist as aides to the puppeteer. These contraptions are not for sale; the vast majority are custom built as a private initiative to the specifications of the particular puppeteer. Usually, the characteristics of the filming location are what demand and inspire unique solutions to the challenges of the production. With that, the most important factor in the design of the wagon is the need for its wheels to be as silent as possible, as even the most believable performance will lose credibility when accompanied by the sound of squeaking wheels.

THE USE OF A CAMERA IN HIDING THE PUPPETEER

In addition to building hiding places for glove puppets' puppeteers, it is important to know that there are other hiding methods which allow for the filming of puppets without having to hide the puppeteer at all. This filming method requires the camera operator to cut off the bottom of the frame at the seam between the puppet and the visible part of the puppeteer's body. Long scenes cannot be filmed by this method because, at some point, the viewer begins to feel the need to see the full picture. However, short scenes can be filmed by this method with no trouble at all.

Filming a puppet operated by an unhidden puppeteer

USING THE FOREGROUND TO HIDE THE PUPPETEER

One of the problems of filming with an unhidden puppeteer is the inability to hide characters' height disparities, especially those of puppets in relation to humans. Any attempt to balance these disparities risk the revelation of the puppeteer.

In these cases and others, it is possible to use a hiding method erected near the camera rather than near the characters on film. Often, the artistic team is required to design scenery which includes a large variety of logically justified objects that are situated near the camera purely "by chance." These objects hide the lower part of the frame and can include large potted plants, a bush, playground equipment, a fence, a bookshelf, and the like.

Filming a puppet and an actor with a foreground object

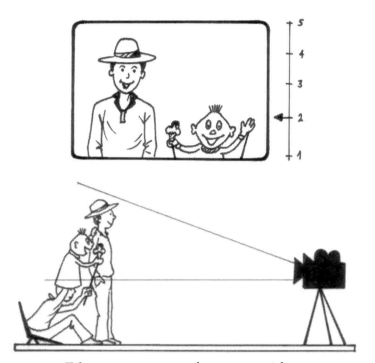

Filming a puppet and an actor without
a foreground object

There exist tens of other techniques in addition to the three basic techniques used in the film and television worlds, and on which I have expanded in this chapter. These begin with gigantic body puppets operated by two or three puppeteers and include marionettes, finger puppets, black light theater, shadow theater, or any technique in which a puppet, object, or prop is brought to life by a human actor. Though these techniques are more common in the theater world than in that of television, a basic understanding of their methodologies will help any content creator whose work is connected in any way to puppeteering.

PROPS FOR PUPPETS

Though it may sound strange, knowledge of the field of props for puppets is perhaps the most important knowledge for a puppet screenwriter to acquire. This knowledge can save content writers the trouble of having many excellent screenplays vetoed when it turns out that they are impossible to film.

Sometimes, actions that seem to the writers to be simple or trivial can turn out to be very complicated to execute when the character in question is a puppet. Props used by human actors are usually clear and simple. A human actor who is required to take a bite of a piece of apple cake or a jam sandwich will be given the real thing. A puppet made of cloth, fur, or any similar material, cannot touch anything liquid or greasy because the ensuing stain will not be easy or even possible to remove. In fact, it is almost impossible to clean stains off of these puppets at all. Therefore, puppets that need to hold staining foods are usually made from synthetic materials such as colored sponge, sculpted latex, colored polystyrene and similar materials. When the puppet puts food into its mouth (like *Sesame Street's* Cookie Monster, who puts food into his mouth and even chews it), the food is made according to particular recipes which won't harm the puppet. An additional problem in the creation of props for puppets is one connected to the operation of the puppet. Everyday actions involving props that a human actor can do with no problem at all can prove to be extremely problematic for a puppet.

Closing a button, eating out of a jar with a spoon, writing a word in a notebook, spreading something onto a piece of bread with a knife, peeling an apple and other similar actions become complicated when they are supposed to be executed by a puppet. Herein lies the significant difference between rod and glove puppets. Inside the hands of a glove puppet are the hands of a puppeteer, of course, and a glove puppet, therefore, has no problem holding objects. Props made for glove puppets can be made from materials benign to the puppet and shaped and sized more or less similarly to the same prop made for a human actor. In this case, the only difficult problem with which the puppeteer is faced is that of coordination. This is because the puppeteer observes his actions on a video monitor. On the monitor, every time the puppeteer moves to the right, it appears as if he is moving to the left and vice versa. When the puppet needs to execute an action requiring the use of both hands, the action must be synchronized between one puppeteer's right hand and the other puppeteer's left, turning a simple action like hand clapping into something requiring much practice.

As opposed to a glove puppet operator, the rod puppet operator's hands are not in the puppet's hands. The puppeteer holds narrow rods which operate the puppet's arms. He can raise or lower the puppet's arms, but he cannot make it grasp or let go of objects. Sometimes, a prop can be pre-attached to the puppet's hands with double-sided tape, a safety pin, a stitch, Velcro, or the curling of the puppet's fingers around the object, such that the puppet can hold a phone receiver, an umbrella, or a pair of binoculars. Of course, in order to arrange for the puppet to grasp the object or to let go of it, filming must be stopped. Sometimes, the prop is fitted with its own rod and is held by the puppeteer in a manner which gives the illusion that the puppet itself is holding the prop.

Using one object is relatively simple. Below is a screenplay that demands the use of many props, making it complicated to film. Take into account that these are rod puppets and that they are therefore incapable of grasping objects, necessitating the creation of props which are themselves controlled by rods. Each time a puppet hands food or an object to another puppet, the puppeteer is, in fact, the one to do the "handing over" by manipulating the rods which are connected to the object. He takes it out of the hand of the giving puppet and puts it into the hand of the taking puppet.

The set in question is one designed for puppets alongside human actors and therefore requires that the puppeteers work in kneeling positions behind scenery objects (a bench, in this case).

THE SANDWICH TRADE

As opposed to the original screenplay, in this version, numbers were substituted for the puppets' names in order to make the technical process more easily understood.

Puppet #1 sits, as it were, on a park bench, behind a picnic table. Her lunch bag is on the table and she is searching through it.

Puppet #1:
(Disappointed) What? I don't have a banana? (She looks into the depths of the lunch bag) What's that? A hard-boiled egg sandwich? But I don't like hard-boiled eggs. (She searches the bag) Hang on... I have an apple here. And I do like apples.

Puppet #2:
Good morning, Puppet #1.

Puppet #1:
Good morning, Puppet #2. (She looks at his sandwich.) What do you have in your roll?

<u>Puppet #2:</u> *(Disappointed)*
Hmm... I have cheese and tomato.

<u>Puppet #1:</u> *(Jealously)*
Yeah. If I also had cheese and tomato in my sandwich,
I'd be happy.

<u>Puppet #2:</u>
What do you have in your sandwich?

<u>Puppet #1:</u>
Hard-boiled egg.

<u>Puppet #2:</u>
Interesting.. Actually, I like hard-boiled eggs. If I had a
hard-boiled egg in my roll, I'd also be happy.

<u>Puppet #1:</u>
It's true. What a pity that you didn't get a hard-boiled egg in
your sandwich and I didn't get cheese and tomato in mine.

<u>Puppet #2:</u>
*Right. It really is a pity. **(With a flash of understanding)***
Hang on, so maybe we should trade?

<u>Puppet #1:</u>
Trade what?

<u>Puppet #2:</u>
Trade sandwiches. Instead of saying, "What a pity" and
feeling sad, we can trade sandwiches!

<u>Puppet #1:</u>
***(Enthusiastic)** Yes!! What a great idea! Let's trade!*

Puppet #2 and Puppet #1 trade sandwiches.

<u>*Puppet #2 +Puppet #1:*</u>
Enjoy!

They are about to take a bite of their sandwiches when Puppet #3 walks by, sad, holding a balloon attached to a thick plastic stick.

<u>*Puppet #1:*</u>
Hi Puppet #3. What happened?

<u>*Puppet #3:*</u> *(In despair)*
I was at a friend's birthday party, and I got a purple balloon, and I don't like purple balloons. I only like red ones.

<u>*Puppet #1:*</u>
Don't be sad. Instead of saying, "What a pity" and feeling sad, think about it. Maybe you can do something!

<u>*Puppet #2:*</u>
Yes, maybe you can trade your balloon with someone who does like purple balloons!

The Sandwich Trade – illustration.

<u>Puppet #3:</u>
Like whom, for example?

<u>Puppet #1:</u>   (remembering)
*Like me!! I like purple balloons. Would you like to trade
your balloon for a cheese and tomato sandwich?*

<u>Puppet #3:</u>
Yes, for sure! Let's trade!

<u>Puppet #1:</u> (waving a balloon)
*Now I have a delicious apple and a wonderful balloon.
Woo hoo. What a beautiful balloon.*

**Puppet #1 waves the plastic stick happily, which detaches
the balloon that then floats upwards.**

<u>Puppet #1:</u>
Oh no, my balloon... my balloon flew away!

<u>Puppet #2:</u>
What a pity. You really had a pretty balloon.

<u>Puppet #1:</u>
*Never mind. Instead of saying, "What a pity"
and feeling sad, maybe we can do something.*

<u>Puppet #2:</u>
*What? What? Who will want the stick of a balloon
without the balloon?!*

**Suddenly, Puppet #4 appears from inside a garbage can,
which is behind the picnic table.**

Puppet #4:

*Did you say the stick of a balloon without the balloon?!
(Wistfully) Oh... once I had one of those sticks, but I threw it
away because it had a balloon stuck to one end. And if
there's something I can't stand — it's balloons.*

Puppet #1:

*Really? So do you want to trade? I'll give you this stick
without a balloon, and you give me something else that you
don't need.*

Puppet #4: (sadly)

*I don't have anything to give you. **(Puppet #4 thinks and
then remembers)** Hang on. **(disgusted)** This morning I got a
fresh banana, and I can't eat it because I only like rotten
ones.*

Puppet #1: (happy)

*A fresh banana?? That's exactly what I love and want.
Do you want to trade?*

**Puppet #4 passes the banana over in disgust and takes the
stick.**

Puppet #4:

*With pleasure. Yuck. Who would believe that there are
people out there who like fresh bananas.
Horrible, horrible... it's just horrible.*

- The End –

The only way to understand the complications involved in the operation of the puppets in this scene is to try to imagine, in parallel to the dramatic action being played out above the picnic table, what is happening below it: the actions of all the puppeteers in addition to their assistants, including the timing of their entrances into and exits from the frame and, of course, the unique way in which the props function in the scene and the way in which they are handled.

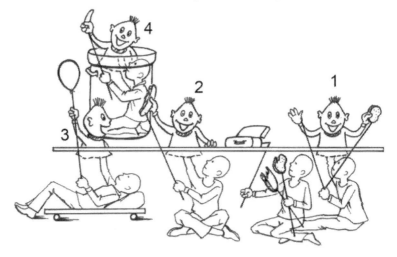

The positioning of the hidden puppeteers
and their assistants in the scene The Sandwich trade

Realizing the scene *The Sandwich Swap* requires intricate choreography and close cooperation among the six puppeteers hunched under the picnic table. A stage-by-stage description of the actions of the four puppeteers and an assistant follows:

Puppet #1, a rod puppet, cannot grasp objects. It cannot take out a sandwich from its lunch bag. Therefore, the lunch bag is attached to a very narrow rod, allowing the puppeteer (or the assistant) to tilt the bag in different directions and in doing so to change the bag's position on the picnic table, according to the needs of the screenplay.

Puppet #2 joins the scene. It is holding a roll with cheese in its right hand. (The sandwich is made of latex, of course.) The puppet appears to be holding the roll in its hand, but the roll is attached to a very narrow rod since it will need to be passed to Puppet #1.

When Puppet #2 proposes a trade to Puppet #1, the puppets come close to each other and appear to trade sandwiches under the table. This is so that the viewers will not witness the lack of arm movement on the part of the puppets. Now, Puppet #2 is holding the roll with cheese in its right hand while the puppeteer's assistant passes the hard-boiled egg sandwich to the left hand of Puppet #1 with the help of a narrow rod.

Now, Puppet #2's operator raises its right hand (which is holding the cheese roll) toward Puppet #1 in order to appear to offer Puppet #1 the roll in exchange for Puppet #1's sandwich. At the same time, the puppeteer's assistant grasps the roll's rod in her empty hand and, with perfect timing, the puppeteer and the assistant hand over the roll to Puppet #1. The assistant then places the roll's rod into the (real) hand of Puppet #1's operator in a way that makes it appear to the viewer as if Puppet #1 is now holding the roll.

This takes us up to the first trade. Puppet #1 and Puppet #2 have exchanged sandwiches.

Puppet #3, who appears to be holding a balloon stick with a purple balloon attached, now joins the action with the help of a wheeled platform. In this case also, the balloon has a particularly long rod attached to enable the puppeteers to easily hand the balloon over to Puppet #1.

Now, Puppet #1 offers to trade with Puppet #3. That is, to give Puppet #3 the roll and to get the balloon in exchange. Since Puppet #2 is situated between Puppets #1 and #3, it will be the one who executes the handover, from the perspective of the viewer. However, the real action will be done by the assistant who will take the roll from Puppet #1, using its rod, and will pass it, in cooperation with Puppet #2's operator into the right hand of Puppet #3. Puppet #3 will appear to put its hand down for a moment so that the handover can take place under the table. Puppet #3's operator will hand over the balloon in exchange for the roll to the puppeteer's assistant who will pass the balloon into Puppet #2's hand. Puppet #2 will then hand it, as it were, to Puppet #1.

Puppet #3 now leaves the scene (with the help of the wheeled platform) and the puppeteer's assistant is now free to release the balloon's thread which is at the end of the balloon's rod. The balloon, filled with helium, is released and floats upwards, toward the ceiling of the studio and Puppet #1 is left holding a stick without a balloon.

Meanwhile, while the viewers are still occupied with the balloon's "escape," Puppet #2's operator carefully lowers the sculpted egg sandwich under the table and switches it (before the camera returns and catches the action), for another sculpted egg sandwich from which several bites have been taken, such that when the viewer sees the puppet again, it seems as if the puppet has eaten about half the sandwich.

Puppet #4 now joins the scene (popping out of the garbage can situated behind the picnic table). Puppet #4 appears to come out of the garbage can, however it eventually joins the others at the picnic table with the help of a wheeled wagon. From this point on, everything is more simple. The puppeteer's assistant hands the balloon-less rod over to Puppet #4 and receives the banana in return (in an identical handover to that achieved earlier with Puppet #3). The banana is made of plastic and its bottom half is connected to a narrow rod, of course. It is handed over to Puppet #1 and the taxing scene finally comes to a close.

Props Designed for Puppets

It is reasonable to assume that a large percentage of the readers of the above description did not really manage to follow the operations of the four puppeteers and their two assistants, and even those who did understand the series of operations carried out in the *Sandwich Trade* scene are still not equipped with the tools to create a similar one.

The description above was designed to expose the reader to the intricacy of the operation of puppets and to the unique design of props meant to be used by puppets in a scene. Screenwriters who mean to write scenes for puppets, or for human actors and puppets together, will begin to learn the technical world that exists below the eye of the camera slowly and step by step. This chapter can serve as an introduction for anyone who intends to work in this field.

ANIMATION IN CHILDREN'S PROGRAMS

Animation is the presentation of single, still pictures in a rapid series, giving the illusion of fluid movement on the screen. The word *animation* comes from the Latin, *anima*, meaning *soul* or *breath of life*.

In previous chapters, I described the skills required for the creating of content for children, the ability to invent magical worlds and characters in particular.

I also said that writing for children is unique in its freedom from the gravitational pull of believability as it allows the writer to broach the borders of reality on many fronts. And which genre is more suited to the broaching of the borders of reality than animation?

In this medium, it is simple to write a dramatic monologue for a fly or a worm. And what is more fantastic and wonderful than a world coming to life as it rises from the page? Talking trees, dancing flowers, and a rock band whose members are mice?

From the point of view of a program, there is almost no competition for the freedom that the world of animation grants a writer, and this is connected to the production methods available in this genre. Animation copes with the world of dinosaurs, dragons, monsters, fairies, dwarves, witches, wizards, superheroes and the rest of the magical creatures which enchant children with as much ease as it copes with the portrayal of ordinary people and animals. How can other genres cope with the world of dinosaurs, dragons?

As is well known, children can lie on the carpet for hours moving a toy car, a doll, or even an empty can back and forth while making various noises or murmuring words that the item in their hands is supposed to be saying. This form of play tells us that in a child's world, objects have life. Movies in which we see a group of talking trains (*Thomas the Tank Engine)*, a mischievous and gutsy car that hatched from an egg (*Bumpety Boo*), or a group of toys, all of whom have full human personalities and abilities (*Toy Story*), concretize the fact that from the point of view of the child, the world of animation is a natural extension of her train of thought and active world of imagination. Animation is the natural home of children's content, a world in which everything is possible. And indeed, it is no coincidence that the vast majority of content for children created nowadays is animated.

A survey of the schedules of many children's television channels show that the majority of programs aimed at children and broadcast by children's channels are animated. For example, 83% of CBeebies' programs, the BBC kids' channel, are animated. The American PBS Kids channel also shows this trend, with 72% of shows broadcast for kids being animated. On the Canadian children's channel, CBC.CA/KIDS, 90% of the series for children are animated (!), and on the American Nick Junior channel, only one of eight of their central series' make use of human characters, and even this series (*Blue's Clues*) takes place in an illustrated world where all the characters other than the human ones are illustrated, too.

In earlier chapters, I described screenwriters appropriate for writing children's content as adults with the ability to create worlds, characters, and plots that children love. It follows from this that all a children's animation writer has to do is connect to the child within and to search in the recesses of her imagination for a world of characters who can form the basis of riveting and entertaining plots. These characters can exist in any world the writer cares to imagine: a world that exists deep inside the ground, within an ants' nest; a world that exists in a dinosaur cubs' kindergarten; or a world of chocolate creatures who live in a giant chocolate factory.

Children's animation screenplays, just like children's screenplays in which live or puppet characters participate, are founded on the same three basic principles that form the pillars of content writing for children: **the awareness of the cognitive abilities of children; the inclusion of educational values; and the concoction of enchanting content.**

Just like with other screenplays for children, screenplays written for animation have an educational message at heart that has been drawn from the recognition of a need in the life of young viewers. This need should form the basis of the world created by the film. Freedom from the world of production enables the writer to sail to horizons that a studio production or a production filmed on location could never reach. This freedom can sometimes cause the writer to forget that an added value must stand at the center of the world she creates. An Internet survey of the *About* pages of most of the successful animated series for children reveals that deep values form the basis of all of them.

The creators of *Dora*, for example, describe the goal of their show thus: Everyday, children deal with hundreds of problems. The overarching goal of the series is to: equip the viewing children with a range of problem-solving strategies such as stopping for a moment to think; asking for help when in need; or using previously gained knowledge. These strategies are modeled in every episode of the series.

The creators of *Thomas the Tank Engine* based their animated series on a series of children's books which began to be written in 1945 by Christopher Awdry and the Reverand W. Awdry. On the *About* page of the series, the series' goals are described as that of educating children to the value of hard work, contribution to society, and efficiency.

Underlying the animated series *Bob the Builder* are educational values and goals such as the modeling of problem-solving skills, cooperation, socialization, and environmental awareness. The movie *Toy Story* also has the values of true friendship, group identity, cooperation, and love for the other at its heart.

Therefore, after you have consolidated for yourself the underlying value that interests you (or that answers the need of the program for which you are writing / has been defined by the client), you can finally focus on the real creative process **and create content of a type so beloved by children**. As such, children's writers must get to know these worlds of animation and to learn how to create similar content.

For a film that is supposed to focus on the concept of cooperation, for example, it would be reasonable to create a world of ants who live in a nest deep inside the ground, since the principle of cooperation exists at the basis of these creatures' existence. Or a group of anthropomorphized work tools that lives in a big shed and, clearly, can only fix things when they work together. Obviously, there is no limit to our ability to invent things, but more than any other guiding factor, we must try to think of worlds that will cause viewing children, and the child within us, to open their eyes wide in amazement and pleasure, a world that children will want to visit themselves in response to the stories within it, in order to get to know its characters, some of whom will be models with which the children identify. They will love these characters and will want to behave like they do or at least to imagine themselves functioning in the same situations as these beloved characters.

PRODUCTION RESTRICTIONS
IN ANIMATED FILM

The protagonists of animated films can change shape to the degree that the rules of their worlds allow this. They can float in the air, shrink themselves, split in two, bounce back to their original shape after having been flattened, and more. But apart from this, the rules for writing screenplays for children's animated film plots are the same as the ones for writing for children in all the other contexts I have already presented. In addition to the different writing principles, the classic screenplay writing formula applies here too: **Exposition > First Inciting Incident > Rising Action (Plot) > Second Inciting Incident > Resolution.**

So, in order to create interest in viewers and to make the plot enjoyable, the animated film is in need of a good rising incident as well as all the other effective rules for writing for young children: the principle of rising intensity, the principle of repeating patterns, rhythmic story flow, and all the other tools that help children more easily predict the developments in the plot and that therefore increase their pleasure.

Having kept this in mind, the writer of animation can strap two booster rockets to her back and take off to spheres which were never available in the world of dramatic writing.

In live action films that are filmed in realistic scenery and acted by human actors or even films filmed in a studio with the participation of puppets, the limitations of the production are clear. The writer is aware of all the parameters which contribute to raise the price of the production. It is clear, for example, that allocating too many leading roles or writing scenes requiring too many different, far-flung locations, or writing in too many special effects burden the production's budget. Drama writers for television or the movie industry can, of course, focus on writing for low-budget or high-budget productions. There is no doubt that in live action films, it would behoove the writer to understand the connection between production limitations and the film's budget.

At first glance, it would seem that animation escapes these limitations. The writer would seem to have no reason to keep the number of lead roles to a minimum, given that they are all illustrated. Neither does she have any reason to keep the number of special effects down. Illustrated protagonists can leap from high towers, ride on the back of a dolphin, play tennis on the roof of a runaway train, become invisible, and more. There is no reason not to include far-flung sites in an animated production since the production team does not actually have to travel anywhere. The producer does not have to book ten hotel rooms for a production team which is supposed to film a complicated scene at the top of the Himalayas since the Himalaya scene can be animated in New York, London, or Tel Aviv.

Nevertheless, it would be irresponsible to say that everything is possible in animation and that writing content for animation completely removes the binds of production from the writer. There *are* specific elements and ideas whose use are likely to significantly increase production costs.

The freedom of expression available to writers of animated content is indeed greater than that of the writers of all other screenplays. However, it is important that writers of animation be aware of the types of content that are likely to increase production costs. The truth is that, as a rule, there is some resemblance between the things that increase costs in animation and those that increase costs in a regular live action production. In the case of writing many lead roles or locations, the situation in animated film and regular film is similar. Each addition of a character in an animated film involves increased design costs and the lengthening of production time. This also applies to every new animated film "location" as this requires the designing of additional backgrounds, increasing complication and costs. Additionally, in animation, even when the location has been designed, you must remember that each time the scene is viewed from another angle, design work is involved as well as the animation of a new background, in addition to the extant basic background (not including 3D animation).

Every intricate camera movement complicates and greatly increases animated production costs. Therefore, an animated scene which emulates the movement of a camera around an animated figure is likely to double and triple production requirements compared to the same scene animated with a static camera, as it were.

It is important to understand the connection between content meant for animation and the intricacies of its production. In order to write better and to get everything out of this medium that there is to be had, the writer must acquire a basic understanding of the animation process and a familiarity with the basic range of techniques used in this field.

UNDERSTANDING WORK PROCESSES IN ANIMATED FILM

The screenplay is the starting point of films in general and this applies to animation, too. The screenplay begins with an idea germinating in the mind of the writer, which is eventually converted to the written word. Screenplays written for animated characters are different in one way from those written for human actors: the process they undergo beginning at the moment the writing is finished and onward.

When the writing stage for human actors is finished, the production stage begins. It starts with reading rehearsals and progresses through to working rehearsals. The screenplay awakens slowly and surely. During the rehearsal stage, the creators (the director and the writer) see and hear their creation come to life. They constantly sharpen, correct, and improve the screenplay through watching and listening as the actors act it out. Naturally, every actor brings a unique personal package (character, tone, appearance, etc.) to the role. This package sometimes demands tinkering with the original screenplay to suit the character who plays the role for real. During this rehearsal process, the creators of regular films, as opposed to animation, learn more and more about the screenplay and their insights make their way into the final product.

Anyone involved in film or television production can be witness to the significant difference between the screenplay as it stood during the first read-through rehearsal and its appearance at the final production.

Clearly the process described above cannot take place in an animated film. Animated characters don't come to rehearsals, make suggestions, and improve their performance from rehearsal to rehearsal. Therefore, animated films cannot undergo the refinement process that live action films undergo.

For this reason, animated films undergo different processes aimed at improving their quality. These processes exist in all animated films, without reference to the chosen animation technique, and it is very important that animation writers know them, take part in them, and use them as much as possible in pursuit of an excellent end product.

1. THE SCREENPLAY

As mentioned above, in animation, as in any other film technique, the starting point is usually the screenplay. The screenplay is the film's verbal layout which serves as the basis for the production of the film or television program. Writing screenplays for children's animated films is identical to the writing of screenplays for children's films of any other type. This is true on condition that the writer knows the participating characters' behavior patterns well (as she would if the film were a sequel or an episode in an existing series where the writer has seen other episodes and understands the personalities of the characters and their manners.) Nevertheless, when the writer is in the first stage of developing content which has not yet been designed, she is likely to face a problem. How exactly do the characters she is writing look? It is almost certain that the writer is capable of imagining a clearly defined set of characters born in her imagination, but when this set of characters is finally designed by professional animators, it is certain that they will differ from those she imagined in some way or other. And then, there is a high chance that the look designed for them will not be completely compatible with the words the writer wrote for them.

Writing for human actors is a much easier process. One can usually classify the character by gender, age, appearance, nationality, personal characteristics, etc. However, in animation, the protagonist can be a fish, as stool, a flower or a cloud. Additionally, even human characters that are animated have an almost infinite range of appearance possibilities. The designer can give a character almost any appearance. It is clear that the appearance of the character will influence the way in which she or he speaks, walks, and behaves.

For example, if we take a look at the five characters below, we will see that even though they were all designed on the basis of the same character description, and for exactly the same screenplay, it is clear that each of them has a distinct personality which will need to find expression in future screenplays.

Process of Animated Character Design

Often, therefore, the process of character design begins during the writing process. The writer writes an initial treatment and a nascent screenplay in the knowledge that the screenplay will develop in step with the characters. The writers and the designers balance each other in this way as the writer increases the precision with which the characters are written in compliance with their appearance.

When the first full version of the screenplay has been

written, it has been written for a fully realized character. A character that will speak and act in congruence with the appearance designed for it.

2. CHARACTER AND BACKGROUND DESIGN

The stage of character and background design begins after the screenplay has been written or alongside it. The designer/animator gets an initial screenplay and a written description of the characters and begins the process of design. This is the *concept art* stage and the characters now begin to come into existence.

This is not the final design yet, which will come at a later stage. But at this critical stage, the writer's content begins to take shape. In the Concept Art stage, the animator begins to experiment with visual renderings of the characters' physical and behavioral descriptions.

The animator's design should emphasize the character's chosen characteristics, such as pride, shyness, courage, confusion, gluttony, or any other trait. In this process of cross fertilization, the writer, designer, director, and the rest of the creative team come to understand how the lead characters will look.

This stage of the proceedings resembles the casting stage for a film or television show in which the creative team searches for the right actor to portray the characteristics written for the character.

The illustration below is an example of the depiction of a group of animated friends. These friends meet in the neighborhood park and get involved in a joint adventure every day.

They include (from left to right):

Neighborhood Friends

A kite, who isn't really part of the group, but always appears at times of crisis and solves the group of friends' problem.

A tiny, spoiled mouse. Since he is the smallest of the group, everyone always has to look out for him, take care of him, and help him. He loves this status and uses it to his advantage.

A bird who serves as the *brains* of the group. She is the one who always has the ideas and finds the solutions. She is naïve and always sees things as they are.

A cat who is pampered and a little sly. Would like to be seen by his friends as innocent, helpless, and shy. He is none of those things.

A little fly who is convinced that he knows what to do and when to do it better than anyone else. He would like to be seen as someone who is smart and knows everything, though, of course, he is nothing of the sort.

A befuddled puppy. Loves to run and to retrieve objects when asked to do so and when not asked. It is very important to him to be seen by the group as a trustworthy and loyal character on whom one can rely (even though he is exactly the opposite of this).

Some of the foundational characteristics of the characters were demanded by the client television channel — for example that the characters would be portrayed by animals.

This is because designing characters to look like humans sometimes actually causes children to have difficulty identifying with them for trivial reasons such as their possessing different hair or skin color, different facial characteristics, etc. A group of child-like animals, however, can give a generic expression to the entire population of the world's children, however they may look.

The characters are examined on many fronts in the design process. Are they compatible with the character the writer created? Would they be interesting to their target audience? Do they answer to the technical needs of the movements of the character? (It is clear, for example, that the movement needs of the fly are completely different from those of the puppy and the cat.)

Additionally, the design is examined for its compatibility with up to date trends and, sometimes, with the possibility of turning it into a successful brand name that will lead target audiences to want to buy products adorned with its image.

At the same time that the characters are being designed, the backgrounds are being designed too. This stage greatly resembles the scenery building stage in a studio production or the stage of choosing a location in movies filmed on location.

Integration of Characters and Backgrounds

At this stage, the visual characteristics of the world in which her characters will exist continue to become clearer to the writer: the general feel of the design of the film, the park or street in which the characters usually meet, the hues of the backgrounds matched to the different colors of the characters, etc.

Similar to the writing process, the character and background design process is also done in stages. This allows for the incremental shaping of the different elements to which various creative team members contribute, leading to the writing of clearly defined and well-integrated characters.

The design process is a long search on the part of the animation's creators for the characters and the backgrounds that perfectly meet the needs of the given content.

3. THE STORYBOARD

The storyboard breaks up the screenplay into a series of illustrations. In the process of drawing the storyboard, the story of the film is told through a series of illustrations that resemble a comic strip. The screenplay is broken down into illustrations that describe what will be seen in the film in the order of plot events. It presents places, characters, expressions and actions from the different points of view that correspond to those that are planned for the final film.

The storyboard is a multi-purpose work tool in the planning stage — and not only in the world of animation. Storyboarding in film and television is done in parallel to other development processes such as rehearsals with actors, planning visits to different locations, and many other planning and building processes which cannot be done in the case of animated content. For this reason, the storyboard of an animated film is much more detailed — its role in the process of predicting the final character of the film is much more significant.

In animation storyboarding, each minute of the film is broken down into a large number of illustrations. Every motion is broken down into sub-motions and every camera angle change is divided into transitional perspectives. In the storyboard presented below, for example, a scene of 30 seconds only is depicted in seven illustrations.

1. A bird enters, stops, and crouches down.

2. Looks to the left, whistles, and goes back to looking straight

3. A mouse enters, tries to jump, and doesn't succeed.

4. A dog enters - jumps over the mouse and the bird - does a somersault in the air, and sits. (The mouse keeps trying to jump.)

5. A cat jumps in over the mouse, the bird, and the dog, and sits down. (The mouse still doesn't succeed in jumping.)

6. A kite enters and swoops around. The mouse sits, disappointed.

7. The kite picks the mouse up above all the others, and puts
it down at the end of the row.
The kite rises. (TILT UP) The logo appears.

The content of the scene is extremely simple: The bird suggests that all the friends play *Leap Frog* and everyone is enthusiastic about the idea. The mouse goes first and does not succeed (because he is so small). The puppy tries next, leaps, and manages to jump over the bird. Then it's the cat's turn. She manages to jump over the bird and the puppy. Meanwhile, the mouse has been continually trying without any success. Along comes the kite that grabs the mouse by the tail and helps him to skip over all his friends.

In a regular film, it is reasonable to assume that the storyboard creators would not have broken down each movement or each character into its elemental parts. They would have been satisfied with one illustration to depict the whole scene, if any.

A ten – twelve minute animated film's storyboard is likely to include 120 to 200 illustrations, depending on the film's degree of complexity. A non-animated film's story board tends to include a maximum of about twenty illustrations. The storyboard is also meant to help us, the writers, to understand how our screenplay has been translated to animation. Acquiring good skills in using this tool will help us to improve and focus our screenplay during the production process.

4. ANIMATICS

The most significant substitute for the rehearsal process in regular films is the animatic (which is sometimes called the videoboard). An animatic is a movie animated on a very low technical level which serves as a kind of draft for the final product. The creative team tries to imagine the final film through the tool of the animatic. In a regular film production, the animatic could be compared to the filming of a rehearsal without scenery, costumes, props or lighting.

The length of the animatic is identical to the length of the final movie and its sound track is usually comparable to the final sound track and used as a guide track. The guide track's voices are not usually the voices of the actors who will eventually voice the film and the music can be sketchy too. Often, the storyboard illustrations serve as the basis for the animatic. The storyboard's illustrations are laid down against the background of the movie's guide track in the space of time it would take for the scene to play out in the final version. The creative team tries to feel the cadence of the film's plot development in this way.

Sometimes, the creative team prefers to use more sophisticated animation in the animatic, incorporating movement of characters in order to more closely parallel the finished product. When the budget allows for a greater degree of sophistication, the animatic becomes correspondingly more sophisticated. For example, it has become common for color to be included in animatics where once this was rare.

The animatic is a very important tool, not just for the animation team but for us, the content writers, too. With it, we can assess the degree to which the created characters and backgrounds match the content we have written. It is reasonable to guess that someone who has never seen an animatic will have trouble understanding this explanation. The best way to understand an animatic is to watch one. And since, naturally, a printed book cannot include video clips, I warmly recommend that anyone who hasn't seen an animatic do so with the help of the Internet.

It is sufficient to enter the word *animatic* into any search engine and you will almost certainly be presented with a variety of sites on which you can watch the various animatics of quite a few projects. I have no doubt that watching several of these clips will contribute more than anything I have written here to your understanding of the nature of this tool.

In my experience, I can say with certainty that this stage is the last one in which it is still possible to correct content mistakes and conceptual problems in all areas — the design, the cadence, the language of film, or animation. Therefore, this stage is critical. It is important to remember that all the stages of production that follow the animatic have already passed the point of no return!

Usually, when problems are revealed at the animatic stage, a new animatic is created through which the defects of the previous version are corrected. The creative team keeps working on improving the animatic until it has gotten results that are complete and satisfactory, allowing work on the final animation for the film to get underway. It is important to note that all the stages presented here apply to all animated productions, regardless of production techniques.

5. ANIMATION TECHNIQUES

Animation can be accomplished with different techniques, the four most common being:

- **Classic**
- **Stop motion**
- **3D**
- **Cutouts**

Classic Animation

This is animation drawn by hand. In the past, animators drew their illustrations on celluloid. The celluloid sheet was placed on backgrounds that had been previously drawn and then filmed with a movie camera, one frame at a time. After filming each frame, the celluloid sheet was replaced with a new one in which the character's position was slightly advanced. In this way, the illusion of movement was created incrementally.

Nowadays, some things are also drawn by hand, with a digital pen on a computerized surface or with conventional tools, the picture then being scanned and entered into computer memory. The number of illustrations required when using this method is enormous (about 24 for every second of film). It is therefore the practice to divide the work between a head animator and assistant animators. The head animator usually draws the key frames and her assistants draw the intervening illustrations. Key frames are ones in which a significant change in the scene is depicted. For example: 1. The protagonist runs toward the ball. 2. The protagonist kicks the ball. 3. The ball hits a window and breaks it. 4. The protagonist runs away. These four pictures constitute the key frames. The pictures between them are called the in-betweens and are drawn by the assistant animators. In essence, the in-betweens are a copy of the key frame with a small change in the position of the legs, arms or any other thing that is supposed to move in the action of chasing a ball.

Another significant process which exists primarily in classic animation is cleanup. In this process, the cleanup person goes over all the lines drawn in the animation and makes sure they are uniform. Sometimes, in the process of drawing, the animator draws the character with thick lines or with thinner ones.

The cleanup person makes sure that the lines are even since a difference in their thicknesses can lead to the illusion of flickering in the picture. The last technical stage after cleanup is that of *coloring in*. In this stage, the *colorers* fill the spaces between the defining lines with the appropriate colors. In this way, a red shirt will be colored in each frame with the same red shade, etc.

The use of computers greatly eases and simplifies the processes of classic animation, but only on the technical level. In essence, classic animation remains as it always was, and its quality still remains dependent on the skills of the animator, the designer, the colorer, and on the magic of the world which has been created by these artists.

The transition from typewriters to word processors did not influence the *content* of the documents written with these tools, and the same can be said about animation created with modern technology as opposed to that which was created in the past. The transition to computerized tools simplifies the work and makes it more efficient, but there is no connection between the use of computerized drawing tools and the skill of the illustrator or the design talent of the animator.

Stop Motion Animation

As opposed to classic or 3D animation, which take place in the insides of a computer, stop motion animation is filmed in physical settings. In classic animation or in 3D, we just imagine reality, whereas in stop motion, reality is filmed.

In contrast to all other animation techniques, stop motion requires a film space. The world of the film is built in this space — a physical world made of real things such as modeling clay figures, dolls made of felt, or any other object which the animators intend to bring to life.

There is a camera connected to a computer in the film space. The characters are moved in front of the camera a millimeter at a time. Every tiny movement is captured on camera and stored in the computer's memory.

Rony Oren, Modeling Clay Animation Craftsman during
Stop Motion Filming (Photo credit: Yossi Aloni)

The object is moved a tiny bit each time and is filmed in its new position. Then it is moved again and filmed again, eventually giving the illusion of smooth motion.

If a toy car is placed opposite a stop motion camera, and the car is advanced by a centimeter or two between each shot, by the time the filming is done and screened, the car will really look as if it is moving of its own accord. Stop motion animation is usually filmed in special studios which allow for work in almost sterile conditions since even a tiny change in the work space or the lighting can negatively impact the resulting film.

For every minute of stop motion film, about 1000 separate shots are filmed, in each of which the animator moves the characters according to a previously prepared, tightly planned schedule. On a good filming day, for a simple scene in which two physical characters are involved, about thirty seconds of animation will be filmed. It is clear from this that one of the biggest problems with which stop motion animators must deal is the difficulty of keeping the filming conditions stable. The film crew must maintain their cameras in exactly the same positions for large stretches of time, and all the lights, sets, and characters on set must be accurate to the millimeter. Any unexpected change (like the unintentional moving of a camera or a light) is likely to generate the need to reshoot a whole scene, and a number of weeks' work goes down the drain.

Many types of animation which serve the world of children's film can be included under the heading of *stop motion*, beginning with the animation of objects, where they appear to put themselves into some kind of numerical or shape-creating order on screen, through to modeling clay animation where modeling clay characters or bodies are easily shaped to depict different positions, motions, and even facial expressions. or doll animation for which unique dolls are designed with a flexible metal rod inserted so that the animator can bend them into different positions, make them "walk," move their limbs, their heads, etc.

Clay Animation

Doll Animation

Object Animation

Three-Dimensional Animation

I once spoke to an animator friend who told me that, from his point of view, the main difference between classic animators and three-dimensional (3D) animators is that classic animators create the illusion that their characters are moving whereas in 3D animation, the characters actually move! Another friend, a classic animator immediately responded by saying that in his opinion, the problem with 3D animators is that they have lost the ability to distinguish between reality and fantasy... Of course, the argument got fiercer, but to understand the depth of these claims, we need to focus a little bit on understanding the technical stages of creating 3D animation.

Three-dimensional animators need to use computer programs that imagine structures or other bodies in a three-dimensional space, and the characters created for 3D movies must be made with these programs. The first stage of the development of a 3D character is the design stage. Reference artists, occasionally called concept artists, sometimes help with this stage. This artist designs the character and background with a free hand. Here, as with any other animation process, the reference artist designs the characters and the backgrounds based on the initial screenplay and on the basis of the descriptions of characters and place provided by the screenwriter.

The reference artist's task is over at the point where the creative team feels that the characters and backgrounds live up to their expectations. The computer work begins from then on.

The animated character moves to **the model stage** which takes the character, as drawn by hand, and turns it into a computer model. In essence, this is a kind of digital sculpture. This process of sculpture takes the character on the page and sculpts it into a computerized, mono-chromatic, three-dimensional body. As opposed to the drawn character, depicted by the reference artist from only or two angles (whichever angles the reference artist chose), the 3D model can be seen from any angle on the screen since it now exists in an imagined reality in the computer's "imagination."

After the modeling stage comes the **rigging stage**. At this stage, a virtual skeleton is built for the character — the rigging looks like a net which is spread over the whole character. The rigging provides the animator with a means of moving the character. With the rigging in place, the character should be able to displace itself, move its limbs, and articulate different facial expressions. During the rigging stage, the character is given joints or elements which allow it to move its limbs separately or simultaneously (like eye rolling, leg movements, neck movements, mouth movements, etc.).

When the rigging stage is over, the **texturing stage** begins. The animator in charge of texturing is the one who gives the character its overall color and the look of the material which covers it, such as fur, scales, or smooth skin. For example, if the character is a panda or a Dalmatian, the texture artist must match the spots or the variations in fur shades to the illustration as it stood in the reference stage. If you look carefully at the picture of the character in the rigging stage, you will see that there are thousands of tiny squares between all the coordinates of the grid. These are called *polygons*. The overall texture of the character is usually the result of the filling in, by hand, of each polygon in the appropriate texture and shade.

Now the **animation stage** begins. As opposed to classic animation, in which, as I already mentioned, the character is drawn anew each time it needs to be seen from a different perspective, in 3D animation, the computer holds each character and each background in its memory. Without any difficulty, the animator can choose from which camera angle the character should be seen or choose the background against which the action will take place. Similarly, the animator can choose the way in which the characters and backgrounds will be lit. The method of moving characters is also up for grabs. The animator can choose a method similar to that of classic animation in which key frames are chosen and the in between frames are filled in. However, she can also give a *movement order* to the fully designed image on the screen such that the character will automatically move from point A to point B.

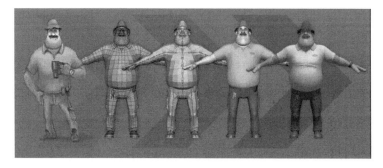

The Process of Designing a Three-Dimensional Character (from left to right):
concept, modeling, rigging, texturing, rendering

And now is the time to return to the comment of my friend the animator who claimed that, "classic animators create the illusion that their characters are moving whereas in 3D animation, the characters actually move!" Indeed... perhaps in most cases they don't actually move, but it is clear that, as opposed to in classic animation, there is no need to draw them again and again and they *do* actually exist, in the computer's "brain," at least.

Cutouts

In the past, paper cutouts were laid on a special animation table on top of which a stop motion camera was positioned. In order to create the illusion of movement, the paper cutouts were moved, bit by bit in exactly the same way that dolls or modeling clay is animated and filmed with a stop motion camera. The work of cutout animation would resemble that of stop motion animation except that here, instead of the cutouts moving parallel to the camera, they move below it.

This work method is no longer used but the principle of cutouts remains. This is why this type of animation is still called "cutouts." The different types of cut out animation are done by computer nowadays. The cutouts that are meant to move are scanned into the computer.

Afterwards, the animator is able to retrieve the cutouts from the computer memory and, with the help of a special program, design the frames.

Cut Out Animation

One of the advantages of this method is the fact that the basic character need only be drawn once and, in order to give the illusion of movement, it can be positioned again and again, with its limbs moved separately. The more the character is broken down into separate elements, the more sophisticated the final product will be. This can be so marked that in some cases, the quality of the animation can approach that of the product of classic animation.

Internet Animation Programs

It is incumbent upon me to add various technologies that are taking pride of place in recent years over the four basic animation processes mentioned above. These technologies have mainly developed in response to the needs of the Internet.

Posting animated film on the Internet required a solution to the heavy weight of video attachments. In response to this problem, different programs based on vector graphics were developed. These contributed to the significant reduction of the weight of attachments. It is important to understand that, on a visual level, all these Internet animation programs work by similar principles to the various cut out methods,. that is, the breaking down of the characters into different body parts in a way that prevents the animator from having to draw the character again and again in different positions but instead to simply have to "move" its limbs. These programs include many other technologies that simplify the work of the animator, such as automatically drawing in-betweens and easily filling in surfaces to be colored in.

How To Decide Which Technique To Use

The determining factors as to which animation technique to use are usually artistic and economic.

Clearly, **classic animation** is usually considered preferable by many animators because it is possible to attain a final product of very high quality. On the other hand, there is no doubt that it is also the most expensive technique since it requires a higher number of hours and a higher level of drawing ability than any other technique. The advantage of using stop motion arises from the magic held by the materials used. In stop motion, the filmed material is not imagined through illustration or by a computer but actually filmed as is. As such, a character made of steel wool, wood, fabric, modeling clay or any other material will broadcast the feeling of the real material from which it is made and will not look like an illustration or imagination of itself. Nevertheless, stop motion work is much harder than any of the other three techniques since it is actually filmed on location and requires physical work.

As opposed to the technique of stop motion which takes place in a real setting and is actually filmed, the technique of **3D animation** is completely virtual and sets the recreation of stop motion reality through computing as its goal. Many children's television series which used to be filmed in stop motion are now filmed with 3D techniques due to the ability of these techniques to effectively resemble the stop motion end product. Young viewers almost cannot tell the difference.

The fourth and last technique is that of the **cut out**. One can choose this technique for a variety of reasons — economic and artistic. This technique, unlike any of the others, is cheap to produce and efficient such that a lot of work can get done in a relatively short amount of time. The artistic quality of the end product is dependent on the skill of the creator of the film and the amount of time invested in the animation.

A writer who targets her content at animation must know the advantages and disadvantages of the animation techniques used to produce her creation. Mastery of animation techniques will allow the writer to connect better to the animators of her work and their partners, and will ensure that she writes content appropriate for the chosen technique.

A familiarity with these media also fosters an understanding of the budget issues involved and the connection between the content she writes and the complications and costs of the production, such that she will become a partner in the decision as to the benefit of including various content elements in the production or not.

Most importantly, an understanding of the components of the medium and an understanding of the visual language of the various techniques will allow the writer to produce the best of her imagination and writing in congruence with the best of the techniques for which she is producing her content.

DRAW ME A SHEEP
OR
HOW TO JOIN THE
CHILDREN'S MEDIA
INDUSTRY

Writing guides of various kinds usually end with chapters in which the author gives all sorts of advice to readers on how to gain entry into the workforce. They deal with subjects such as why it's important that your screenplay cover be more eye catching than other screenplay covers; how to join the regular staff writers of daily television shows; how to deal with rejection; how to find an agent; and more. There is no doubt that these issues are important ones, though in my eyes, most of them belong to the world of media for adults, a world in which a group of adult producers chooses a few screenwriters to write screenplays for adult viewers.

I have no problem with the world of adults, and some of my best friends who belong to this world can be my witness. However, I have always tried to examine children's content from the point of view of a child. Antoine de Saint Exupéry described this best in the first chapter of his story, *The Little Prince*. He tells of how he went around his whole life with a small drawing in his pocket which he himself had drawn at the age of six — a picture of a boa constrictor that had swallowed an elephant.

Antoine de Saint Exupéry writes that the adults to whom he showed the picture always thought it was the picture of a hat whereas children understood immediately, and without any difficulty at all, that it depicted a boa constrictor that had swallowed an elephant...

This is how he describes his relations with the world of adults: "In the course of this life I have had a great many encounters with a great many people who have been concerned with matters of consequence. I have lived a great deal among grown-ups. I have seen them intimately, close at hand. And that hasn't much improved my opinion of them."

Whenever I met one of them who seemed to me at all

clear-sighted, I tried the experiment of showing him my Drawing Number One, which I have always kept. I would try to find out, so, if this was a person of true understanding. But, whoever it was, he, or she, would always say: 'That is a hat.' Then I would never talk to that person about boa constrictors, or primeval forests, or stars. I would bring myself down to his level. I would talk to him about bridge, and golf, and politics, and neckties. And the grown-up would be greatly pleased to have met such a sensible man."

Unlike Antoine de Saint Exupéry, I do not walk around with a picture of a boa constrictor in my pocket, though when I am asked to assess a screenwriter who wants to write for children, I suggest that we watch a short film or children's program that has captured my heart. Watching a film together cannot bear witness to the writing talent of the person sitting next to you, but the twinkle in her eye (if there is one) can prove, without a shadow of a doubt, that first and foremost, she understands and loves this world of content.

Some will watch the film with polite patience, some try to look interested, some feign enthusiasm, and there are some who have a look in their eye that makes you feel like you are in the company of a curious and genuinely enthusiastic child. The official reason for the meeting is forgotten for a moment and they become instantly addicted to the journey to the past that I am offering them.

"Draw me a sheep," asks the Little Prince of Antoine de Saint Exupéry at the beginning of the book. The Prince is not satisfied with the first sheep drawn by the author because she seems to be ill. The second sheep is not acceptable to him because she resembles a ram, and the third is too old. In the end, the author simply draws a box with breathing holes which, for the Prince, hits the nail on the head. Now he can imagine how the sheep inside the box looks for himself, and he is happy with the picture.

In my opinion, this is the essence of our job as children's writers: to draw a sheep for the child; to invent a story for him; to really be able to see the world through the eyes of a child; to identify with his pleasure, desires, and needs; and to use our greatest skills to that purpose. None of this is to say that I am not aware of other programs that are built on other formulas altogether — programs that broadcast aggression, violence, and evil. The inclusion of these programs on broadcast schedules is astonishing, and this book does not address that kind of content.

Children's television and film producers who do faithful work are supposed to represent the taste and needs of the viewing child while taking moral responsibility for the chosen content. In this spirit, producers of high quality children's content locate the writers most suited to writing for this precious target population. The goal of this chapter is to suggest to the reader ways of joining the various children's media industries. These ways identify the needs of the child along with the needs of the broadcasting bodies or producers of children's content.

When all is said and done, children are the ones who will vote with their feet and determine what is their favorite content. They are the ones who determine if a film or a new program succeeds or fails and if its hero will become a superstar or remain obscure. However, before content can be judged by children, the responsibility for choosing recommended content for production lies with the program's management team: the editors, head producers, directors, and head writers. These people use their professional judgment in choosing creators who are likely to create the product which most accurately answers the needs of their target audience from a large pool of candidates.

Understanding the considerations of the program directors and other professionals I have mentioned is the key to entering the world of work in this field.

1. CONSIDER YOUR PROFESSIONAL SKILLS

A few years ago, a young writer came to me to propose her writing skills for a children's series I was editing. This writer had become known at that time thanks to an excellent screenplay she had written for a student film (not aimed at children), which she also directed, and which won accolades and prizes. I asked her if she knew the series for which she was interested in writing. She answered that she did and that she had even written an episode, on her own initiative, as a test case. I looked at the episode and could not hide the boredom it engendered in me. The writer understood that I was not enjoying the episode she had written and was quite surprised.

"This is not what you're looking for?" she asked in surprise.

"Not really," I answered, "it is a little boring for me."

"That's true," she said, "it's also boring for me, but that is what you're looking for, according to my best understanding."

"Why would we want to produce a boring series?" I asked in amazement.

"I have no idea," she answered. "I watched one of the episodes in your series, which, in fact, did not interest me very much, and I wrote as similar an episode as I could. I thought that that is what children like," she said.

"But if the series is boring to you, why do you want to

write for it?" I insisted.

"The truth is that I don't really want to," she answered, "but everyone has to support themselves somehow..."

At the beginning of the chapter, I described the experience of watching films with potential writers. I singled out the ones with whom watching the film was like watching it with a curious and enthusiastic child, as opposed to those for whom the film held almost no interest. Enjoying children's films is no guarantee that any given writer will be skillful or successful, but the ability to enjoy children's content is critical to our ability to assess ourselves as children's content writers. Someone who enjoys excellent children's programming will not allow himself to write mediocre material that he himself will not enjoy.

The ability to enjoy content aimed at children motivates the writer to aspire to the creation of high quality content. Children's content writers must always remember the pleasure and excitement they feel when they watch high quality children's programming or the pleasure and excitement that they used to feel as children and which they still remember to this day. As such, when you are writing a screenplay, you should always be asking yourself if this would be a film or program that you would want to watch. This essential test question will force you to take a personal stand as to the quality of the content and will stop you from being patronizing — something that happens from time to time to children's content creators.

This attitude sometimes generates an "I'm not interested in this, but children will be" attitude, as if it were possible to write content that is interesting to children without holding any interest for its creators.

Therefore, I wholeheartedly recommend that everything you write be put to the *Me* test. Ask yourself, "How much would this film I have written interest me?" "Will the actors enjoy acting in it?" "Will the director enjoy directing it?" "Will my audience of children actually enjoy watching it?" Only after you can honestly answer *yes* to all these questions should you continue with the process of selling your product to whomever you have chosen.

2. WHAT ARE CHILDREN'S CONTENT PRODUCERS LOOKING FOR?

In order to be able to answer this question, put yourselves in the shoes of those who make decisions regarding which screenplays to accept and which to reject. The decision-making process of children's program producers is complicated by a range of parameters. The first is based on the catalog of content which exists and is available to them. Any proposal which resembles or reminds them of an existing program will usually be vetoed at the outset, and in order to avoid proposing content which will be vetoed immediately (and in order to save you aggravation and anguish), it is important to know what content already exists in the market.

I remember a meeting with a talented writer very well. He showed me his proposal for a wonderful series which he had developed lately. It was for a series where all the characters would be animated hats — a police officer's hat, a firefighter's hat, a builder's hat, etc., who all live in a city of hats. The writer had already written several sample episodes and brought along a few songs in draft form. His surprise was extreme when I showed him another series, though not very well known or successful, which *also* took place in a city of hats populated by a host of animated hats. Therefore, in exactly the same way that you would do a background search before registering a patent, conduct a thorough search of the field to make sure that you are not working for nothing. It is true, though, that there are times when we make a conscious effort to replicate a previous success. In these cases, we take a successful creation, try to understand the reasons behind its success, and then try to replicate it in slightly different form. Given my experience, I strongly urge you not to do this because I know of only very few cases in which this strategy bore fruit.

The constant aspirations of decision makers in this field is to identify new trends or needs in their target audience which other people have not yet identified or responded to. A few years ago, for example, educational institutions began to promote a campaign tackling the problem of obesity in children. Obesity comes of an imbalanced diet and insufficient exercise, of course. Identifying this social problem inspired several content producing bodies to initiate programs addressing the need for healthy eating and encouraging children to get involved in sports and movement. In a short while, children's channels all over the world were showing series dealing with these issues.

Broadcasting channels follow new trends with great interest. These could be a new children's game which has suddenly gained popularity, new dolls about which children are enthusiastic, new literature, music or stage productions that are capturing children's hearts, or current social phenomena which demand a reaction in children's content such as the increase of violence in society, the decrease in the status of children's books, etc. The identified issues are carefully examined and passed on as briefs to development teams with the goal of finding them a series appropriate for production.

In parallel to the search for new trends, content producers also examine current school syllabuses in an attempt to produce new and up-to-date answers to children's daily needs. Old solutions are constantly reexamined and producing bodies ask themselves if current solutions really respond to the needs of children now. Maybe the time has come to create new content or refresh old content in ever-relevant fields such as reading readiness, the improvement of children's cognitive skills, and the treatment of issues that trouble children. Examples of these are moving to a new house, moving to a new kindergarten, or moving to a new stage in life. Dealing with children's fears is another faithful topic — the fear of darkness; imaginary fears; fear of monsters; or existential fears, such as the fear of abandonment and the fear of death. Another fruitful avenue is that of children's daily rituals and all they imply, such as waking up in the morning, going to sleep at night, hygiene, eating, etc.

However, despite everything I've said here, you must not forget that the interest of all these decision makers in educational, moral, or social content takes **second place only!** The child's experience of magic, excitement, and pleasure from the content he watches always has and always will take first place.

A fascinating character, a magical adventure, a new musical experience, or anything that generates excitement will always take first place for decision makers. And because they know that they cannot actually assess content through the eyes of a child, they are happy for any *prophesying* help they can get. They can get this through exposure to new books whose characters are making their way into children's hearts, internet clips that have gotten X number of hits, or even a video of a group of children who are reacting with interest to a screenplay that you have written. With that in mind, I recommend that you avoid passing on family-based advice. If your son refuses to go to bed before he hears the wonderful song you composed for him, it still does not mean that other children will find it interesting at all.

3. STAY UP-TO-DATE

It is reasonable to suppose that even if you are not involved in the world of children's content, you have nevertheless surely heard of films like *Toy Story, The Little Mermaid,* or *The Never Ending Story* and of television series like *The Smurfs, Thomas the Tank Engine, Bob the Builder, Dora the Explorer,* etc. But real familiarity with children's content requires much more than this. The children's content market includes a lot of other content less widely known to the adult population but well known to its target audience.

Of course, you do not have to watch every children's movie on the market or hundreds of episodes of all the children's television series but watching a number of episodes from the tens of leading children's television series and getting to know a respectable percentage of children's movies would certainly be beneficial.

A brief period of Internet surfing on children's channel sites or on sites that sell children's videos will allow you to watch examples of different episodes and quickly learn what is the leading content on the market.

As children's content creators, it is important for you to get to know as many films and television programs as possible that are targeted at your intended audience. This familiarity is important on a number of fronts.

1. It will prevent you from wasting precious time in developing ideas or content similar to content that has already been developed. It does not matter how creative you are; no broadcasting body or production team will show any interest in content that resembles something that is already on the market.

2. Familiarity with as much content as possible can only increase your creativity for exactly the same reasons that writers read as many books as possible in order to improve their writing, or painters expose themselves to as many other artists' work as possible in order to widen their artistic worldview, or musicians listen to other musicians' compositions, etc. Many young creators who want to write for children know well the works on which they themselves grew up. But they are not at all aware of the wide range of films and programs that have been produced since they grew up and stopped consuming children's content. They are not aware of the changes that have taken place in cinematic language, in the change of pace, in the use of new technologies, the visual developments, etc. As a result, their writing tends to be a generation or two out-of-date. Adult screenwriters know that one cannot write for any particular genre of film without getting to know that genre very well. In order to write a good Western, it is desirable and worthwhile to immerse oneself in the world of Westerns. Similarly, the writing of sitcoms or telenovelas is subject to clear rules and writers of the various types spend a lot of time watching existing series in order to learn the rules of the genre for which they mean to write.

There are genres and types in writing for children too and it is worth getting to know them. They include: the integration of real and animated worlds; different kinds of music clips aimed at children; dramas for children as opposed to talk shows; different program formats; different types of characters; types of puppets; the integration of puppets and human actors; transitions between imagination and reality; and an infinity of situations and ideas that no textbook could cover. No explanations, no matter how erudite, can replace the thing itself: the informal watching of current programming for very young children.

3. Additionally, watching other people's content can only boost your inventiveness, enrich your imagination bank, and serve to sophisticate your visual expression skills. The group of personified pickles that you saw in one series will only improve the group of personified potatoes you are inventing for another. Insufficiently interesting plots can only help you raise the level of quality of your own work. And the wonderful plots can only help you set the level of quality of your work where it behooves it to be.

4. Regular surfing on game sites for children of your target audience's age will also help you solidify your understanding of the world of content for which you are writing. When writing for children, it is necessary for you to view the world from a different point of view. It is a point of view in which time has a different meaning and in which concepts such as *funny*, *sad*, or *scary* will be projected onto situations that would not register in an adult as having those properties. Surfing on children's game sites will help you lower your mental age level, and it will enrich your imagination with imaginative content from the world of children. Of course, a large percentage of children's game sites are a natural extension of children's television channels. These Internet sites widen the world of television by transforming it into an interactive experience with the help of the web. The televisual content of the channel expands

and spills over into the world of web games. And so, in addition to the game experience, you will be exposed to a variety of leading television personalities who star in these children's channels and will learn their characteristics.

4. RELATED FIELDS OF CONTENT

In my experience as a lecturer on writing for children, I can say that the percentage of people who are suited to writing for children among the students who have completed various university level writing courses is very low. Usually, writing students are young people whose own childhoods are far behind them and who are not yet interested in the next generation. It is true that a young parent, interested in using a newfound screenwriting knowledge in order to build a bridge to his or her child's imagination, sometimes makes his or her way into this group. And there are also the very few, shy writers who approach me at the end of the course to ask with shining eyes if I can look over a children's book draft, a children's play or a screenplay which, inspired by the course or by their own imaginations, they have written. The number of these writers — those who are enthralled by the world of children — is extremely small.

Children's television channels are also aware of this phenomenon and they therefore search for children's writers in parallel fields. Children's content producers try to identify potential talent in writing for children in creative professionals who do not necessarily come with a screenwriting background. These can be children's authors, children's playwrights, actors whose professional development has been in children's theater and who view themselves as potential creators of content, creative kindergarten teachers, children's Internet content creators, and even talented children's event clowns who are interested in integrating into the writing field. All these people have a deep knowledge of their target audience as a common denominator. As such, if the field of scriptwriting really speaks to your heart, go ahead and make your way to the various production specialists and offer them your services. If you really want to write for the children's field, do not limit yourself to writing exercises in the first stage. Try to get involved in related fields. You can work as a production assistant or researcher, you can organize focus groups in kindergartens, etc. These jobs will help you make your way to the head writer, editor, or other decision makers in the production crew. This is the time to remind you that the knowledge you need to acquire in order to write scripts for children is not the kind that is learned in screenwriting courses. Children's content writers usually develop professionally in the context of workshops offered by the various children's production departments of the children's television channels. These workshops are not offered at fixed times and they are usually offered during the development of new children's series.

Potential writers are usually invited to these workshops. These are people who are somehow connected to the world of children. The workshops are designed to develop all aspects of the series and often include lecturers who are professionals in related fields such as psychologists, didactic advisors, etc. In the course of the workshops, the participants will be asked to write a good number of experimental screenplays. These screenplays will be test cases for the head writers and producers as to the talent of the workshop participants and will help them choose a writing team. There is no doubt that taking part in one of these workshops can be a significant shortcut for anyone who wants to write for children. Try to stay in constant contact with leading channels or various writers' forums so that if and when a workshop is offered, you'll be able to take part in it.

Participating in other fields related to children can also be useful. Children's film festivals, puppet festivals, animation festivals, children's literature conferences, etc. are appropriate places for you to start to find yourself. These festivals usually include meetings or master classes with limited participation where you might meet high ranking professionals in different children's fields or in related technical fields. The market is full of opportunities. You just have to make an effort to find them. Everyone knows that opportunities do not happen by themselves. In the words of Francis Bacon, "A wise man will make more opportunities than he finds." So, if you want opportunities, go out and make them.

5. COMMERCIAL SAVVY

As someone who has been preaching the importance of values and educational content in children's programming throughout this book, I must admit that it is a little difficult for me to present the issue of commercialization and its connection to content that is written for children. In my work with ethical broadcasting bodies and bodies not inspired by a profit motive, I learned that, for the most part, the primary motivation for these bodies is the quality of their written material and the degree of interest it is likely to arouse in the child who will eventually view it. Nevertheless, I have occasionally met certain broadcasting bodies who assessed material according to an additional criterion — that of its commercial potential. That is to say, how much would the written material be compatible with the sale of spin-off products such as dolls, action figures, games, and accessories? It would be hard for me to claim that this criterion would be the deciding factor for these bodies, but when you are about to make an offer, it is worth making sure that you understand each other's expectations in this regard and that you assess the importance of the commercial angle in your offer. Despite the reserved way in which I am presenting this issue, it is important to stress that the commercial aspect of the industry is not negative in and of itself. There are quite a few programs in which spin-off products play a significant part in the spreading of the values of the broadcasts. In programs aimed at the acquisition of various skills, such as math, science, or language, different spin-off products can help children practice the skills they learned when watching the program. Non-educational spin-off products increase children's pleasure in the experience. There is no doubt that a child who carries his favorite television-program-inspired action figure around with him continues to draw pleasure from it even when the program is not being broadcast.

Nevertheless, there are series and films in which commercial products are part of the general economic strategy. In these ventures, spin-offs are released right alongside the series or the movie. The process of product development influences the content of the film to some degree and the commercial emphasis of the production is significant. As content writers, it is incumbent upon you to get to know the field of game development. You can accomplish this when you are watching any children's program on the Internet in any case. After viewing the program, go into the sales page of the website and take a look at the products offered there. It is reasonable to suppose that one or two visits to web pages of this nature will help you understand the connection between content and sales better.

6. STANDING OUT AND TRIAGE

For many years, I was the content director for a children's channel and I shudder to remember the piles of proposals that were heaped on my desk. Tens of proposals for programs of different types: children's cooking programs, yoga for children, music and movement programs, drama proposals, animation series, etc., etc.

Clearly, I didn't stand a chance of getting through those heaps. Nevertheless, my belief that somewhere, deep inside the heaps, some kind of wonderful idea was hiding, motivated me to dedicate quite a lot of time to reading these proposals. At first glance, they all looked the same; they were all written on paper and bound in plastic. In order to divine the differences, it was necessary to sit and read dedicatedly, to dive into the world of characters invented by the writer, and to try to understand what stood behind the hundreds of words that the proposer had written.

There is no doubt that it is difficult to discern a good proposal among an infinity of proposals. Therefore, it is important that the person who tends some kind of proposal imagines to himself how it will look in the midst of an enormous pile of plastic folders, bursting with proposals for different series, some of which will even resemble the proposer's program.

In essence, try to imagine an unbelievably cute chick taking a stroll on your desk.

Then, try to imagine eighty more unbelievably cute chicks, similarly hued, who are also taking a stroll on your desk. Now your chances of identifying the first chick are eighty times lower.

Let's move from imagination to reality: Try to imagine a content director reading one proposal and then another and then another and then another... And now, after having read five proposals, he gets to yours. Now try to imagine the mood your reader is in when he approaches your proposal. He has already read five other proposals, the majority of which did not teach him anything new. He is therefore interested in getting to the most important issues that underlie your proposal without having to wade through cumbersome introductions. He wants to understand as quickly as possible:

- What is the idea?
- How is it unique?
- How does it answer the needs of its target audience?

It is important to understand that the fewer words your reader has to read in order to get to the essence of your proposal, the better. Only in the next stage, when he has understood the essence of your idea, to the degree that it is actually new, unique or stirring, and it has captured his heart, will he be willing to delve deeper and to read the details of your proposal: the dialogue, the character descriptions, and the structure of the series.

The folder in which you place your proposal should also be unique in some way. A unique external design, like a special binding, unusual proportions, or, principally, unique illustrations designed to burn the image of your proposal into your reader's mind, is a good idea. Of course, this is on condition that the distinct aspect of your proposal is in good taste and faithfully serves the content of your proposal.

And all this is just in the first selection stage, before your reader has looked at the minutiae of your proposal. To this day, I remember a proposal whose subject was the environment. The writer had bound his proposal in a used cardboard which had been cut out from a used cardboard box. This binding emphasized the idea behind the proposal and also served to differentiate the proposal from the other ones on my desk. Another example of a proposal I remember is one with pictures of children in different professional uniforms on the binding. The proposal was one for a program dealing with the realization of children's dreams and the children were seen on a fishing boat, in a chocolate factory, and on a model's runway. In a different case, the tender of a proposal came up with a particularly creative idea: He included a clip of kindergarten-aged children listening in wonder to his description of the plot of the television series he was proposing. Of course, I have come across many more presentation ideas that supported the proposals within them. Some better, some worse. But I never came across an idea, however good, that managed to sell a mediocre program or film. On the contrary. Terrific packaging of a mediocre idea only serves to increase the reader's disappointment since the greater the expectation, the greater the disillusionment.

"Draw me a sheep," demands the Little Prince of Antoine de Saint Exupéry at the beginning of his book. In my opinion, that is the essence of our job as children's content writers — to use the best of our skills in order to create high quality content that will directly serve the tastes of our audiences. And in order to do that, we must take a step back and see the world through children's eyes. We must become the children we once were.

As Antoine de Saint Exupéry writes in the dedication to his childhood friend Leon Werth and to all the readers, which appears at the beginning of the book: **"All grown-ups were once children — although few of them remember it."**

i   Korney Chukovsky (1882-1962) is one of the most important Russian writers and poets for children. He is also (and primarily) known as a literary critic who wrote about children's linguistic development, whether in his nonfiction books (***From Two to Five)*** or through his literary creations, which have become beloved classics throughout the world. Among his books are: ***Barmaley, Limpopo, Right and Wrong, Fly Boldly Buzzing***, and more.

ii   Jean-Claud Carrière (born 1931) Screenwriter and cinema personality who worked under the aegis of directors such as Buñuel, Wajda, and others. He wrote scripts for outstanding works like *The Discreet Charm of the Bourgeoisie, A Harlot High and Low, The Return of Martin Guerre*, and others.

iii   From Proverbs 6:6, "Go to the ant, oh sluggard, consider their ways and gain wisdom."

iv   Limbo is an accepted television concept constituting a kind of undefined, neutral space.

© **Contributors**

SCRIPT WRITERS AND COPYRIGHT HOLDERS:

1. **Measuring Love** - *Shahar Sitner / Courtesy of* **HOP TV**
2. **Its Cold Outside** - *Courtesy of* **Subtext Ltd**
3. **We Don't Want to Sleep** - *Haim Idisis / Courtesy of* **HOP TV**
4. **Bert & Ernie at the Beach** - *Courtesy of* **Sesame Workshop**
5. **Important Things** - *Haim Idisis / Courtesy of* **HOP TV**
6. **The Fire Engine** - *Courtesy of* **Sesame Workshop**
7. **Planet Earth** - *Hanan Peled / Courtesy of* **Israel Educational Television**
8. **Boy or Girl** - *Courtesy of* **Subtext Ltd**
9. **Boys Can't** - *Haim Idisis / Courtesy of* **Sesame Workshop (& HOP TV)**
10. **Making a Mountain Out of a Molehill** – *Yoram Sachs / Courtesy of* **HOP TV**
11. **The Identikit** - *Haim Idisis / Courtesy of* **Noga Communications**
12. **The Spoon** - *shahar sitner & Bar Ben-Yossef / Courtesy of* **BFTV**
13. **The Sandwich Trade** - *Shiri Zuck / Courtesy of* **Sesame Workshop (& HOP TV)**

PHOTOS AND ILLUSTRATIONS:

1. **Measuring love** - *Grandma Bali, Chuck, and Grandpa.* / *Courtesy of* **HOP TV**
2. **We Don't Want to Sleep**- *Zoom, Peewee, and Milly* / *Courtesy of* **HOP TV**
3. **We Don't Want to Sleep**- *Mr. Mortimer* / *Courtesy of* **HOP TV**
4. **Bert & Ernie** / *Courtesy of* **Sesame Workshop**
5. **Piney** / *Courtesy of* **Sesame Workshop (& HOP TV)**
6. **Noah** / *Courtesy of* **Sesame Workshop (& HOP TV)**
7. **Abigail** / *Courtesy of* **Sesame Workshop (& HOP TV)**
8. **Human-looking puppets** / *Courtesy of* **Puppet Productions (& HOP TV)**
9. **Puppets that look like animals** / *Courtesy of* **Sesame Workshop**
10. **Creatures** *(Known also as Monsters)* / *Courtesy of* **Sesame Workshop**
11. **Puppets in the form of objects or humanized plants** / *Courtesy of* **Sesame Workshop**
12. **Body Puppet** / *Courtesy of* **HOP TV**
13. **Glove and Rod Puppets** / *Courtesy of* **Sesame Workshop (& HOP TV)**
14. **Alan the All Powerful - The Antihero** / *Courtesy of* **HOP TV**
15. **Victor** *the Angry Telephone* **Alan** *the Schlemiel superhero, and* **Holly** *the Pampered Flower* / *Courtesy of* **HOP TV**
16. **inside the crib** – *illustration* / *Courtesy of* **BFTV**

17. *Large body puppet operation* / *Courtesy of* **Sesame Workshop**, *Illustrated by* **Dudy Shamay**
18. *Large body puppet operation* / *Courtesy of* **HOP TV**, *Illustrated by* **Dudy Shamay**
19. *The operation of a glove puppet by two puppeteers* / *Illustrated by* **Dudy Shamay**
20. *The use of a video screen as an aid to the operation of a puppet* *Illustrated by* **Dudy Shamay**
21. *The operation of a rod puppet by one puppeteer* / *Illustrated by* **Dudy Shamay**
22. *Raised set for puppets only* / *Illustrated by* **Dudy Shamay**
23. *Raised set for both puppets and human actors* / *Illustrated by* **Dudy Shamay**
24. *Puppet operation on a realistic set* / *Illustrated by* **Dudy Shamay**
25. *Moving Platform Allowing the Movement of a Glove or Rod Puppet* / *Illustrated by* **Dudy Shamay**
26. *Filming a puppet operated by an unhidden puppeteer* / *Illustrated by* **Dudy Shamay**
27. *Filming a puppet and an actor with a foreground object* / *Illustrated by* **Dudy Shamay**
28. *Filming a puppet and an actor without a foreground object* / *Illustrated by* **Dudy Shamay**
29. *The Sandwich Trade – illustration.* / *Illustrated by* **Dudy Shamay**
30. *The positioning of the hidden puppeteers and their assistants in the scene The Sandwich Trade* / *Illustrated by* **Dudy Shamay**
31. *Props Designed for Puppets* / *Illustrated by* **Dudy Shamay**

Bibliography

Child Development / L. Alan, Robert G. Cooper, Ganie B. Dehart / McGraw-Hill, 1992

Children's Humor / Paul E. McGhee, Antony J. Chapman / John Wiley & Sons Ltd, 1980

Comedy - Techniques for writers & performers / Melvin Helitzer / Lawhead Press, 1984

Comedy writing / Milt Josefsberg / Harper & Row, 1987

From Two to Five / Korney Chukovsky / University of California, 1971

The Secret Language of Film / Jean-Claude Carrièreii / De Vries, 1969

The Growth of Understanding in the Young Child / Nathan Isaacs / WLE/ Israel, 1968

Dialogue with children / Edna Katznelson / Kinneret / Israel, 2005

Story (Substance, Structure, Style and the Principles of Screenwriting) / Robert McKee / Gordonbooks / Israel, 2005

Child development/ f. E. A. Schmidt / National Hashomer Hatzair kibbutz Publications / Israel, 1987

Piaget guide for teachers and parents / Peterson and Felton Collins / Brother publishing house / Israel, 2003

Childishness / Zohar Shavit / Open University / Israel, 1996

"Laughter" / Henri Bergson / Rubin Mass Ltd / Jerusalem, 1998

Playing and Reality / DW Winnicott / Am-Oved / Israel, 1995

Literature for young children / Miriam Ruth /

Teacher's Treasure / Israel, 1969
The Meaning and Importance of Fairy Tales /
Bruno Bettelheim/ Modan / Israel, 2002
The world of play / Uri Rapp / Israel. The Ministry
of Defence Publishing / Israel, 1980
Small philosophers / Adir Cohen/ Amazya / Israel,
2008
Psychology of Child and Adolescent / Paul
Solberg/ Magnes Press / Israel, 2007
Psychiatry of Child And Adolescent / Shmuel
Tiano / Probook (Dionon) / Israel,1997

Printed in Great Britain
by Amazon